R.W. Holder has worked in industrial management since 1958 with British, European, Irish and American manufacturers. He spent many years at the head of quoted companies, and in semi-retirement remains involved in the manufacture of such diverse products as textile machinery, telecommunication equipment and pet food. He is also Chairman of a transport and storage company.

He has lived in the same Somerset village for forty years. He is married with five children and many grandchildren.

Also by R.W. Holder:
THE FABER DICTIONARY OF EUPHEMISMS

Thinking About Management

R.W. HOLDER

WARNER BOOKS

A *Warner* Book

First published in Great Britain in 1992 by
Bath University Press
This edition published in 1994 by Warner Books

Copyright © R.W. Holder 1992

A CIP catalogue record for this book
is available from the British Library.

ISBN 0 7515 0485 8

Typeset by Solidus (Bristol) Limited
Printed and bound in Great Britain by
Clays Ltd, St. Ives plc

Warner Books
A Division of
Little, Brown and Company (UK) Limited
Brettenham House
Lancaster Place
London WC2E 7EN

Contents

vi   *Contents*

'There is much to be said for failure.
It is more interesting than success.'

Beerbohm

Foreword

by Sir Kenneth Cork, GBE, D. Litt.

I have been asked to write a foreword to Bob Holder's book on management. Over the years I have read many books on management, with quantities of advice, but I have never read a book as good as this one; nor as entertaining, or as well packed with information.

As this book shows, Bob Holder has been in many companies, and he has put into his book many of the lessons he has learnt. He refers to everybody from Shakespeare to Dryden to Bacon, and various other specialists, all to accentuate his points. Every Managing Director, Chief Executive, and Chairman (particularly the more idle Chairman), should have this book on his desk. This goes for budding people too, who aspire to these outstanding positions!

Every chapter covers a multitude of incidents from Bob Holder's experience; some where things went right; some where things went wrong. Bob Holder travelled widely, and he travelled with extraordinary people, from a famous Scandinavian pop singer to Harold Macmillan. He often used these opportunities to gain an insight into other people's jobs, and all this tends to make the book entertaining.

When you first open this book, you will be tempted to read

it right through, but DO NOT. Read a chapter a month, or two a month, and make a note of the points which affect your business, and the things you did wrong, and do not be conceited! You will find yourself listing many things you did wrong, or could have done better, and many things you have neglected to do.

This book tells you about the things you ought to be doing: thinking, plotting, planning and checking. I have always said that if your Chief Executive is busy, you should sack him. His job is thinking, and that is what he is paid for. Bob Holder takes this much further, so even my definition would not go far enough in saying what your Chairman or Chief Executive ought to be doing!

Most important businessmen are asked to make speeches or to present papers on business, but few provide as much amusing material as there is here. Bob Holder avoids a boring recital of do's and don'ts and gives us instead something which is vital and interesting.

I cannot recommend a book of this sort more. It's the only book on management which is both readable and truly instructive; it may well help to put Britain back on the manufacturing and commercial map. I congratulate Mr Holder on his achievement.

CHAPTER 1

Contemplation and Analysis

'The man who does things makes many mistakes, but he never makes the biggest mistake of all – doing nothing.'

Franklin

* Benjamin Franklin is a happy choice for our first quotation, a man who understood that you need to stick your neck out occasionally if you want to achieve anything. Not many fifteenth children of first-generation immigrant tallow-chandlers go from poverty to wealth, obscurity through adversity to distinction, as he did. That experiment with the kite in a thunderstorm would alone have won him immortality, although the next two people to try it were less fortunate, both being electrocuted on the spot.

* By such a thin string does history hang. Who would have drafted the Declaration of Independence, signed the fateful treaty in Paris and written the United States Constitution if Franklin had not been around?

The late and likeable Joe Hunt – Sir Joseph to give him his correct title – told me once that making money was not difficult: the problem was holding on to it. As he had risen to be Chairman of the large engineering company where in his childhood his deserted mother had cleaned out the latrines, nobody could accuse him of having had an easy ride. He was to prove his point

1

at the age of 64 when his circumstances became straitened and yet he quickly contrived to restore his fortunes.

This book isn't principally about making money, although if you pay attention to the advice and warnings it contains, you may well improve your prospects. There are a number of legal ways of becoming rich, of which inheritance or a judicious marriage are the least demanding. If neither of those routes is open to you, the surest way is to hold shares which increase in value as the fortunes of a firm, or its image, improve. If you manage the firm, you are in a position to see that it is run in such a way as to bring about that improvement. Owning a lot of shares in one company can be dangerous too. Exceptional growth nearly always demands exceptional risks. I don't want to discourage you from gambling, but I intend to help you improve the odds.

The rewards of managing a large firm amount to much more than building up an equity stake or having plenty of cash, although many of us would settle for that. You drive a grander car than you would if you were using your own money. Your health insurance also covers your wife* and family, with a tax-free death benefit of four times your salary to soothe your widow's grief and enhance her prospects. What else do you want? Share options, to make you richer still? A flat in town? A private aircraft perhaps, although when you learn the incidence of crashes among light planes you may be driven back to the rigours of travelling on scheduled services in the first class.

Then there is the public recognition, if you like that sort of thing: the travel, until it palls; and the excitement caused by the endless succession of crises, until you become weary of that along with all else but the salary cheque and the seat in the Lords.

You may have noted that I talk about a large firm, not

---

*In accordance with literary convention and to avoid the inelegant use of language, the male gender may also import the female.

necessarily a successful one. Once you are installed, you will be unfortunate if you are disturbed in the enjoyment of your privileges so long as you achieve or distribute enough to keep your shareholders and colleagues satisfied. To do that, it is not necessary for the organisation to grow but it must remain solvent and independent. If it is taken over after a contested bid, you may be humiliated by instant dismissal with compensation for loss of place and face, quickly finding another outlet for your ability, another cow to milk. But if the company goes into receivership, the heavens fall in – no salary, no car, no job, no pension, and no savings if you had invested heavily in the firm. You will have joined the founder of Corinth at that stage in the cycle of his toil when he is once more at the foot of the cliff in the underworld, with the stone lying there, waiting to be rolled upwards from the bottom.

Like Sisyphus, you will also find yourself alone.

I have twice reached a summit of sorts, and once seen the stone roll down. The errors I have made are so painful to recall that sections of what follows have been written under sedation. However unfair on society it may be to profit from the mistakes of others, I am going to tell you how to avoid doing things which might impede the progress of your rock up the cliff, or most of the way, and how to keep it up there once you've made it.

Most writers of management books profess to instruct you how to achieve wealth, success and a measure of distinction (although the causation is unproved) by references to theories of management. The examples I will be giving you are all factual, usually of things which went wrong. My ambition is limited to explaining how to avoid overreaching yourself or, in plain terms, how not to go bust.

The editor of a leading publisher of such books told me that, when considering publication, she had constantly to remind herself that nobody in fact read them: the odd paragraph here and there, the bold type or the underlined text. Hence the staccato style, the block diagrams and the algebraic formulae which students respect without understanding. You will find none of these devices here. On the few occasions I think you might find a set of figures or a list useful, it has been consigned to an appendix. There will be no footnotes. To benefit from this book, you must keep reading.

I try to steer clear of the temptation to tell you how smart I was, on the few occasions when I could build up a case of sorts. I both enjoy and learn from books written by, or ghosted for, 'achievers'. They deal with real people and, within the constraints of the laws of defamation, actual events. As with the Gospels, the delay in setting the record down can result in an incomplete and often contradictory account, but the gloss is there, along with the attempt to deify.

You can enjoy a private game with these books by adding up the number of times the author is 'often asked' a certain question. It happened to Armand Hammer twice on one page. The only thing I am often asked is the way to an incomprehensible address in a strange city in a foreign language. My Spanish phrasebook covers directing strangers in Madrid to the Prado Museum but elsewhere I am usually at a loss. And to do justice to the Prado, I'd have to stand in the same place all day, risking sunstroke or arrest.

I have kept a journal for years, mainly as a business tool. It can be important to refer back to what was said or done, where and by whom. Such a record, made at the time, is accepted in evidence, and its existence may once have deterred someone from suing me for a large sum in damages, his word without a contemporary record against mine with. The only disadvantage of a journal is that it reveals you were never as smart as you thought you were by hindsight. Most of my anecdotes relate to failure rather than success because management tends to involve more the containment of failure than the exploitation of success. Anyway, failure can be more instructive than success, because business success is the avoidance of failure.

That's enough explanation. If you decide to read on, I cannot guarantee that it will make you richer, but it will certainly help you stay clear of receivership and that, believe me, is something.

The question a businessman should ask, at the outset or as soon as he thinks about it, is exactly what does his operation consist of or, in starker terms, what business is he in. Engrossed as we become in the functions and tribulations of management, many of us go through an entire career without posing this basic question. Yet you must know the answer before you move to the more advanced problem, where do we want the business to be in a year's time, or in three years' time.

You are unwise, apart from major project development, to try to look further ahead than three years, beyond which guesswork can turn into fantasy. The five-year plans promoted by authoritarian planners have to rely on extrapolation at the far end, quite apart from any element of political optimism. With every passing month, each imponderable becomes less susceptible to accurate prediction. Just as wartime couples, separated for three years, grew apart for six, so your competitors will be doing unexpected things to affect the market in ways which you certainly and they probably cannot at present conceive. As will emerge from much of what follows, the world of business is dynamic, and if that comment seems trite, you are already wiser than most.

Stating in these terms what business you are in calls for more than a brief trade classification. Haulier, ironmonger or telecommunication engineer will not do. You have to go through the chore of bringing together your monthly, quarterly and annual management and statutory accounts; lists of your shareholders or proprietors; your sales and promotional literature; your management chart and personnel details. You must identify your customers (actual, potential and past), your markets, your competitors, your sources of finance. Then you must think about the picture which emerges.

You should set about the exercise as though you were hoping to buy the firm yourself, using your own money or credit. That concentrates the mind: about the quality of individuals, the threats caused or the chances given by your competitors and the precise nature of the resources available to you. If you have been managing through conventional controls, most of the information you need should be available in some form or another, although some of it will become out of date every day because you are operating in a climate of constant change, with unpredictable things happening all the time.

I joined the engineering firm of Avimo Ltd as a director, one of two, in 1958. My main qualification for office was that I could speak French, unlike the 250 other employees, and the French proprietor spoke no English. It was not until 1961, with the wolf lifting the latch at the door, that we were forced into making a fundamental analysis of the business.

* Avimo was a wartime phenomenon. Located in Taunton, the only sizeable West Country town to escape bombing, it had prospered on an open order book at cost-plus for everything from small instruments to Spitfire fuselages. When the kissing stopped in 1946, it had developed formidable optical, mechanical and electrical skills but no products and no marketing organisation. The North Koreans came to the rescue in 1950 and the last of the contracts arising from that 'police action' were still stumbling through the production line a decade later.

* The company had tried to use its resources to create unwarlike products of which one at least, a self-photography device, failed through lack of marketing skills rather than its design or potential demand (which has been good news for the people who now dominate the market with a similar system). Having lost money on this, on high-speed cameras, on a small car, even on a lawn mower,

the firm went from one customer to another accepting contracts in a random way for things as diverse as mechanical tape-readers, reflecting telescopes, automatic soft drink dispensers, refrigeration absorption units and garbage grinders. Despite a few contracts for military, nuclear and aircraft instruments, by early 1961 it was going bust.

* Once we had made a formal analysis of where we stood, we realised that alone among the hundreds of other similar enterprises spawned by the war, we possessed optical skills and the specialist tools, jigs and fixtures to cash in on them. There was a plethora of jobbing mechanical engineers, jostling for sub-contract work, and a shortage of optical firms.

From that acorn, belatedly planted, an oak tree was eventually to grow, but we had to travel to the brink of disaster before we recognised it.

Normally you can only decide what business you want to end up with by planning its evolution from where you are now, starting with the resources you possess and the way in which they are at present deployed. If, for example, you are running a ferrous foundry, you may dream of retailing mobile homes because your neighbour seems to do well out of that and cuts his grass from a ride-on mower while you have to push yours. The practicalities are that in the short term you can automate your pouring, or move to more exotic metal formulae, or control the nickel content more efficiently, or put two patterns on a plate where you had one previously. If you can afford machining centres, you might even expand your sales by machining for your customers what you have cast. But that's about all, unless you decide to sell out or shut the place down.

The analysis may throw up something so vital that failure to act will cause the firm to fail. It might be the raising of more equity capital, the disposal of uneconomic assets, the shedding of labour or the recruitment of someone with special skills. In the case of the Norman Aeroplane Company in 1988 it was achieving the type certification of the Freelance aircraft.

> * In 1987 Norman, which saw itself one day wearing the mantle of the pre-war de Havilland in the world of general aviation, had type certificates for its Fieldmaster and Firecracker aircraft, both hard to sell, but had still to certificate the Freelance for which major prospects had been opened up through the decision of Cessna to pull out of the single reciprocating engine high-wing monoplane market. Norman's funding was sufficient for the company's plans so long as a type certificate for Freelance was obtained by February, 1988. There were many conflicting demands on the design, prototype and certification skills of the small company. It was providing a service to lessees of Field-master in approving and installing modifications; it was tidying up drawings for the production of that aircraft in Yugoslavia and trying to sell Firecrackers in Australia. Its presiding genius, Desmond Norman, was continually on the move, seeking orders around the world. But nothing should have had priority over certificating Freelance.

> * When there was still no type certificate for Freelance in July, 1988, Norman went into receivership.

Your analysis will also tell you the true margin on each of your products. You may indeed be surprised to find out that some of your activities are irretrievably loss-making, receiving overt or hidden support from others, or your bankers. Beware the plea that the loss-maker is making some contribution to overhead recovery, for which a case of sorts can usually be made out. On close examination, you usually find the extra overhead would not be incurred without the presence of the loss-maker. When you identify a loser, or find the whole concern is in loss, there are only four choices open to you:

increase volume without increasing fixed costs

reduce costs, fixed or variable, without losing volume

increase prices without losing sales

get out of the business.

You may be able to come up with a policy which contains elements of the first three choices, but outside these options there is no cure for a loss-making operation and even if you can fool your bankers or proprietors to fund your deficit, it only ends in tears.

My family firm, founded by my grandfather, survived the Great Depression but came to grief because its management persisted in subsidising a loss-maker to the detriment of its only profitable line.

* E. Holder & Co. Ltd made collars and cuffs when shirts were only changed on Sundays and washed on Mondays and men affected no deodorants. By the 1960s it had two types of product, bed-jackets and trimmings.

* The small-bore revolution in central heating (where the proto-type pumps were built by Avimo, as it happens) raised the temperature in British bedrooms, if only literally. By and large, the women who wore bed-jackets were married to husbands who could afford central heating. It was not hard to show that all the profits made on the higher margin and potentially huge trimming business were being frittered away on the labour-intensive gar-ments which were rapidly going out of fashion.

* My father, the Chairman, was a local dignitary and in that role it was noble of him to retain people in work, although they would have found better paid jobs in the electronic factories developing in the town. As a manager, he starved the trimmings side of resources so that, when the bad year for trimmings arrived, the business collapsed, to be saved from receivership only by a favourable sale of its freehold premises.

* Then or later almost all the employees lost their jobs. I can't recall that my father became less of a pillar of the community after the debacle.

Another business from whose experiences we may try to extract some benefit is the old Fairey Company about which you can learn more, along with the others cited, in Appendix III. When in 1970 I joined the company, then under threat of receivership, we looked at each of the manufacturing subsidiaries and came up with some unpopular decisions, most of which proved right. The case of Fairey Marine will allow me to make two further points.

* Fairey Marine made power boats for fair-weather sailors who didn't like paying and Olympic class yachts for real sailors who couldn't. It made no return on its capital and generated no cash.

* We saw that we could offer the existing hulls and power plants of the pleasure boats, with almost no modification, to the paramilitary market which was developing as the colonial powers retreated from the Persian Gulf, West Africa and other parts of the globe, taking their police, fishery protection and customs services with them. We borrowed a few soldiers, photographed them leaping ashore with determined mien and there we had our warships. Since then, Fairey Marine may have looked sideways once or twice but it has never looked back.

So to another teaching device, aping an innovation by Moses which seems to have withstood the ravages of time. Where we stumble across some fundamental truth which might help you on your way, we will emphasise it by recording it as a Commandment. These Commandments are listed in Appendix IV, and you can cheat by looking at them now.

In reorganising Fairey Marine, we put into practice both the First and Second Commandments. The First is – Never sell a new product to a new customer: an old customer is more likely to help you through a burn-in phase on a new product, whereas a new customer will be intolerant about the defects of anything not fully developed and proved in service. The Second Commandment is – Always look first for a customer who isn't spending his own money. Whether or not he has a budgeted expenditure to achieve, a spender of the firm's or public money is never as price or value conscious as someone paying from his own pocket.

Let us suppose that your analysis and investigations are complete. Instead of letting things drift on as before, you must decide how to allocate your resources so that everything you do makes a satisfactory contribution to the whole. Your resources are always finite. If you protect laggards, it will be at the expense of survival or of expansion elsewhere.

I don't intend to bother you with many metaphors, but the imagery of the room with a number of exits is apposite. Some of the exits may have doors, and some of the doors may be locked. If you want to get out, it is easiest to go through the holes without doors, then through the doors which are open, then through the doors which are unlocked, then to find a key to unlock a door and, in extremis, to pick the locks, if you know how. Despite the availability of more convenient means of egress, many of us in our businesses continue to bash our heads and shins against the walls without looking for the doors, and then wonder why we are still in a box.

Beyond the doors, to pursue this imagery, lie the markets. Nothing happens in industry until you sell something which customers want to buy, at the price you need and delivery you can achieve. It is no use having a unique selling proposition if you don't know how to interest your customers in buying it. We will be looking at selling and marketing later, along with all other aspects of management we can think of. An example of what can happen if you develop products without customer interest plagued me from 1975 to 1977.

* Fairey Electronics possessed an encryption system so rapid and secure that none of the accepted decoding devices, whether depending on computer aids or the detection of magnetic signals from relays, was able to crack it. A potential customer in South America transmitted only zeros at over 12,000 characters a minute for two weeks continuously, and experts in Washington were unable to read what was being sent. We were using a pseudo-random signal generator, with oscillators to avoid the tell-tale signals given off by magnetic relays (whence the transmission from lead-shielded rooms in embassies). You could leave the machine running day and night, with a trigger of letters telling the recipient when the burst of message was being sent, and when the device was reverting to gibberish. At full speed, the encryption pattern was repeated only every 126 years.

* Despite demonstrations, we failed to sell a single system and even if we had, there would have been a further mountain to climb when it came to obtaining export licences for equipment rather more secure than that which NATO had at the time. When Racal bought the company, it sold the finished inventory within months for more than it paid for the entire business. Racal was in the telecommunication business, and Fairey wasn't.

Some clouds have silver linings. At the time of the Falklands War it helped the British to be able to read what Galtieri's people were saying amongst themselves. Of course, if they had paid notice earlier to the same source of intelligence, there wouldn't have been a War at all, and once started, it wouldn't have been necessary, after intercepting her orders, to sink the *Belgrano*.

In planning where you want to go, then, you start from where you are, using the resources you have to your hand. You address your mind, in the business area you already know, to which customers are likely to want to buy from you at the time when you have something ready to deliver, developed, tested, tooled, in production and profitable. The snag is that, at the same time, and all the time, you have to keep the existing business going. But if you have an objective, you can nudge the organisation gradually in the direction you have chosen rather than drift with no purpose other than survival and a quiet life. When at last you have scaled the peak, it will almost certainly prove to be a false crest, but a crest for all that.

If there are short cuts to success and expansion (different things which you must remember to keep apart) they have eluded me. I was indebted to my predecessor at Avimo for showing me one of the things not to do.

* I mentioned that Avimo made instruments for the nuclear industry. With Stalin not long dead, there had been little thaw between the Great Powers keeping the peace with their thermo-nuclear bombs. We manufactured the ionisation chambers, which were used to detect sudden increases in levels of radiation such as might herald a Chernobyl or World War III. Running late with deliveries to the Atomic Energy Authority because of a lack of special felt with which the instruments were filled, the General Manager sent out to a firm of local builders' merchants who supplied roofing felt. That contains tar.

* The national Red Alert happily did not lead to an immediate reprisal, but it was enough to kill off Avimo's relationship with the AEA.

Following accepted literary practice, we have been introducing to the reader most of our characters in the first chapter, albeit at the expense of too many anecdotes. And the real villain, Stone-Platt Industries, has yet to appear with the rest of the supporting cast.

Before we move on to accounts and financial control, do not forget the gems which have been scattered here and there, the Commandments and the list of the only four things you can do when you are faced with a loss-making business. Asking you to consider where you are and whither you think you are going sounds like an agenda for a revivalist meeting, but perhaps you should be thinking about revival: the alternative, the preachers tell us, is damnation and a regime which would seem to involve considerable personal discomfort over a protracted period.

And nothing said yet about hard work? No, and for good reasons which we will come to later. Thinking is more difficult, and more important.

CHAPTER 2

Accounts and Accountants

'At many times I brought you my accounts,
Laid them before you; you would throw them off,
And say you found them in my honesty'
                                    Shakespeare

* It would be presumptuous indeed to add any note about Shakespeare, the sage, philosopher, humorist and poet whose genius effectively fixed and established the English language, the world's most versatile method of communication: easy to learn at a functional level, grammatically simple in use but capable of infinite subtlety and complexity with its double sourcing from German and French. How strange that his plays were committed to paper by two others and how appropriate that there should be a memorial to them in the City of London.

Even if it were possible, like the princess with her frog, to turn ourselves into accountants with a few magical pieces of advice, there is no need – and we would have to weigh the dire prospect of not being able to turn back. You can hire competent people who spent years ticking columns of figures and running up excessive audit hours for their principals to make them what they are. What we need is a crib sheet, telling us those corners which are most commonly cut in financial reports and how to deter people from trying to bamboozle us.

Figures are the language of management. In the past someone will have used them to tell you less than the whole truth; if you read on from here, not any more.

Our primary object is not to go bankrupt. That means we must not exhaust our credit or run out of money. In any business cash is the ultimate verity. It is the one figure in any set of accounts which cannot be smoothed, distorted, massaged, misstated, wrongly transcribed, put into a computer or lied about without the truth emerging fairly soon. It is the figure we should check first. In the simplest case, we verify it by counting the till but for most of us, we reconcile our bank statements with our cash book. The prudent manager sees the cash figures weekly, the nervous one daily.

Nobody ever failed in business while he was solvent but many petitions for bankruptcy have been filed and receivers appointed when a business looked as if it was still profitable but had run out of money. Solvency, the ability to pay your debts as they fall due, is an inflexible concept. Most of us operate on the basis of cash supplied by someone else, in the form of equity or a bank loan. If we manage our affairs so that we can meet our liabilities as they come up, we can continue trading. Few of us do not remember wintry conditions when we had to skate on thin ice, surviving an ominous crack or two. But once the ice breaks, which it can do with little warning, we are through, and finished. The water will be horribly cold and the other skaters will keep well clear.

In businesses like travel agency or mail order, cash can deceive you, because you tend to get paid in advance of providing the service or goods, which is why so many of them fail. Providers of other services like haulage don't get paid in advance, but at least they don't have to finance inventories. Manufacturers face the complex equation; apart from cash they have the full works – debtors and creditors, sales and purchases, wages and overheads, finished goods, stocks and work in progress. Cash is the fixed point from which is constructed the reporting triangle of balance sheet, cash flow and profit and loss account. If the other figures look right but cash is out of line, you had better start digging. In 1984 we dug too slowly and not deep enough.

* Bridport-Gundry owned Brownell and Company in Connecticut, making in New England many of the products developed by its Dorset parent. Month by month the amount of cash stayed out of line with the other figures – profit, working capital and inventories. The cash had to be right so something else was wrong.

* Even after a full regular audit and stock count, the figures smelt bad. We therefore laid on an intermediate audit, which involved the expense and disruption of another physical stock-taking. Everything came out as before. The auditors sent us a bill for $25,000.

* We still knew something was not right and kept looking. By checking the figures on stock cards, we discovered that the senior accountant in Brownell, worried about its performance and his job, had been systematically inflating the amounts of work in progress fed into the computer. As he had previously worked for the auditors, he knew their procedures. When they went to lunch, leaving papers in an unlocked office, he had increased the quantities on those stock cards which they had physically checked, adding a digit to inflate the total number of items recorded. Thus 540 balls of twine in a batch might be shown as 1,540, and valued accordingly. The profit overstatement was found to be $357,000, almost exactly what we had seen as the cash shortage.

* The bad consequences were:

> we had to tell our shareholders that we had reported inflated figures

> we had been paying taxes in America on fictitious profits

the accountant had spent so much time juggling with the figures that he had neglected his proper duties

the distortions had led to bad pricing and investment decisions which were to dog Brownell long after the event.

* The accountant left. So far as we could judge, he had not committed any criminal act. The auditors were changed too. The $25,000 fee was not paid.

Having checked the cash position, turn to debtors and creditors, or in more appropriate American speech, receivables and payables. Debtors should turn into cash within a predictable time. Even slow payers tend to be regular and you soon get a feel for how things should be. If debtors start mounting and cash dropping, check that the goods have really been shipped and accepted by the customer at the invoiced date. You may then find that your production manager has decreed that even the shortest month should have more than 31 days.

If a good payer starts taking his time, see if you have overdelivered or shipped early. In either case he won't pay until it suits him. You may find that a shipment has been rejected, which will involve rectification or an argument, leading to delay or non-payment. That in turn will affect profit, which doesn't matter too much, and cash, which does.

You may find out that people are not paying because invoices are being sent late, which is an inevitable consequence of trying to introduce a new computer. The customer has not been born who complains about not being asked for money on time. When he receives a statement, he will take his normal credit from then rather than from the delivery date. At the year end you may decide to slow up the paperwork, to reduce your tax bill or give you a good start for the next year; but that is a decision you must take, not your accounts clerk.

Creditors and accruals take care of themselves; the ones you need to watch closely are those suppliers who can shut you down if you upset them by consistently slow payment, and then demand cash in advance. The others will start shouting if they are treated too badly. Because in the end it affects cash, you need to know what is owing in total, how much is overdue by periods and how much is in suspense. Leave the details to the bean counters but occasionally look at all the incoming mail yourself. That will tell you how good a payer you are.

If an excessive amount claimed by creditors is in suspense because of delays in your goods inwards procedures, you may have to increase your resources there, or make your inspectors work harder. Few things are more frustrating than to see a line stopped in a factory because materials have not been released to production.

Nothing should enter the factory unless it corresponds to a numbered order, especially if, as with fuel or chemicals, you are paying by direct debit. The order should lay down quantities, prices and delivery: the goods received note and the inward inspection report should be reconciled with the order. If they don't, the supplier's invoice should not be cleared for payment.

Wages and salaries are a major cost but, apart from ghosts on the payroll, you should have little to worry about. Too many individuals are out there checking their wage slips to allow mistakes to go undetected. There used to be scope for conserving cash by hanging on to deductions from earnings under the taxes known as PAYE or National Health Insurance. That is now not merely counter-productive but positively dangerous. There are penalties for late payment, as with VAT, and directors have a personal liability for any deficiency to the Revenue if the business fails.

Depreciation is a blessed item in any profit and loss account because it is a minus which does not involve the actual payment of cash. Whatever is debited in the one place comes back in another, through the cash flow, as a credit. You will come across attempts to modify the impact of depreciation on profit and loss, as when machinery has been delivered but not commissioned and the accountants want to defer making a charge until the asset is producing a return. That does no harm, except perhaps to overstate profit, and there is no tax penalty in playing those games as the Revenue uses its own rules about depreciation, regardless of what you choose to do in your accounts.

So, to sum up thus far, ignore depreciation. Your deliveries should tie in with your debtors and in due course with money received; your purchases will be reflected in your creditors, accruals and money paid out. Wages and salaries have too many monitors out there to tolerate any errors. We will come to stocks in a moment. Cash is cash – what the cash book says and not what the bank thinks it is. The two figures can differ either way, according to what uncleared cheques are floating around. If your cash book tells you that you are over the limit, you can take small comfort from the fact that the bank doesn't know that yet. Within five days it will, or sooner.

With stock and work-in-progress, the certainties, such as they are, cease. These are the pools in which the piranhas lurk. If you detect a pattern of rising stocks, falling debtors and diminishing cash, someone may be producing goods for which there are no immediate customers, rather than facing nasty decisions like redundancy or showing losses. The stock valuation will include a percentage for factory overheads, which you would be better off not incurring if you can't sell the product. In an extreme case, producing unsold goods can so deplete your resources that you lose room for remedial action, which is more or less what happened to the mighty Stone-Platt Industries.

* Up until the early 1980s, Platt Saco-Lowell was one of the world's largest makers of textile machinery, with several factories in the United Kingdom, a large plant in Spain, another in South

Carolina and various other operations dotted around the globe. Along with many exporters, the firm suffered from the early-Thatcher recession, when the strength of sterling played havoc among those manufacturers who had virtually no home market.

* Short of other work, the management in Lancashire was so confident of receiving a vast order for fitting out an entire textile mill in Saudi Arabia as a turn-key operation that it put the work in hand and paid handsome commissions in advance to plausible middle-men. At the holding company, we saw stocks rising and cash vanishing as the machines were built, packed and stacked. Whenever we met, the mirage of the order was in place, no closer and no more substantial.

* Even those directors who believed in the fixers should have worked out what sterling at $2.40 was doing to the competitiveness of British manufacture, what the fall in oil prices was doing to Arab purchasing power and what specialist suppliers of individual textile machines were doing to the old turn-key concept. When Stone-Platt got round to the hard decisions, cash had run out and the patient proved too sick for surgery. You will read more about it later and in Appendix III.

As our former friend in Brownell showed us, if you wish to mislead, there is no need to tinker with figures which can easily be verified. The killing ground lies in stocks and work-in-progress. Whether you intend gentle massaging or downright fraud, this is the place where you go as poacher, and where you look as gamekeeper.

I once gave the winding-up address at the residential course for National Westminster Bank managers at Heythrop Park on the theme 'How to cheat your banker'. I told them that, when it comes to valuing work-in-progress, directors do not even have to cheat; they can simply 'take a view', and by so doing mislead auditors, shareholders and bankers alike; and sometimes themselves too. The manager who first invited me to speak there has risen to dizzy heights, within the bank and outside, not excluding the royal tap on his shoulder. I was asked back to give the same talk twice more and it is gratifying to note that the bank itself, in some disarray over its own liquidity in those dark days, seems to have been doing much better lately.

When you know your business, bought-out items and raw materials are relatively easy to control, not least because you can go into the stores and count them. If people want to cheat over them, they have to fall back on overvaluation or incorrect classification. No auditor can tell one semi-conductor from another or which components have a discrete shelf life. On the edge of honesty is delay in writing down redundant or slow-moving stocks, or keeping items of inventory at cost when the current price has fallen.

Things like nickel, steel scrap, electronic components and commodities fluctuate in price wildly, sometimes from week to week. Most of the time it is sensible to ignore these movements when preparing management accounts, so long as you remember to to pick up material cost increases to pass on to customers. When an audit comes round, you use the current figures and, as with unhedged currency movements, you can have some nice surprises or nasty shocks.

The joker in the pack will always be the value of work-in-progress. If you do a physical stocktaking, you have to arrange for everything to be counted, and then valued, using material content, added labour and an agreed manufacturing overhead. Any change in overhead rate is classified as a change in accounting practice, which the Revenue will argue about and the City suspect. Even with a computerised production control system, it is wise to do a physical check, to sort out all the programming and other errors of the previous six months. If a rolling or continuous physical stock assessment tallies with the computer print-outs, you are running an exceptional operation, or an uncomplicated one, or you are a very lucky person: probably all three.

A danger in estimating inventory by adding a notional overhead percentage to standard hours or direct hours booked is that you will fail to pick up discrepancies. How efficient were your productive hours? How do you treat consolidated batches of components built in advance of order cover to increase efficiency? What about scrap and rectification? Eventually you have to reconcile reality with the estimates by physical counting.

Naturally, the way you check inventory depends to some extent on what you are manufacturing. In a short cycle process, like extruding creamed and centrifuged latex into elastic thread, you have a door-to-door time from bulk raw material to packed product of 12 hours, and you obtain an accurate stock every week. But if you are making military electro-optical instruments, with up to 300 piece parts involving as many as 20 operations each, and housing some 80 pieces of glass which, after machining, may have faults you cannot detect until final assembly, there is no simple solution. The production cycle for each instrument may be seven months and for a batch, up to four years.

Firms do get work-in-progress somewhere near right immediately after valuing what has been physically counted, even in aircraft factories, and it is hard to manage effectively if you are living with inbuilt errors. The scope for getting it wrong, or fudging, is great. Only if you have a constant feeling for cash will you detect a dangerous error creeping in before serious damage is done.

Although you may feel you know how best to monitor your business, it may help to compare what you are doing with what I suggest you should be doing. Every figure reported to you should be an actual, apart from stock movement, the amount by which inventory has been calculated to have gone up or down in the period under review. The first period uses the value of inventory at the year end check; after that we reduce the figure by the amount we deliver more than we produce, and increase it if we produce more than we deliver. We still have a wild card, only one, and it is face up on the table.

As already suggested, cash should be reported weekly, with an estimate as to what is forecast over each of the next four weeks, and then perhaps for three months after that. With forecasts, handwritten figures are preferable to typewritten, and both to computer print-outs, because that increases the possibility that the compiler has thought about it. Some of the most revealing information you will read is the accountant's footnotes explaining why cash differs from previous forecasts. Few of us take pains to conceal why somebody else's default has made our life more difficult and our previous predictions inaccurate.

You need to see the other key figures every month. Set a date – perhaps 8 days after the month end – and insist on having the report by then even if there are blank spaces. Apart from the obvious, ensure that the debtor report highlights any change in your bad debt provision. Bad debts are multiple disasters: you lose a customer, you lose profit and you lose cash. On top of that, they play hell with your VAT returns.

The monthly report should tell you the numbers employed against budget under the various categories – direct, factory indirect, sales, development and administration. Here you need to watch for a shortage of direct workers, which means your overhead recovery may be inadequate. The employment of temporary staff or high sub-contracting may indicate the inefficient use of labour.

Overtime payments should be broken out as a separate item. Overtime is not all evil; it allows trained people to be used flexibly to meet surges in demand. Excessive overtime is inefficient and you need to be awake to the various stratagems used by employees to ensure that overtime is institutionalised. Even when you detect abuses, you may elect not to end them, or not immediately.

When things are running smoothly, you can pick up a summary of overhead expenses in the monthly profit and loss account. Bear in mind that fluctuations in overhead, even reductions, can hint at bad news. If agents' commissions fall in an export business, overseas sales, usually at better margins, will be down. Watch out too for virement, so beloved of the civil servant, whereby a cost overrun on a development project, for example, gets tucked away in the drawing office overtime premium.

Managers tend to know their forward order books before seeing management accounts. If you are selling capital goods, it is important to know the value of uncleared orders, where you are waiting for buyer credits, import licences and suchlike, if only to ensure that obstructions are shifted as soon as possible. Obviously there is no formula for the perfect length of order book. In the sewing thread business, we had to supply the shoe trade the same day but building the Dungeness B nuclear power station took a lot longer.

We will be looking at capital expenditure later. At this stage, remember that it normally involves an outlay of cash which will not turn into income quickly. You will have a formal system for the release of each item of capital expenditure, even when it has been budgeted. The cost will appear in the cash forecast and, if things look really tough, you may be able to postpone the purchase or switch to leasing. If you find out how to put off the purchase of company cars, please let me into the secret.

All this information can be gleaned from the monthly profit and loss account, the balance sheet and the cash flow statement. We have already noted that these three sets of figures form the sides of a triangle: if the corners don't meet, the figures are wrong. To recapitulate, our bête noire, inventory, appears in the balance sheet as a sum and in the profit and loss account as an increase or reduction in the cost of sales. Obviously the figure for stock movement has to reconcile with the balance sheet value or we wouldn't have our triangle.

Insist, if you dare, on figures for period 12, even if that involves consolidating periods 1 and 2 in the new year. It is instructive to compare management accounts for period 12 with the audited accounts for the year. If they look similar, you have a good management accountant and a well-run business.

Once you've been involved in it, management accounting is no more than common sense. It remains a jungle for many managers because they let the accountants dictate what is presented and how. In Appendix I you will find a facsimile of a weekly cash report and sets of monthly and quarterly accounts prepared by a well-managed company. If you are already seeing as much information as concisely presented as this, you needn't have read this chapter.

Most of us are not clever enough to run businesses over the long term unless we have all this information presented to us in ways which we can readily understand. Hunch and hearsay can pull you through the good times, but they won't do when recession is about. The purpose of management accounts is not to tell you what has happened but to alert you to what might happen in time for you to do something about it.

Every figure should tell you something, whence our Third Commandment – Never ask for any figures which are not also necessary in running the business. And our Fourth – Never let an accountant circulate any accounts which the rest of the management cannot understand. Leave that to the auditors.

Accounts have the reputation of being boring and I have to confess I don't find it an easy subject to write about. Before you turn away, glance back at Shakespeare's words with which we prefaced this chapter. If they bring you accounts, don't throw them off. You can't rely on honesty these days.

CHAPTER 3

Budgets

'His budget with corruptions cramm'd,
The contributions of the damned'

Swift

* Anyone who penned the above lines should have been a production manager rather than a man of the cloth. If in funds and the Republic of Ireland, you can today see the Dean's likeness on the £10 note. To such expediences are countries driven when they reject royalty. As the satirist was received in Dublin with insults and looked upon his life there as a state of exile, he might not have been too happy with this posthumous honour.

Budgeting is a tedious function and a game in which there are only losers. When you get it right, the credit you receive will be grudging, tinged with the insinuation that you should have set your sights higher. When you get it wrong, which is most of the time, you can expect kicks and abuse.

Bear in mind that budgeting is work managers have to fit in additional to the trivial round, the daily task. Give them a standard format to follow and a series of assumptions – on inflation, wage increases and the like. Then they may not waste time on parallel guesswork and you will receive a set of documents prepared on a common basis. It does not help to

27

burden them with learned articles on economic forecasting or to call for too much detailed scheduling.

Because budgets have to be expressed in figures, we can easily fall into the trap of thinking that the entire process is the responsibility of accountants, a delusion which a Financial Director will foster. Handing over the compilation of budgets to accountants is like asking stokers to con a ship.

Most of us see budgets as instruments against which we can be measured, or against which we can judge others. There is the additional temptation to use them as pacemakers, the carrot which hangs just beyond the reach of the manager's thrusting jaw. To use a budget like this is dangerous as well as being unfair. Monitoring achievement should be their secondary function.

The primary function is to provide a mechanism through which you consciously prepare realistic and attainable plans for the future, at the same time having timely warning of approaching hazards. In most businesses, budgeting for a year ahead – the financial year or on a rolling basis – is long enough. You have to give yourself enough time to put in place the resources you are going to need. It is obviously silly to embark on a production programme which calls for ascertainable hours of direct labour without the right numbers of bodies available with the relevant skills: and so too for machine time, space, test gear, power loading, vendors, tooling and all the other ingredients which have to be tossed into the pot. However people still do it, which is better than not bothering with budgets at all, though not by much.

How far ahead of the start of the budgetary period you need to complete the process depends on what sort of business you are in. You may already know that a petrol filling station (to call them 'service' stations is a cruel misnomer) breaks even at a throughput of 1.5m. litres, given the normal sales of peripherals like oil, wiper blades, confectionery and the high-margin junk you sell in the kiosk; and from there on every litre sold will give you a profit of 1.9 pence less variable overheads. Apart from watching your borrowings, especially if you are so unwise as to give credit on a commodity of which more than half the cost is up-front tax, you can leave the budgeting to the end of the previous year without any fear of much going wrong. And you will survive if you ignore it altogether, so long as you watch the cash.

By contrast, a manufacturer with a four times annual stock turn and long lead times on material and machinery needs to complete his budget as far ahead as he dare, but not so far ahead that his opening figures, for inventory especially, are conjectural. If they turn out to be very wrong, the entire budget will be flawed.

We all know management is a blend of experience and common sense. It's a truism therefore to state that without customers you have no business. It follows that the opening batsman in your budget team is the salesman who has to predict how much he can sell, when and to whom, at what prices and in what currencies.

It is a useful discipline to ask the person forecasting sales to write out what has led him to his conclusions. As well as concentrating his mind, it will give you an additional insight into his problems. Normally the volume, timing or mixture of what the sales people want produced is not in line with your facilities or would lead to inefficient working. That is all right, so long as you have time to do something about it. The worst sales forecast is the lazy one which backs on to existing output, with a casual 5% or so tossed in for inflation or growth.

We must factor any good salesman's forecasts generously. If he weren't an optimist, he would never have taken up selling. It is instructive to cross-check by talking to your customers; or even more by meeting agents and distributors, who have a fetish about telling you bad news, especially about your competitors. But don't accept as true everything they tell you.

* On 26th August, 1982 two of us were in Salonika seeing the sewing thread distributors of James Pearsall. We were delighted with the standard hibiscuses lining the street (although we couldn't see why the Greeks had named them after marshmallows) and disgusted by the pollution in the bay. We were given a hard time over the inroads an Italian distributor was making into our Greek market despite our price advantage, due to his superior quality.

* Experience had taught us to keep quiet when this happens. The person complaining will not be any happier to learn that you are supplying the offending Italian with the identical product to what you sell him.

You must guard against people who try to give the appearance of fully using their production resources by forcing their sales projections, and so avoid taking painful decisions. Obviously everyone wants to sell what can be most profitably and simply made. If there is a mismatch between potential orders and production, you may be able to redirect your sales effort to bring demand into line with efficient supply. If however the forecasts say that you cannot market your output because some of the products are obsolescent or unsaleable in their present form or at an economic price, you need to take a fresh look at your production methods, advertising, packaging, pricing, presentation, promotion, discounts and all the other factors under your control which affect demand. If that look reveals only a series of dark spaces, you may have to drop products and face up to various unpleasant realities, not the least of which is the loss of overhead recovery which will knock on through the rest of your operation, unless you can immediately divert the assets to another use.

If the sales forecasts indicate that you are going to be oversold, beyond what your likely resources can produce, you can restrict demand by putting up prices, after inserting earplugs to drown the cries of anguish from the sales team. This is not the kind of problem which drives you to reading management books in the small hours, other soporifics having failed. In any analysis, too many orders leads to more contentment than too few.

If you are an exporter, you need to think about exchange rates because they will affect the pricing policies of your foreign competition. You are certainly too wise to gamble in currencies. There are people who do that for a living, their eyes glued to a VDU from the opening of the market in Tokyo to the closing in Chicago. The economist who writes in bankers' house journals prophesying what will happen to the peseta in six months' time doesn't know. If he did, he wouldn't be sharing his knowledge but stretched out on a sun-drenched private beach in agreeable company, a cool glass in his hand.

We have to buy and sell in foreign currencies. Some things, like aero engines, are sold only in US dollars and selling to customers in the currency of their choice is part of the concept of making it easy to buy from you. If you can match currencies, you save paying the banks their commission on conversion. A matched deal can save $1\frac{1}{2}\%$, and that is all profit. With commodities that fluctuate widely or are subject to cartels, like nickel and fibres, you cannot totally cover your exposure but you can at least ensure that price increases are passed on to customers.

Remember that a currency is worth what it is worth today. The only reliable guide to possible movement is to take a commodity which isn't the subject of forward trading in a commodity market or controlled by a cartel – titanium dioxide, say – and compare the cost in different countries. If it is cheaper today in Swiss francs than Dutch gilders, buying in Switzerland and Holland, it is likely the two currencies will move to eliminate the difference over the next few months.

You have to think about inflation and its effect upon prices when you are completing the sales budget. Most salespeople will be happy to pass on to customers the benefit of old material costs, even though you are replacing the same materials at higher prices. It is difficult in a competitive market to stop margins being worn away by the insidious erosion of inflation, but that is what you have to guard against. Plenty of bodies forecast what inflation will be in the months ahead but, as with all forecasting, nobody knows. Read what they say, make your own judgment and tell people to use that figure, for receipts and for costs. So long as both sides of the ledger balance, you won't come to much harm.

In most manufacturing businesses, projecting deliveries is the hardest thing to get right, but it forms one side of the pair of scales. The other, expenses, has many components – buying, stock levels, people, overheads and all the other elements of manufacture and distribution. Of these, people are likely to be the most expensive, and the hardest to increase or reduce as demand fluctuates. Check that your plans are feasible by looking at your direct hours available. Watch out against working in round figures. 'Our plan calls for 420,000 hours of productive work or 210 direct workers': it doesn't. It may call for 42 skilled machinists, 28 welders, 63 fitters, 6 wiremen and so on. You cannot transfer people from one trade or skill to another overnight, or at all in some cases; nor can you hope to recruit all the extra people you need without paying everyone more money.

Machine-tools are more flexible than people. You can plan ahead, either by buying more, or by finding sub-contractors. When they work shifts, machines don't ask for a premium. When they stand idle, they don't clock on to waiting time. If you have a simple process, like extruding chips to yarn, you know what tonnage you achieve on a 40 hour week, on a double day shift, on 5 day continuous working and on 148 hours. However, for most of us, the conundrum is more complex because every production process develops a bottleneck, usually a complex early operation machine or a specialist finishing process. We may have plenty of spare capacity either side of it, but this is the constraint on our entire output.

The budget should show you what machines you have to procure, and when. An experienced production manager keeps his board advised of what he is going to need in terms of machine replacement and addition, which is a more useful guide than the accountants' rule of thumb, spend each year not more than your depreciation charge.

A manufacturer has constantly to buy new machines to stay in business. If you fail to match your overseas competitors in machinery and tooling, they will bury you because their employees are almost certainly harder working or less well paid than yours. Corporate predators may claw back depreciation as a cash benefit, also pumping up profits by saving on interest and lowering depreciation for a year or two. Leave the prestidigitation of 'acquisition accounting' (undervaluing assets on takeover to produce as profit later) or 'growth by acquisition' (asset stripping) to others; we are trying to create wealth over the long haul, or at least to have a salary cheque coming in next year.

Capital expenditure should include market and product development as well as plant, machinery and specialised tooling. In a business like telecommunications, with test procedures designed to achieve zero defects and interminable field trials ahead of production, the capital costs lie elsewhere than in buying another auto-insert or wave-solder machine. You must also consider, and write off, the cost of training and learning. No-one is strong enough or clever enough to make new customers go on buying old products, as Herbert's discovered with lathes and John Bloom with washing machines.

* John Bloom destroyed the old domestic washing machine cartels

by imaginative advertising and offering a simple machine cheaper. At the height of his success, he took me into his research department at Cricklewood. It was a smallish room in which two fitters were dismantling and examining his competitors' products. Those competitors are still in business, and I believe he is too, not making washing machines but running night clubs in America.

It is inevitable that capital expenditure is the first casualty when the budget is 'unsatisfactory' to a parent company or the board, who may not be satisfied by the best those who know the business can forecast. The Group Managing Director tells you he wants a 25% return on assets with 10% increase in profit and a positive cash flow. As he and the Financial Director are driven away in their limousines, you ruffle through the figures again. If we try to charge more for the product, we'll kill sales, lose volume and reduce margins. We've pared production costs to the bone. If we don't match inflation in our wage increases, we'll have a strike or, at the least, lose our best people. The Group has already taken the credit for a pension contribution holiday. The only places to take the knife are development, marketing, training and equipment. It will screw up the future, but, if that's what they want. . . .

Asking a competent management to revise a considered budget to achieve certain targets is bad enough: demanding arbitrary cuts in expenses is stupid unless people have been accustomed to a haggling regime in which everyone asks too much, knowing there will be cuts all round. Delta had an unsettling experience after being bought by Tellabs Inc. early in 1989.

* The Delta managers had had five years of using their own money between acquiring the business from Mitel and selling out to Tellabs. Faced with re-budgeting immediately after the acquisition, they had neither the time nor the wit to do other than continue the thoughtful and frugal habits which had brought first survival and then success. For its part, the new parent thought it sensible to apply to its subsidiary the cross-the-board cuts to which its own operating divisions were of necessity subjected.

* In the event, the cuts were made, the expenditure was incurred, and the end result for Delta, now Tellabs Ltd, was slightly better than the Irish team had predicted. So in consequence everyone was happy, and some wiser.

Once strands have been drawn together from sales, production and development, you turn the accountants loose. This is what we mean to sell, this is what it will cost to make and this is the capital we plan to spend. What does it all add up to in terms of working capital? How much more will we have to invest in debtors if 30 days became 45, or even 60? What about dividends? We must look more closely than at the month end figures, because cash peaks are not dictated by the calendar. If we need more cash, can we get it, and at what cost?

You should wait until this stage is complete before you permit yourself the indulgence of working out returns on capital employed and on sales, your profit per employee and all those other riveting statistics. Then, after all the sweat, you may find the result of the exercise is not credible, occasionally too good, normally too bad. As you go through the figures, shut down the canteen, downgrade the company cars, postpone one of the CNC's, at least you can reflect that you have built your house from the foundations up, and not from the roof down.

Computer-based spread sheets save time in preparing budgets but are dangerous. Sitting before our screen, we make a simple adjustment to the gross margin, or volume, or selling prices: press the 'enter' button, watch the figures dancing across the screen and, hey presto, all our targets have been achieved without engaging another fitter or postponing our new Jag. The machine has done our thinking for us, even assuming that the modern inhabitants of the Workshop of the World indulge in productive activity between the 22nd December and 3rd January. So to our Fifth Commandment – Never trust computer-based spread sheets.

Once the budget is in its final form, show it to the people whose input created it and let them register any objections to assumptions which they think have been forced upon them. The budget will demand more attention if managerial bonuses are based in part on making the forecast profit and in part by their achieving the result within the working capital predicted. This method of paying incentives (which will be explained to the patient later) keeps managers focused on the budget throughout the year and deters them from taking too rosy a view of life during the budgetary process.

However carefully we plan, most of us get our timing wrong. New machines and processes seldom work when or as predicted: new products usually take too long to introduce: new customers are always more cautious than their buyer led us to believe over his third glass of brandy. Despite all that, by constructing our budget in this way, the management team will be aiming at targets which they have themselves acknowledged are achievable.

You may have to present the budget in its final form to your board. So long as the ratios look satisfactory, do not expect any intelligent comment, criticism or analysis from your colleagues; you will not then be disappointed. Before circulating copies to the people who have to make it happen, have a column showing the previous year's comparative figures inserted for quick reference.

After circulating the approved budget, do not change it, however distressing the experience of seeing how wrong you all were. You will, on a monthly basis, be updating your forecasts, the 'expected result' column, but constant re-budgeting only causes chaos. The bigger the organisation, the greater the chance that the swings and the roundabouts, the optimists and the pessimists, will cancel out. But even the big boys have their problems.

* The Vigilant anti-tank missile programme was transferred to the British Aircraft Corporation at a critical time in its development. Avimo supplied much of the optical and electronic test, guidance and training gear. Without knowing BAC's plans, we could hardly make our own, their orders taking a large part of our capacity. When once I pressed the Project Manager for guidance, he pointed to a crystal ball on his desk, saying, 'Don't ask me. Look for yourself.'

* His Managing Director (Sir) George Jefferson and his Chairman, Lord Caldecot, were destined to become, if not already, leaders of British industry, laden with richly deserved honours and even greater distinction, not excluding, for one of them at least, the selection of an Archbishop. Some of our anecdotes then lead to no particular conclusions.

Budgets, as we have noted, are based on sales projections. The best budgetary information we obtained from BAC in those days came from the salesmen, and it will be to selling that we turn next.

CHAPTER 4

Sales and Marketing

'The precious weight
Of pepper and Sabaean incense take,
And with post-haste thy running market make,
Be sure to turn a penny.'

Dryden

* A British manufacturer between 1956 and 1981 saw himself as feverishly stoking the boilers of the ship of state while ministers steered zig-zag and uncharted courses, exhaled clouds of steam and contrived to waste every alternate shovelful of coal heaved into the clinker-ridden furnaces. How he envied his French counterpart, protected by politicians and civil servants who cynically and consistently pursued the national interest.

* Dryden lived in equally trying times for a playwright. He adjusted to the Commonwealth and Protectorate, to the Restoration and the Catholicism of James II, before failing to clear the last hurdle of the Glorious Revolution in his ageing stride, losing with the finishing tape in sight – his appointment and stipend as Poet Laureate.

* These short character sketches may comfort you in showing that trimming and sycophancy are not exclusively present-day phenomena. Just as 17th-century scholars and clerics adjusted and

38

re-adjusted their beliefs, fawning alternately on King and Commonwealth, so modern businessmen have professed successively to find virtues in the social and economic policies of Macmillan, Wilson, Heath and Foot where others, less perceptive or favoured perhaps, failed to detect any principle or principles on which those policies were based. And the rush to the exits could be heard months before the end of the Glorious (Thatcher) Revolution.

Nothing happens in industry until you sell something. This chapter is not about how to sell but about how to understand and control salesmen. It is headed 'Sales and Marketing' because the two activities, insofar as they are separate, are complementary. You have then also to control people who call themselves marketing experts.

In the popular mind, marketing people affect bright bow ties and employ personal assistants while salesmen wear knotted ties with company logos and have no access to secretaries, in working hours. The marketeer will tell you he does the cerebral part, the strategic analysis and so forth; deciding what the customers will want to buy at the time you have it available to sell, while the reps are merely out there banging on doors and booking orders. The salesman will say that without marketing experience he would be unable to persuade anyone to buy from him. Your job is to bang their heads together.

Some wise people say that you can never understand marketing unless first you have tried your hand at selling. I remember one successful Chairman who thought that was right.

* Spirax Sarco has long been a market leader in control instrumentation. I knew the Chairman in the sixties who had anticipated both industrial and domestic trends, the right products being available just as customers found they needed them. He told me he had not picked up much to forward his business career from his studies at Cambridge. On coming down and unable to find another job in the recession, he had hawked the Encyclopaedia

Britannica from door to door for six months. That was the school in which he had been trained.

Your budget will tell you what your sales team has to achieve. Salesmen are expensive to keep on the road, and even more so in the air. You must be sure that someone actually manages the sales force from day to day – the journeys, the visit reports and correspondence, the quotations and follow-ups, and the administration. Because a good Sales Manager is likely to be anywhere but at his desk – a whiff of kerosene sees most of them instantly airborne – you need to be sure there is always someone in the office managing while he is away, and in most firms while he is there too. Regular customers come to rely on the Sales Office Manager as their eyes and ears in the factory. A good one is a treasure indeed.

Every now and then you need to check up on the way salespeople are planning their trips. In Globe Elastic Thread I tried for years to discourage our multi-lingual continental rep from criss-crossing France, driving frantically and expensively from a customer in Normandy to another on the Belgian border, and back to Rouen to see a third. Travelling salesmen lead a tough life and you have to tolerate some eccentricity. All the same, it's worth going with them occasionally. You may even learn something.

* The same salesman visited customers in the textile region centred on St Étienne. That meant flying to Lyons and visiting both historic cities like Le Puy and distant towns like Ambert. Why then, on my first trip, were we climbing though darkness, fog and ice to the remote mountain village of Yssingeaux? As the minutes passed and my hunger became more acute, so did my disaffection at this irrational deviation.

* I changed my mind quite early in the dinner. On later trips I too found Yssingeaux admirably situated as a resting place.

There is no point in seeing a regular customer too often or wasting time with small talk if he is busy. People travelling from afar have a tendency to hang about, as if the length of their visit has to reflect the distance they have come. If all is well and you have the order cover you need, get down the road, if only to have a break before your next call. Conversely, even the closest customer can be lost if you fail to keep in touch with him, or persist in giving the buyer lunch when decisions are really being made in the drawing office.

Each customer visit is justified if it establishes whether or not there is a sales opportunity. When the target firm is buying the product, but from the competition, you should be able to find out why – price, presentation, quality or just habit. Sometimes it pays to hang in there, with occasional visits, in case the competitor starts slipping. Occasionally you find a buyer in a competitor's pocket; even if you suspect bribery or kick-backs, forget it. Nobody will give you credit for blowing the whistle. But don't squander your resources by allowing people to pound too often on closed doors.

There are four types of market and each of them needs a differing approach if your team is to be used to best effect. By analysing your customers' perception of the product, you avoid spending time and money on activities which won't affect his judgment. You are hunting in a jungle where the rifle is of more use than the scatter-gun. Bridport-Gundry's netting was sold through each of the four markets, by retail, as a commodity, as a branded product and as a component. It is therefore convenient to use netting to illustrate the various approaches a manufacturer can take to these markets.

Retail

Selling direct to the public by a manufacturer, by retail, involves giving the customer a wide enough choice in a convenient location at a competitive price. Cutting out the middlemen when you have manufactured in bulk should result in higher margins. You will find however that retailing calls for skills, overheads, credit management and systems of stock control which are unfamiliar to most manufacturers. To attract customers into the store, you have to carry a wider range of goods than your own. As well as selling the range of netting you produce, skippers will want netting you don't make, knotless perhaps, or treated twisted nylon, which means you end up buying from competitors. And the customer who comes in for nets also wants twine, ropes, buoys, floats, shackles, pins, baskets, shovels, oilskins, filters, pumps, gloves, boots, warps, paint and other bits and pieces.

Unless therefore you have a compelling reason to set up a shop or use mail order, leave it to the experts. If you only sell direct, through your own outlets, you are far more vulnerable to recession than you would be using conventional distribution channels, any fall in retail sales passing directly to your production call-off. With netting, there is a compelling reason to go direct: you won't sell so many of your own made-up trawls, at up to £40,000 a go, if you don't also sell chandlery in the port. Happily for Bridport-Gundry, retail sales take only a small part of the overall production and the Marine Division, which managed the chandlery side, was treated as a separate, and unfavoured, customer by the factory.

You have to find the right site for your shop and, as ever, to study the buying habits of your customers. If you are selling to professional skippers, you don't want weekend yachtsmen cluttering up the store for half a coil of rope. Skippers tend only to shop when their boats are tied up for painting, bad weather or, increasingly of late, quota restrictions. They like to mooch around for hours, chewing the fat, and then take away what they buy. That means providing somewhere they can park.

* Bridport-Gundry's original Lowestoft store was near the quay with a useful private yard at the side. A local firm of solicitors made what seemed a good offer for the yard, to use as their car park, and it was accepted. As the shoals of herring shrank, many trawlers moved away but Lowestoft remained a good centre for the East Anglian coast, with its wide variety of inshore and other fishing.

* Then one day some workmen painted double yellow lines in the road outside the shop. Traffic wardens trawled a fine harvest for a few weeks among the visiting skippers until their overfishing also took its toll and the catch vanished. The local trade was limited to four ships. The shop was sold and it was some years before the company found other suitable premises in the port.

Commodity

Netting is also a commodity, a product which users will buy in bulk from whichever source is cheapest, given reliability and convenience. These sales are attractive to the factory because they often lead to long production runs, and a quiet life. You cannot expect customer loyalty. If he can find the product cheaper anywhere, you lose the business no matter how much wine you pour into the Chief Buyer, and cheaper includes how much credit is on offer as well as marginal costing and subsidising freight.

With a commodity, your sales office needs to know every day what your competitors are up to in terms of availability and price; often they will tell you because they need the same information about you if you are not both going to be crucified by customers playing one off against the other. Your sales office manager requires the alertness of a bookmaker, damping down demand by raising prices when he is overloaded and rustling up work at short notice to fill in empty production slots. Add a VDU tuned in to the money market, a telephone and a fax, and customer visits become social and gastronomic occasions.

There are instances too where a branded product can more profitably be sold as a commodity. There's no point in spending money promoting the brand image and calling on customers if that doesn't increase your sales.

> * Air cargo nets retain the contents of the hold in place so that they don't fly loose if the plane hits an air pocket, rupturing the floor above and causing the rapid and involuntary deplaning of adjacent passengers. So long as they comply with the appropriate safety regulations, airlines can pick up the nets wherever they fly, avoiding problems of freight and duty. Price is therefore the key element in the choice of supplier.

> * The American manufacturer sold by telexing his price weekly to all potential users. The German operated a normal sales structure for a branded product. The French copied the British product, marked up the price and sold to Air France. In England, Bridport-Gundry managed its sales with a single office manager/salesman, offering the refinement of colour coded nets to try to cut down the persistent pilfering by Third World airlines.

> * The American, the French and the British prospered. The German failed.

Branded Product

A 'branded' product need not, for our present purposes, carry a brand name but is an article of general application not readily interchangeable with something being offered by a competitor. Sheet netting, sold in bulk in the condition in which it leaves the machine, is a commodity. You can buy the identical product in England, Norway, Belgium or Portugal; and in the Far East, too, if you can tolerate the inflexibility of ordering months in advance. If you convert the sheets into trawl netting, with its precise mesh-size heat-set to avoid it being confiscated, along with the catch, by Fishery Protection patrols, the product has just about moved over the dividing line into being branded.

We will come to the subject of brands later. Here let us note that coding a product which is being sold for a specific use has a serious purpose beyond mere advertisement. A trawl may scoop up a hundred tons of fish, rock, weeds and rubbish from the sea, the weight being concentrated in the part last to be winched inboard. If the knots in the netting or the twine itself are not properly set, a four-inch mesh can become three, which is bad news when the inspectors pull alongside and get their rulers out.

Some customers really believe you supplied the defective product they return to you. If they've just gone to court for using an illegal mesh size, you need to be able to prove you didn't. Others know it wasn't yours, but try it on. It takes dabbling in US procurement to come across really evil intent.

* Brownell, Bridport-Gundry's New England subsidiary, started supplying camouflage netting to the government, which upset the firms who had been dividing up the business between them. Just before a multi-million dollar order for netting was to be placed with Brownell as the lowest bidder, the authorities in St Louis received from an unnamed source some 'Brownell' netting which was off specification.

* Unknown to the competition, Brownell had woven a single invisible thread into their twine and were able to prove the defective netting hadn't come from them. However in the two weeks it took to sort things out, so urgent was Uncle Sam's need to place the order (which had been kicking around for months) that St Louis had had to go back to the higher bidder. Ah well, that's tough. Don't worry. There'll be another requisition in a year or so. We'll think up another dirty trick next time round. And they did.

Your salespeople have to stay close to customers with branded products, keeping them aware of any changes you may be introducing. The customer also needs stroking by being fed and fussed over: a function of the trade show is to let him have a good day out. If you make a visit with the regular salesman, guard against grandstanding. The buyer may well have saved an order to celebrate your visit but the credit must go to the fellow who pegs away, month in, month out.

You will know that sometimes you have to sell a commodity as though it were branded, especially where a retailer like Marks and Spencer seeks to exercise quality control over every component of its clothing. Elastic thread is the typical commodity, but not in Baker Street.

* The agent which stops rubber thread shrinking when it is washed has a slight tendency to yellow as it oxidises, causing almost imperceptible staining on white garments. You can arrest the process by adding formalin to the recipe, but customers don't like that either. If I talked about the phenomenon of hysteresis, I would confuse both of us. Suffice it to say that Baker Street wanted a property from extruded rubber thread which was only to be found in cut thread, a process where latex is calendered and then sliced.

* So Marks and Spencer continued to use cut thread in their men's underpants. Cut thread tends to roll, distorting the waistband and making the garment less comfortable to wear. If the buyer had been a man, I suspect she would have put up with the yellowing. After one pair from St Michael, I went back to Y-fronts which used extruded thread.

You can give salesmen latitude in taking orders for branded products, except on delivery times and credit. We will deal with 'specials' later. For the most part, you can discourage modifications to your standard product by putting the price up. Sometimes customers are irrational, but you have to take them seriously. If the same shoal of mackerel can only be caught in green netting from one port, in blue from another and in black by the fellows up the coast, do not waste breath by debating with skippers the ocular phenomena associated with piscine colour-awareness. It's no big deal switching from one colour of twine to another. You don't even have to break a machine down.

Component

Now for what, in default of a better term, we have chosen to call components, things which are incorporated into another's specific product or system and not saleable by you in that form to a third party. For the benefit of anyone outside industry whose eye chances to light on this page, we should explain that this is an area of huge demand, where selling is especially important. A power station, for example, may involve 3,000 suppliers or sub-contractors, many of them with their own further network of component suppliers. Many old industries – aircraft and car manufacture, shipbuilding too before we sentenced it to a lingering death by nationalisation – exist on the back of their vendors; and so do modern businesses, like telecommunications and electronics.

The path to having your product selected can be as tortuous as the result can be pleasing. Your people may have to work in tandem with the Buyer or Sub-Contracts Manager, and the design office. The earlier in the project you become involved, the larger the risk but the greater the reward if it goes ahead. Sometimes you have done everything right, having your prototype incorporated in the system and enduring months of modifications and tests only to see the project manager buying a Chinese copy from a competitor, which he justifies as being cheaper in the production run. Of course it is, if you have picked up the non-recurring costs. How he justifies that new car in the park is his business.

Still with netting, the nets which stop your luggage in overhead racks falling out and braining your neighbours are components. So were the nets Bridport supplied for the de Lorean car.

Managing and supervising a sales force is so important that it has to follow a system and routine. By putting customers into the right categories, you can concentrate your effort and minimise expense; use the rifle, to repeat our earlier image. Even if you don't see the visit reports, ensure that they are scrupulously made and properly dealt with. The monthly management accounts will tell you how orders are coming in, and what change of emphasis is needed if they are off budget.

Watch your competitors closely. Place a standing order for their filed accounts and, if they are publicly owned, buy a few shares so as to receive their reports. House magazines are especially valuable because they contain more of the truth than other publications, employees being harder to hoodwink than shareholders and the City.

So far we have been looking at selling in our home market principally, to non-government customers and ignoring 'specials'. That leaves a minefield untrod, in which lurk agents, distributors, licensees, stockists and all manner of surprises. We also need to address our minds to contractual conditions.

CHAPTER 5

More about Selling and Marketing

'... use your own tongues;
Let every eye negotiate for itself,
And trust no agent.'
                    Shakespeare

Many of us have to sell abroad because our home market is too small to allow us to manufacture efficiently. Only a masochist starts attacking foreign markets before he has mopped up demand at home and driven out as many imports as he can, which is why so many quite large American companies do not export at all. Over here, it is not a strategy which will lead the Queen to think about you on her birthday, but, if you can afford to adopt it, you will spend many more nights in the comfort of your own bed, for which there is much to be said.

No businessman would pronounce anything as daft as 'Exporting is fun'. When Macmillan and I shared a VC10 to Canada many years ago, I observed he was travelling in greater style than I was. I still have the BOAC Flight Guide which he autographed, stacked appropriately beside some Lido programmes from the Champs-Elysées and other memorabilia of a demanding life frittered away in hard stations. Young people unthinkingly say they want a career which involves travelling and meeting people, by which they do not mean as a ticket collector or lorry driver. The seasoned traveller wants to stay home and meet nobody, although some contacts are unavoidable and others even stick in the memory when time has thankfully erased the catalogue of delays and diversions, drab lounges and plastic meals which the years have accumulated.

I now recognise on screen the actor I chatted to on the way to New York; he had been genuinely delighted to meet someone who knew neither his face nor his name. I don't think I would identify again the Scandinavian pop singer who unburdened herself to me on the way to Copenhagen, although my children said she was more famous than royalty. My favourite encounter was with a sales engineer, again in mid-Atlantic; learning that I lived in Somerset, he asked me if I knew Margaret Holder. There was, it transpired, a plausible explanation for his being familiar with my wife.

You are unlikely to succeed in supplying an overseas market on a regular basis unless you have somebody on the ground to keep his eye on things for you. The time may come when you set up your own local organization but until then you need a third party to handle the product and be quickly available to the customers, whether as agent, dealer, factor or stockist.

The Bard, as usual, is on the ball when he tells us to use our own tongue. So long as you have someone in the firm totally at ease with the native language, you should aim to deal with the customer direct. For most British firms, that means the customer's first language must also be English. In other cases, however good your customer's English may be, it is a question of good manners and good sense to obtain the services of a fluent linguist. Other nationalities than the French also worry about this. Speaking the language is alone sufficient reason to use an agent. Even if you have a salesman who passes for a native, your technical staff and others visitors will need help on their trips from someone who can interpret, knows the product and has an interest in seeing it sold.

Overseas travelling is expensive in both time and fares. A good agent helps keep the cost down as well as sorting out the inevitable documentation problems. Simply by being there, with a local phone and fax, he provides a degree of comfort to indigenous customers. If your product has technical applications, ensure that he is well trained and updated. The more commission he earns, the more time he can afford to devote to your affairs. A good agent is a predator who needs regularly to catch game, a vampire who needs constantly to taste blood.

Theatrical agents are a byword for unreliability and we will never know whether Shakespeare was speaking from experience when he wrote 'Trust no agent'. Possibly he had been fobbed off with 'Don't call me – I'll call you' once too often. You can place most confidence in an agent who makes a living handling only your product. When he has other lines, watch out for conflicts: he may just be using you as a filler, or a lead for his other principals. If he has been recommended by a customer as a condition of placing the order, pay attention to the alarm bells.

I had a costly and unhappy experience when I trusted an agent for whom our product was peripheral to his other activities.

* Globe used in Switzerland an agent whose main business lay in promoting the sale of another type of textile to the same potential customers. Indeed his consenting to represent us came over as something of a favour, based perhaps on the days his predecessor and mine had spent between tee and green. As the agent refused to deal with our European rep, the quarterly tour fell on my shoulders.

* On my last trip, a major customer brought up a complaint over

quality. I need hardly tell you that a customer who uses your product in an application for which it was not designed or which is outside the specification will not take that as an excuse if the product proves inadequate. If you know that is likely to happen, you refuse to supply, but in this case I didn't know until I was in the buyer's office and facing the complaint. There was no question: the thread, uncovered and in that particular application, was imperfect.

* The buyer said he would never order from us again unless I agreed there and then to raise a credit note to cover the cost of the entire consignment and the damaged material. The agent backed him. I foolishly and weakly agreed.

* Soon after we found out that the firm had decided to get out of that particular business anyway and would never have placed more orders. I hope the agent hadn't known that. We still fired him.

I made four mistakes. I should never have kept on an agent with a conflict of interest, especially when he refused to deal with our rep. I should have given the factory a chance to look at the complaint before conceding any liability. I should have limited the damage to the cost of the thread. And I shouldn't have gone myself, leaving no Jorkins in the back room for my Spenlow to consult before conceding anything. It's an old, and nasty, trick, screwing your supplier on a bogus claim when trade is bad or you have already decided to get out.

When a potential customer tells you that you must appoint a specific agent, especially if he names a domestic competitor, you should walk away. Unfortunately with Dassault and the F1 I didn't.

* Recording speed through the sound barrier is a tricky business because static vents, which factor the pitot reading, cease to function as the bang approaches. We discovered in Avimo that a certain configuration of static vent on the fuselage much improved the readings. I duly explained this in St Cloud and the device was

the only British equipment selected for the aircraft, conditional on our appointing our French competitor as our agent and licensee.

* After delivering the prototypes I don't think we received another order or any royalties, although when I came to make F1's in Belgium some years later, I seem to recall they all carried compensated static vents.

* My guard had been lowered by some subtle flattery. When I was leaving St Cloud, the engineer said his goodbyes in perfect English. I suggested that we might more profitably have conducted our affairs in that medium during the past couple of hours. 'Ah, no,' he replied. 'You are the only British or American engineer who has ever introduced his product to me in my own language.'

Never neglect a good agent because he is out of sight. Above all, and this should be our Sixth Commandment – Never try to bilk an agent of his commission. A rider to that is to be chary of trying to reduce his percentage even when it seems disproportionate to his effort or involvement. If you really cannot afford to pay a certain rate of commission and still stay in the market, talk it over with him. The common proposition that you should never pay more to an agent than your own profit is an emotional rather than a logical reflex. A successful agent is seldom short of principals, and you will be lucky to be one of them.

You should try to ensure that your agents operate under the same disciplines of planning and reporting as your employed salesmen. Never pay commission except on the basis of achievement, and then only after the customer has paid you. Other than when you ask him to visit your factory or attend sales conferences or exhibitions, do not volunteer to pay his expenses. If he cannot finance his business, he is unlikely to be the right man for you. However much you use him to chase up bad payers, insist that any cash he receives is banked in your name.

The appointment of an agent is much too important a matter to be delegated to a junior salesman. It may well be reasonable to give him the exclusive right to represent you in a territory or for a product, so long as the conditions are spelt out in advance; indeed, a competent agent will be reluctant to invest his time, experience and money building up your business without that kind of protection. You try to get away with non-exclusivity if you can; if you cannot, make sure that the operative law allows you to terminate the agency without penal damages or ongoing commitment. You have to retain the facility to stay with your customers even if you fall out with the agent, or to change agents.

Occasionally you will be pressed to pay commission in advance. Your salesmen have been persuaded that the Lebanese gentleman operating out of the Ritz and leaving the barman £5 tips is cousin to a clutch of Arabian princes and emirs. The moment you make a contribution to the sweeteners he has to disburse on your behalf, the order will be yours. It is certainly true that one of the signs that you are in the running for a big order in many parts of the world is this jinni whose appearance can be as sudden as his powers are magical. He will know the number of the tender and the amount of your bid. Unless you retain him with a large sum paid in a hard currency outside his home country, you will lose the order. You will even hear from the close relative of an African president, whose lectures on moral issues to the West in general and Mrs Thatcher in particular brought tears to the eyes of every bishop in the land. (We declined to forward £10,000, lost the order and the firm which took it went bankrupt later.)

What these characters tell you is often true. Pay up or else. Stick with else. Never pay commission in advance. As usual, I was to get it wrong.

* On a trip to Jordan about something else, I was asked to see if I could unblock an order for military equipment worth about

£1.8m. A prominent lawyer persuaded me that a retainer to his firm might help to move things in the right direction.

* I returned convinced – rightly as it transpired – that the wheels were indeed turning again. It was less satisfactory to discover that three other agents had already inserted themselves into the deal, to a total of 19% of the price. As Her Majesty was funding the purchase anyway, it must have seemed like Boxing Day to our desert friends.

(Not all trips are tedious. We left London on a Friday after a day's work, did our business on Saturday morning, visited a deserted and wholly fascinating Jerash in the afternoon and dined in state that evening. On Sunday we went to Petra, flying back overnight by Baghdad to restart work in London on Monday morning. We had also managed, so it transpired, to set in motion the recovery of a multi-million pound debt for bankers who had written it off.)

The Seven Deadly Sins represent eternal truth. Avarice and gluttony reveal themselves in inverse proportion to the maturity of the society in which they are observed. However severe the sanctions, bribery is endemic in business conducted outside Northern Europe, North America and the Antipodes: and present in those regions also, especially when people on fixed incomes are in a position to spend other people's money.

Those of us intending to remain in business without having to conduct it from the Costa Blanca or a prison cell are careful not to allow our firms, or ourselves, be tainted by offering bribes or accepting kick-backs. Naturally you deplore paying extortionate commissions or consultancy fees, even though they are added to the selling price. What the recipients do with those fees is up to them. In the days of Exchange Control, the need to reveal such payments to the Bank of England put some gloss of legality on paying bribes by proxy. These days, unprotected by bureaucracy, ensure that all about you behave with caution and outward propriety.

We observed earlier, in passing, that Bridport-Gundry supplied nets for the de Lorean car. Along with many others, the account remained unpaid.

> * The $17½ million paid by the gullible British government to develop the two-seater sports car was transferred abroad, and then misappropriated, with a gloss of legality because of Bank of England approval. As Sir Kenneth Cork remarked (*Cork on Cork*, Macmillan) 'Accounts were certified yet the whole misappropriation was successfully concealed ... So when questions were asked outside the company the answer was given that it had received Bank of England approval.' (Sir Kenneth's book is a rattling good yarn, larded with sound advice. I much regret that he did not live to see the publication of this book, about which he was so generous and enthusiastic.)

The world of the fixer is unsavoury, unfair and dangerous. We sold six lifeboats to the Shah's Iran from Groves and Gutteridge without any bribes: the Admiral responsible lost his job and the contracts manager his head. Perhaps our probity, and theirs, contributed to their dire fate. Avimo, with Ministry of Defence approval, supplied an African general with one hundred times the recommended scale of plotting boards for his single battery of guns, at double price less 50% commission. The general's action, and ours, was to be deplored, yet less harmful to the human condition than that of the minister in the same country who drew funds for high quality American rice, bought inferior grain in south-east Asia at a third of the cost and sold it on his controlled market at the higher price. That earner was worth a quick billion or two in US dollars. If you are so much as suspected of indulging, however unjustly, in that kind of business, it is essential to get your loot and your body offshore without undue delay. So long as you remain in exile, your life will be safe, provided you stay clear of packing-cases in remote airports. Dead men tell no numbers of Swiss bank accounts.

You cannot remain unaware of corruption whatever your business; and, at a certain level, you cannot stand totally aloof from it either, any more than Henry Ford could eventually ignore body styling. People are greedy, and greed is a condition which culture, comfort or affluence may temper but will not extinguish. The more the sophistication, the greater the sophistry.

You don't believe me? You would if you had been manufacturing surgical sutures, in James Pearsall, with its consequent insight into the behaviour of those most respected and upright members of our community, the medical profession. Have you never wondered how, ill-paid as they claim to be, the members of the British Medical Association can afford, spouse on arm, to congregate in far-off, albeit agreeable, climes for their conferences and such? Why does the National Health Service, starved as it constantly tells us it is for funds, pay up to eight times as much as its European counterparts for pills, potions and consumable stores? What drives the surgeon to reject a less expensive product, flinging it angrily across the Health Service theatre floor, while he uses nothing else in those operations for which he is paid privately? What motivates the general practitioner to prescribe proprietary medicines and proscribe the unbranded alternative which would suffice, at a fraction of the cost? Why, if things are as bad as the doctors claim, is there so much resistance to change?

The boundaries between greed, corruption, bribery and theft are not capable of fine definition. The best a manufacturer can do is to distance his firm, and himself, from overt impropriety. This applies especially in the United States where, despite draconian laws to the contrary, business can be rough, dirty and corrupt.

We seem to have drifted into a series of insalubrious but

cautionary tales, the telling of which has been muted by the laws of libel. Let us reflect that, with such rich pickings in prospect, con-men are sure to gather around the kill. You only succeed as a con-man if you are plausible; the con-agent will therefore be extremely convincing. He has however one distinguishing mark, his absolute necessity to secure cash up front.

I have seen tough and experienced businessmen tricked by these rogues, among whom I give the palm to a Frenchman in the seventies whose entourage and patter hooked a manager in Fairey and would have caught a second in Bridport-Gundry, had I not listened to his asides during a meeting in a London hotel. (You don't always let on what languages you understand.) When you allow yourself to be tricked by these people, you pay twice: you waste money and you effectively cut yourself off from a potential market.

There is no formula for finding the right representation. Ensure that someone has at least thought through what you are looking for in terms of location, skill, technical support, contacts and so on. Sometimes the people in the Embassy can help you, or the British Overseas Trade Board. More often you will be approached at a trade show or, as we have noted, receive a recommendation from a customer.

You now know what to look out for and what to guard against. When you employ a good agent, cherish him, if only for his scarcity value.

CHAPTER 6

Still more about Selling and Marketing

*'Let the measure of your affirmation or denial be the under-
standing of your contractor; for he that deceives the buyer or
the seller by speaking what is true in a sense not understood by
the other, is a thief.'*

Jeremy Taylor

* Jeremy Taylor, Doctor of Divinity, was one of those men of the
cloth who, like Mr Norris, lived in stirring times. Laud must have
had a roving eye because Taylor, like other young clerics in those
years, received his notice and favour, including a recommendation
to a fellowship at All Souls, despite his Cambridge birth and
education. Being created a Doctor by royal mandate in 1642, he
was bound to the royal cause and army by gratitude as by
conviction, his soldiering coming to an end when taken prisoner
before Cardigan Castle in February, 1644–45. After brief incar-
ceration, he surfaced teaching at what might today be termed a
crammer's at Llanfilhangel-Abebythych and it was in that remote
and improbable spot that he wrote the sapient lines quoted above.

* Taylor found himself in London at the time of the king's
execution and on hand to receive not only the royal watch but also
a few pearls and rubies from the ebony case in which the king kept

his bible. He was still there in 1654 when Evelyn heard him preaching. Perhaps he should have kept quiet because he soon found himself behind bars in Chepstow Castle, and again in the same prison for a few months in 1655. Yet when he decided in 1658 to remove himself to a parish near Lisburn, Cromwell granted him a safe conduct 'under his sign manual and privy signet'. No doubt the Protector knew what he was doing when he sped the passage of the unrepentant episcopalian to 'that sweet land across the Irish Sea'.

* Come the Restoration, Taylor found himself Bishop of Down and Connor, Prochancellor of Trinity College and called upon to preach in Dublin on the great occasions of state. In his diocese, however, he was to meet only contention and strife until he died in 1667, being no more able to reach an accommodation with the Scots/Irish Presbyterians among his flock than are the other occupants of that beautiful country today.

We postponed our consideration of the dilemma created by the 'special', along with that of conditions of sale and selling to government. With Taylor's admonitions on integrity ringing in our ears, let us look at these three aspects of selling seriatim, the specials first.

For our purposes, a special is a product outside the standard production range either sold as a one-off, a single example; or in usually limited production for a specific application. We have noted that many industrial products and projects rely on a large number of suppliers and sub-contractors. Many of these will be selling specials, items designed, developed, tested, tooled and manufactured for a single end use. Do not confuse specials with own-branding – packaging and labelling a product so that it leads the buyer to believe your customer produced it himself; that causes no problems because the differentiating processes come at the end of the production cycle. Own-branding is good news insofar as it increases demand for a standard product. Specials may or may not be.

Before accepting an order for a special, you need, as ever, to marshal the facts so that the risks and opportunities can be assessed. Your check sheet reads as follows:

Is the item to be supplied for an existing firm project or are you being asked to devote resources to a speculative venture?

If the venture is speculative, what is the competition your customer is likely to face?

How much of the non-recurring costs – development, tooling, test equipment, field trials, prototypes and so on – are you going to be expected to carry or amortise?

What is the likely production call off, at what rate and over what period? (You need to know this if you are amortising fixed costs. If all else fails, take the customer's estimate and divide by five.)

Will your product remain proprietary to you or will your customer start looking for a cheaper source when the venture develops?

Are there any plans for oversea manufacturing or licensing?

What will it do to your cash flow?

How would it affect your market position if you turned the order down and let a competitor in?

How badly will it hurt if the project fizzles out and would there be anything to salvage from the wreck?

If you decide to go ahead, ensure that you incorporate in your product every casting, circuit board, lens system or other component which you already have, curbing the natural penchant of the drawing office to start with a clean sheet of paper. Defer any tool design until the drawings are sealed. And authorise only minimal work to be done before you have an agreed specification. We nearly came to grief over that when enthusiasm replaced caution in Delta Communications.

* In some American hotels the room telephones have rotary dials

and the switchboard cannot tell from which extension a call is being originated. The operator can ask, but won't always get the right answer. The billing problems include not being able to charge for calls, charging them to the wrong room and arguments with people who cheat.

* Delta was owned 30% by Mitel in Canada. Mitel had a US subsidiary offering a piece of equipment which, combined with a Call Logging Indicator (CLI), would identify the extension originating the call. Delta had the technical capability to develop the CLI. As these hotel switchboards were obsolescent and being gradually replaced, we had to hit the market fast. The salesmen in Delta's customer, based in Washington, wanted quick delivery; their technical people, away in Florida or Texas, had higher priorities than agreeing the specification for a device to be made in Ireland. Ah well, it's a sister company. We can't let them down. Delta had spent IR£200,000 before the salesmen found the product was less saleable than they had hoped, and didn't work with every switchboard in the configuration in which it had been produced. Had Delta built it to specification? Nobody could say, as none had been agreed. Was there a contract, without a specification? Not really.

* The Managing Director of Delta and I flew to Dulles, went to an hotel, agreed and signed a contract, went back to Dulles and flew home again. A stewardess trod on my unshod toe when I was asleep on the way back, which later provided a souvenir, of a sort. We managed to get paid for most of our CLI's but I believe there is still a stock of them available out there, if you're looking for one.

Avimo carved out its position in the guidance, control and test instrumentation for guided missiles by hazarding £500 to design a monocular sight for the prototype Vickers Vigilant anti-tank missile when Vickers' own optical subsidiary declined to do it on a risk-sharing basis. As you might expect, not all our speculations were so fortunate and later, when we broke every rule, we were made to suffer.

* After the early Comet fatigue disasters, the plane survived as the basis of the Nimrod, in maritime surveillance. To measure the wind speed at sea level and drift, the crew dropped a smoke flare and observed it through the belly of the aircraft. This required a rotating unit-vision instrument, the On-top Drift Sight – effectively a nine-foot telescope built to an aeronautical specification with a revolving head.

* Unit-vision (seeing things the same size) calls for magnification of a tenth. Roll a bit of paper and look down it for yourself, if you doubt me. More of a problem is all-round vision because when you rotate the object glass, the image topples. What with one thing and another, we were being asked for a quite complex optical system. Unfortunately our salesman was not sufficiently technical to realise that.

* The buyer told him that our main competitor would supply the sights at £1,800 each, including development and tooling. He took the order at a fraction less for some 18 instruments. In those days companies didn't renege, and de Havilland was buying various other things from us too. The gear train alone cost £1,800.

* If we'd known what Marconi was to get away with as contractor for the AWACS system on the same project, we might not have been so stoical. At least the On-top Drift Sight worked.

The painful lesson was still being learnt month by month when I received a telephone call on Saturday, 26th March, 1969, summoning me to Burbank for a meeting at 10 o'clock the following Monday. These days we think nothing of picking up tickets at the airport and arriving in a distant land with no currency and two pairs of underpants. Then there was no plastic, but I still made it. The anecdote which follows shows that even the slowest-witted can learn from their mistakes, so long as the mistakes have been sufficiently painful.

* When the Lockheed 10-11, later known as the Tristar, was being developed, Avimo had quoted for some of the instruments. There were close links in those days between British aeronautical suppliers and American aircraft design offices because most design teams over there were led by refugees from the Sandys persecution of the aircraft industry. This particular project leader came from Bristol and was delighted to tell me we had won the contract for the pitot and pitot-static heads.

* In the meeting they produced the contract. We were elevated to being 'participants' in the programme. Read on, cut the garbage, and you learn that all non-recurring costs are to be amortised over the first fifty production aircraft, and the supplier will only be paid when Lockheed has had its cash. They couldn't see my problem. Rolls Royce had signed up on identical terms.

* My people were sorry when I came back empty handed. My wife sold her few Rolls Royce shares for 34/6d. Lockheed almost went bust too. If we'd been really smart, we'd have bought back into Rolls Royce for a penny.

It pays from time to time to review your products, looking for specials which have insinuated themselves into the standard range, or standard products where demand has fallen to the extent that they bear all the characteristics of specials. The false strength of sterling in 1981 brought foreign elastic thread pouring into the United Kingdom just as it was becoming ever harder to export from Globe. To survive, we had to double the output with half the labour force. That could only be done by ruthless standardisation, which would allow week-long runs on the extruders making tonnes of a single type and colour of thread. We reduced the number of standard lines from 55 to 17, the number of 'whites' from five to one , even eliminating what the trade felicitously calls 'white white'. Within weeks we were back in profit. Why hadn't we acted sooner? That's a good question.

In any sales negotiation, there is only one chance to agree the conditions, which is before you book the order. You are better off with a lower price and security of payment whatever blandishments the customer may offer to entice you into becoming his supplementary banker, or worse. Who pays for insurance and carriage, the acceptance of penalty clauses, inspection, packaging and a host of other items have to be settled, but the core of it is cash. Nothing is so irrecoverable as a bad debt.

Ideally, we manufacture everything to order and hold no completed goods anywhere. In this imperfect scheme of things, we are lucky to get away with holding stocks in our own premises against expected orders. Some products, particularly spares, bulky commodities and short-order goods, have to be readily available for customers who are too remote to depend on service from the factory. If the distributor won't pay to hold them, you may have to live with consignment stocks.

Consignment stocks of spares are not too damaging because the margins are high and you can always divert them else-where, so long as there haven't been too many 'shrinkages' – better known as theft. Most distributors will accept as much inventory at your expense as they can comfortably store. You need to keep it at the minimum, and to ensure that sales are regularly reported. Every time you take physical inventory, you will find discrepancies. Before trusting consignment stocks to distributors in places like the Philippines, Panama or Pakistan, consult a psychiatrist. You should leave charitable giving to Oxfam and the other do-gooders.

You need to be sure of your customer before you trade at home on open account, and doubly sure if he is abroad. Indeed, our Seventh Commandment is – Do not give open credit to foreigners. We have already noted that it is unwise to run currency risks and we can save bank commissions by matching material purchases with sales. An unconfirmed letter of credit is worth very little. If confirmed, the confirmation must be by a bank in a reliable country, not merely by one with a familiar name. Barclays Bank in Lagos as confirming house is just another Nigerian bank, and you know what that means.

To collect on a Letter of Credit, its terms must be scrupulously complied with. The commonest problem is getting extensions for late delivery even if the customer has failed to send his inspector or there are no available ships. The Russians don't like Letters of Credit and you will normally be safe accepting their promise to settle through the Norodny Bank in London, so long as payment is not expressed to be due 'two weeks after the goods have arrived' somewhere. Once they have disappeared into the vastnesses of Mother Russia, or even across the dockside at Tilbury, you have no means of telling when the condition has been fulfilled.

Cash in advance speaks for itself. Cash against documents is comforting but there are three traps to guard against.

Ports like Bombay become clogged. The master decides to cut his losses and push on to Singapore without unloading, carrying your goods with him.

The goods are off-loaded but the customer decides he doesn't want them or cannot afford them, which leaves you with inventory rotting in some distant shed and demurrage accumulating by the hour.

The nominated carrier, the state, the bank and the customer are a single entity. The carrier hands over the goods without getting the documents signed and the bank refuses to pay. (When it happened to Globe in Poland, it took a threat to the Commercial Attaché of cancellation of a credit line for £100 million to persuade the bank in Warsaw to pay up.)

Do not overlook the advantages of air freight. The packing is cheaper and your documents get signed off at a home airport.

Selling abroad, and especially exporting capital goods, will involve bid, advance payment and performance bonds. Although bid bonds are a costly nuisance, they have the virtue of being discharged quite soon. An advance payment bond is naturally covered by the cash you have received; all the same, the bank will deduct the amount from your overall facilities. A performance bond is a running sore. Some governments, like Nepal, never seem to discharge them; others use the bond as a pretext for screwing spares and maintenance services out of you long after the equipment has been delivered and commissioned. You may find the liability of the bond hanging over you for years, reducing your credit and costing you fees, only to have it called unreasonably; the bank has no option but to pay up and debit your account.

Where long-term credit is involved, insure payment with the Export Credit Guarantee Corporation. If you cannot get cover, leave it alone. You will possibly have to accept 5% or 10% of the risk but if there is talk of a recourse agreement, walk away. And don't leave it to the eleventh hour, as Bridport-Gundry did once.

* I don't like jointly-owned companies: it is difficult for a minority shareholder to exercise proper control. That is why I did not find out the terms on which a company jointly owned by Bridport, a boat builder and an engine maker was proposing to sell a fully equipped trawler to the Gambia. I had supplied vessels before to that part of the world, with all the hassle arising from subsequent breakdowns due to total non-maintenance. However, with ECGD backing the deal, it seemed safe enough.

* Late in the day, too late to draw back, I was asked to hold a short board meeting to approve a joint and several recourse guarantee to ECGD. As our content of the deal was about £10,000 out of more than £350,000, the proposition seemed unattractive. 'But we've already agreed it,' I was told. 'Why then do you need my board's resolution?' I replied.

* ECGD reluctantly accepted several guarantees, each party's liability limited to its sales value. I then had to sell this to the other two chairmen. The boat was delivered, and not maintained. When the bills were unpaid by the customer, the guarantees were called. The boatbuilder ended up in receivership.

If you intend to sell to government, you must learn to live with waste, frustration and stupidity. The Americans say an elephant is a mouse built to a military specification: with the British, it is a camel and a horse. You need the requisite inspection approvals, then to get your name on tender lists and after that, patience. Do not bother about trying to sell to foreign governments because this is one area in which the EC flouts its own rules. The first priority of a public official is to avoid controversy or making decisions, which he does primarily by ensuring the file is in order (or lost, in extreme cases). If you keep your paperwork straight and deliver to specification, even if you deliver late, all will be well.

A government contractor has to obey the rules. If you become too efficient, you will be penalised the next time your costs are investigated; your overhead rate will be lowered and you will be paid less in future. Your object is not to improve the article supplied but to supply what has been ordered. Boats are not made for rocking. Nobody will thank you for criticising a poor design originating from a government development establishment. Do that and next time they may forget to send you the enquiry.

You may receive a design contract, or the design parentage of something someone else has designed. That will give you an advantage on production orders both for home and export markets. To keep the peace, you must learn to bite your tongue. If the Fighting Vehicle Research and Development Establishment was determined to produce a battle tank too heavy to cross Dutch bridges, you may deplore seeing the market handed over to the German Leopard, but you need your share of the action: keep quiet and pray there won't be another war. And when a visiting general asks for the profile of the turret on the prototype to be two inches lower, don't bother to tell him or anyone else what 6 months of redesign of the sighting instruments alone will cost.

I know things are better, or worse for contractors, after the scourge of my old friend and successor as Avimo Chairman, Sir Peter Levene. Let us end then with two tales from the past, to show what he had to contend with.

* Avimo had in 1962 an order for some 200 off Apparatuses Illuminating Dial Sight, a small bronze box which held a battery and bulb, to be clipped on to the no. 9 Dial Sight of the 25-pounder field gun so that the gunlayer could read the verniers at night. Our rather officious Chief Inspector insisted on seeing that the device worked. It didn't. The specified battery didn't fit.

* We applied to the Inspection branch for a Concession or Production Permit. They turned us down, suggesting we talk to the Design Establishment. They refused to amend a drawing which had been used for producing the 'store' to everyone's satisfaction for 18 years. The Contracts Branch were not interested. Production Branch wanted delivery, whether it worked or not. The Supply Reserve Depot complained that they already had surplus stocks and the user, the Royal Artillery, confirmed that they still favoured a candle in a jam jar, just as I used to, in the gunlayer's number 3 seat on night shoots twenty years earlier.

* So we delivered to drawing. It wasn't specifically why we parted company with the Chief Inspector but we couldn't afford both his pay and his conscience.

* We also made the mark 9 pitot-static head for the V bombers. It was bad engineering practice to mill out the static slots around the circumference of the tube instead of punching them because the more metal you removed, the weaker the tube became. Although

not the design parent responsible for drawing changes, we pointed this out to the Ministry, verbally and by letter. If a tube broke while the aircraft was on automatic pilot, the false indication of loss of airspeed would cause the nose to be depressed, quickly turning into a dive from which there might be no recovery.

* The wreckage of the V bomber which crashed off the Isle of Man was recovered from the ocean at great cost, along with the bodies of the crew. After that the design of the pitot-static head was changed. Nobody knew about the letter we had sent and there was certainly no trace of it at St Giles Court.

Happily, it took only 24 hours to approve Raychem's suggestion that anti-radar chaff might be released from the air brakes of the Harrier, once the Falklands War had broken out. The ability to combine physical and electronic evasion techniques no doubt saved several lives and aircraft.

As we have noted more than once, selling consists of making it easier for the customer to buy from you than from your competitor. Easier, or cheaper, when it's their own money; easier, or more reliable, when you are a supplier to another firm; easier, or avoiding personal risk, if selling to a bureaucrat. Selling is where it begins, but production is what brings in the cash, and that is where we go next.

CHAPTER 7

Production

'The best of queens and best of herbs we owe
To that bold nation, which the way did show
To the fair region, where the sun did rise,
Whose rich productions we so justly prize.'

Waller

* Waller, like Dryden, Jeremy Taylor, Milton and other sages from whom our quotations come, pursued his career in the tumultuous years of the mid-17th century. He had the advantage, as an Old Etonian, of being able to abandon his allegiances and his friends with greater élan and less remorse than those of humbler education.

* Some of his better lines were in praise of Oliver Cromwell, on whose demise he penned a less favourable piece which he entitled 'On the death of the late usurper, O.C.' You might have thought that it would have been wiser to keep the quill unsharpened for a month or two while the dust settled but there were no television chat shows then which would transmogrify the nonentity into the celebrity, a talent being a coin rather than the adulation of your peers. The pen and the pulpit were the only devices through which the ambitious might attract attention.

* The Restoration saw Waller back in the fulsome address

71

business. When the Merry Monarch complained that, as a poem, the royal panegyric was inferior to that accorded to Cromwell, Waller replied, 'Poets, Sire, succeed better in fiction than in truth.' This wit so tickled the King that he found Waller a seat in Parliament, not for him a novel experience as he had first sat in the Commons at the age of 16.

* How, we may ask, did Waller, even with the advantage of superior schooling, foresee the emergence of Japan as the industrial super-power? He was not to know that some of the 'rich productions', far from being 'justly prized' are an infernal nuisance. He obviously never tried to read on a train near someone with a 'Walkman'.

Organising and controlling production calls for skills, experience and character greater than are needed for any other management job. The accountant can take his holidays whenever he pleases, so long as he is around during the last of the audit; the designer is seldom seen anyway and, if looking out of the window, is credited with being inventive; the salesman travels the world at his whim. Yet the wretched production man cannot escape for a day, or even an hour, because something is always going wrong. He has the ultimate challenge of dealing with a commodity which is unprogrammable, unreliable and unpredictable – people, whose labour he has to turn into value. He operates under legislation which Murphy enacted on a bad day.

Even when he contributes to the production of the budget, which is seldom because he has little time to spare for meetings, he is expected from above to achieve a programme based on theory; while from below he is contending with the chaos introduced by organised and disorganised labour. As he walks through the shop, he needs to recognise each piece part of every component, sensing before the computer tells him that something is running late. Talk to him in his office and he will break off, alert as a deer at the approach of a hunter, because the thump of the CNC nibbler has ceased for upwards of ninety seconds. His judgment on manning, shifting, batch sizes, tooling, bonus systems, wage rates, recruitment, training, intermediate inspection stages, buffer stocks, machine utilisation, make-or-buy and so on will ultimately determine whether you avoid scrap, satisfy your customers and make profits.

Even when the goods are passed off, packed and in the loading bay, somebody will want to change the programme – to unpack everything, introduce modifications and still meet the original delivery date. Those of you who have for a period of your lives run a production shop will never be as other men. Too many of my friends in production have suffered stress illnesses and early deaths. Although I didn't do it for very long, I'm not feeling too well myself.

Despite his burden, you may well acquiesce in paying your Production Manager less than other senior staff: after all, he didn't go to a public school, did he? What does he need a car for, spending every waking hour in the factory? If you still take him for granted and underpay him after reading this chapter, I hope he walks out on you.

Especially if you've never done the job yourself, you, the boss, must constantly bear in mind what production involves. You need to protect your Production Manager by ensuring that the budget is attainable with the resources he has to hand; and that any additional resources are available in good time. You must stop sales people placing unreasonable demands on the shop, either by promising unrealistic deliveries or accepting changes to programme without prior consultation. You must silence carping criticism from accountants, whose job it is to provide information on which management decisions can be made, not to seek scapegoats or rewrite history. Above all, and hardest, you must see that the firm is run in a way which gives the Production Manager time to relax and think.

Where a factory is involved in a continuous process, or churning out the same product for several different customers, organising the shop floor may be less bothersome. The Production Manager still needs to be around for most of the time to deal with plant breakdowns, power cuts, absenteeism, material shortages, quality problems and the various other snags which emerge from hour to hour. In most factories however life isn't that simple. Even a product so mundane as continuous filament nylon sewing thread can lead you into thousands of product permutations, when different counts, strands, lengths, coatings, shades, packages and labels are taken into account.

We all make the mistake of accepting production forecasts based on what might be achieved in the best of all possible worlds. The production environment is not the best. When Virgil conducted Dante through the Inferno, they never even reached the circle reserved for production managers.

One of the commonest pitfalls is the assumption that labour can be recruited to provide the direct hours called for in the programme. We have all grasped at last that there is no pool of skilled workers available anywhere in the United Kingdom. Some of us still assume that, with politicians banging on about a scandalous rate of unemployment and demonstrators demanding the 'right to work', there are unskilled people out there looking for jobs in factories. As ever, we find the truth the hard way.

* Bridport-Gundry makes camouflage netting by manually adding scrim to nets on set patterns. The contracts are lumpy, so that there is either no work or the need to put on double shifts. The job is simple, boring but relatively well paid. Salesmen take orders from around the world on the basis that so unskilled a workforce can be readily recruited. When there was a surge in demand with tight delivery dates in the summer of 1986, all the expiry dates on

letters of credit and penalties for late delivery seemed acceptable.

* Even production for once saw no problem. After all, the statistics told us there were 470 unemployed people in the Bridport area. Among these, 82 were interviewed as being suitable for this particular job. Of the 82, 9 agreed to work shifts. The others were not prepared to face the changes of lifestyle involved by getting up at five in the morning or missing the pub and the television in the evening, however attractive the shift premium. The firm eventually met its deliveries by bussing students on vacation from 35 miles away.

Occasionally some mandatory external requirement will introduce the need for a production change so difficult of achievement that the company itself is permanently weakened.

* The early stages of The Norman Aeroplane Company's move to Wales went well. The new labour force bettered times on the manufacture of detail parts for the Fieldmaster production and were achieving them on sub-assemblies. Even the wing, which had incorporated elements in its design so as to attract government funding, went together well, despite being a pig to assemble. (We will not pursue here the reasons why a designer chooses an inferior solution in order to achieve government support: common sense and bureaucratic practice are not good bedfellows.)

* Between the design of the prototype and production, the Civil Aviation Authority changed the safety margins which applied to the wing. With the first production set completed, the next two in their jigs and details for the rest of the first batch manufactured, tests revealed that the wing needed strengthening. The design and stress offices achieved this by calling for additional heat treatment to spars and stub ends.

* After this further heat-treatment, the components became almost impossible to machine without distortion and, when machined, difficult to drill for rivets. Despite prodigious efforts on the shop floor, funnelling the best labour to this section at the expense of

progress elsewhere, the Fieldmaster programme proved incapable of achievement within the time and cost budgeted, causing the directors to return to shareholders for further finance, and contributing in part to the eventual failure of the company.

The 19th-century polymaths who fathered the Industrial Revolution trained sufficient all-rounders in their own image to take us into the 20th century. Education at the fitting bench and lathe gave way to the Grammar School, which produced able, disciplined and well taught youths, working as apprentices by day and attending technical classes in the evenings, acquiring by that route the knowledge which their predecessors had picked by example and experience. When we adopted the Comprehensive system, we laid concrete on the seedbed. The progression from apprentice to skilled hand, to chargehand, foreman and shop-superintendent has been stopped. Yesterday's social tinkering with education decreed that factory workers were an underclass. Today we can't attract apprentices or persuade skilled men to assume the role of chargehand. In this respect at least, I would rather not be around British industry tomorrow.

Already your Production Manager therefore is likely to be the least qualified among your senior managers. Where others flaunt their degrees and professional qualifications, he may do well to boast a Higher National Diploma. He will do his job better if you demonstrate by your behaviour and personal support that you consider him in no way – status, perks, pay, board membership – inferior to any other member of the team.

You must ensure that all functional managers have the authority they need to carry out their tasks. This is especially true of the man running the factory. Watch out for financial people who want to take over personnel, or salesmen who cast covetous glimpses at estimating. We will be looking later at who should report to whom: at this stage, suffice it to say that you should not fudge the issues by allowing someone to generate a family tree where dotted lines of partial responsibility lead to the fostering of bastards. As in life itself, disputed parentage leads to a blighted inheritance.

If you think I am giving Production too much of a build-up, take a look at your management accounts and add up the overall items for which your Production Manager is responsible, and the number of people; then compare these figures with the corresponding ones for your Sales, Financial and Development Managers. At the least, this should persuade the driver that the cart has four wheels.

As we have noted, the hardest task of the Production Manager is to manage people. The personnel function, or Human Resources if you wish to go mid-Atlantic, is a barrel of bran into which we will thrust our arm more deeply at an appropriate time, in the hope of extracting some goodies. Happily the tendency among personnel managers to see themselves as a kind of industrial probation officer, casting the employer as the baddie, seems to be in decline although, in the quiet of their private bowers, many still fantasize about being a power-broker between the 'two sides', men and management. Further reflection may remind them which side writes their pay cheque.

There are some formal functions – pay records, statutory returns and the like – where personnel needs to liaise with the company secretary or financial management. When it comes to appraisals, accident reports, hiring, disciplining, issuing warnings, wage negotiations or firing, the boss has to be the Production Manager.

So too with maintenance and security. Company secretaries are often underemployed and there is a temptation for these functions to pass into their control to give them something to do. This may not be harmful if you confine the remit to maintenance of buildings, although you may well find that the temperature in the office block has been raised to enable men to work in shirtsleeves and girls in summer dresses at the expense of shutting down the heat setting plant for want of steam. Mechanical maintenance has to be a production responsibility unless you accept that a squeak in a typist's chair is more important than a seized bearing in your only planer.

Inspection, or Quality Control as modern parlance demands, is a function within a sequence of events leading to delivery of a product and payment by a customer. In some industries – nuclear, aircraft, explosives and the like – the inspectorate must be sufficiently independent that it cannot be coerced by Production. Elsewhere, it is merely another activity, or series of activities, on the job card which has to be properly carried out so that goods can be delivered, lying within the ambit of the Production Manager's authority.

Most Chief Inspectors see things that way. Sometimes a Production Manager will twist an arm too often or too harshly and you have to intervene. If, as with the episode of the Apparatus Illuminating Dial Sight, you decide your Chief Inspector is an inverted Scrooge, always waiting for something to turn down, or persistent delay in passing off goods is leading to poor delivery, you have to authorise the Production Manager to replace him. This may not be as simple as just sacking him and appointing someone else.

Manufacture of anything to do with aeroplanes, nuclear reactors, military hardware and other potentially dangerous or highly technical products is subject to the supervision of outside bodies like the Civil Aviation Authority, the Nuclear Inspectorate and the various bureaucracies set up by the Ministry of Defence. Your inspection arrangements will have been vetted by, and the firm may enjoy delegated powers from, the outside body. The approval or delegation is normally to the Chief Inspector personally, and not to the firm. If you allow him to be sacked without clearing your lines first, you may lose the approvals or delegated powers. As with all dismissals, it pays to record the sequence of misdeeds leading to the rupture, so that you can show why action was taken.

I have not interspersed the foregoing paragraphs with edifying tales drawn from life, as is my wont, not because of a lack of them but because of a plethora. During the week in which I first sketched out this chapter – a week in which I was also drafting a Prospectus (to save lawyers' bills) and settling a legal action (in which my side was entirely in the wrong) – a number of incidents happened on various shop floors of sufficient concern that I came to hear about them.

* Those wing stubs on the Fieldmaster proved incapable of machining within the limits required and because the wing was on the critical path, the project was effectively stopped until a solution was found.

* Nets are made out of monofilament yarn, twisted twine or braids. Bridport-Gundry decided to reduce its reliance on outside twine suppliers by buying a new twisting machine from Germany for £80,000. Procurement was reduced in line with the capacity of the new machine to produce on a double day shift. Because of staff shortages, the machine was only running on single shift, with knock-on effects through the netting shop.

* A customer for braided parachute cords bought them to length. Somebody decided to measure and cut them before treating them. As cord shrinks during treatment, the customer had no product and Crewkerne Textiles had a pile of expensive scrap.

* In the foundry at John Williams we had gone over from manual to auto-pouring. The Italian engineers who supplied and set up the machine had gone home. A gas vent repeatedly blocked, leading to imperfect castings. To accommodate the auto-pourer, much of the manual line had been demolished. By reverting to manual on the emasculated line, we were still losing 1,500 moulds a day, with all that meant to our customers' car production and our costs.

* A Digital Trunk Translator in a Central Office – an international telephone exchange – was picking up spurious tones which were actuating its alarm system, making it effectively inoperative. The main contractor to whom Delta supplied it and who had overall responsibility for the system, had failed to keep a scientific record of the defect. The user, British Telecom International, cannot permit even a partial shut-down of the exchange so that normal detective work can be undertaken. The cause could be underground trains running deep below the building, a software design error, a manufacturing fault, a spurious signal from overseas, a defect in the equipment supplied by the customer: almost anything.

* An accountant from the parent company, newly converted to Just in Time, decreed that Halls, Barton was carrying too much wire in stock. Over a third of the rope-making machines were now stopped, despite clamant customers, due to shortage of raw materials.

Next week some of these problems will have been solved and some will still be around, to be joined by others. A Production Manager faces a new set of exam papers each week, knowing that there are no right answers, only questions set from outside the syllabus. In two of the examples above, the ultimate blame lay with design, and in a third, with a foreign machine supplier. It still fell to the Production Manager to sort things out. Kicking his backside may relieve your frustration but is otherwise counter-productive. Things will be resolved quicker and at less cost if you understand the environment in which they are taking place.

Because output is measured in figures, people tend to look upon production as some kind of mathematical trick: you have the raw materials, the bodies, the machines and the orders, which means that the right substances have to come out of the end of the tube. That will only happen if the Production

Manager also has the feel of things, sensing trouble like an experienced driver, using all his senses and his peripheral vision.

To understand and support him, you too should walk the shop floor when you can, having given notice of your arrival and asked the factory manager to join you. If you spot something wrong, tell him later. If people spring from immobility to action when you appear, that's a bad sign, especially if they were reading an adult comic like the *Mirror* or the *Sun*. You have to point out any safety infringements on the spot but if you hand over your ear muffs to someone using a pneumatic drill without protection, don't expect to see them again. I now have no alternative to hearing speeches at weddings.

After such a build-up for the Production Manager, let us end with some warnings. Batch sizes should be determined after careful thought before launching the product. If the factory is running late, it may catch up by cutting the batch size, but that is uneconomical and leaves you with the headache of a split batch. Larger batches involve less setting time, require proportionately less labour but come though more slowly. If batch sizes are changed after launch, you end up with excess costs, redundant work-in-progress or late delivery. To make his life easier, a Production Manager may try to consolidate batches before loading the shop, or to cut them when things are running late. At least make sure that someone else knows what he is doing.

The same holds good for certain production materials, like electronic components, where delivery is slow or the price falls rapidly with volume. Every electronics manufacturer has a store full of redundant resistors, capacitors, semi-conductors, diodes, hybrids, boards and so on called up by Production to save a penny by spending pounds, to balance unbalanced stocks or to provide a buffer against purchasing delays. To avoid this happening, Production should be allowed to buy no more than is budgeted and planned.

We have talked of the difficulty of recruiting people to work shifts. Shift supervision is even more of a nightmare. Unless the process dictates the rate of production, shift working is less productive than day work even when properly supervised. You cannot expect your best supervisors to be at their posts from 6 a.m. to 10 p.m., or indeed for any hours outside the working day, although most of them are. When you can, look in yourself to see how the late and early shifts are doing. I used to park my car in the yard of a factory near the station in Taunton when I went to London, often returning by a late train, when I would look in on the evening shift. The Shop Superintendent told me that car was worth the output of four men.

To repeat the message, your Production Manager is, and must be treated as, a full member of the team. He will be the hardest to replace if you lose him. He needs time to plan and think, like any other manager. You can best help him by understanding the job he has to do. If you've had to do it yourself, these few pages will have been no more than glimpses of the obvious, albeit rarely seen in print. For the rest of you, it's not too late to change your ways.

CHAPTER 8

Buying and Sub-contracting

'... sulphurous and nitrous foam
They found, they weighed, and with subtle art,
Concocted, and adusted, they reduc'd
To blackest grain, and into store convey'd.'
                                        Milton

* Many people today think of Milton only as a mouthwash, the poet having suffered the fate of Walter Scott, hallowed among the literati, but unread. This is unfair on Milton because, unlike Scott, some of what he wrote is still readable.

* We may question his judgment, however, a Puritan who married a seventeen-year-old Royalist in 1643. Perhaps he was hedging his bets, the King appearing to have the upper hand at the time. It was tactless to spend much of the honeymoon developing a treatise on divorce, even one which was to go into a third edition. We should not excuse him on the grounds that he found his wife a stupid girl: that, along with other personal qualities, is best investigated before the knot is tied.

* He later became Secretary to the Council, in effect to the great Oliver himself, in which labours he was assisted by Andrew Marvell who demonstrated there was poesy in the bracing Hull air long before Philip Larkin came on the scene. Marvell's 'To His

Coy Mistress' strikes a closer chord today than Milton's religious apologia, written in retirement, poverty, disgrace and the enjoyment of a third wife. This lady was not stupid, we are told, although she was not sexy either: but by then the poet was, like Love itself, blind.

* This chapter is about getting things 'into store convey'd', preferably without being adusted in transit. 'Adusted'? Another misprint? No, parched or scorched, as in 'the Libyan air adust', to draw once more from Milton's inkwell.

Before pressing forward, a reminder of what we are trying to achieve may be timely. The object is to stay in place, to avoid bankruptcy, to keep receivers and administrators at a distance. We are not presuming to suggest how the various functions in a manufacturing concern should be performed, and particularly how to manage procurement; such claims belong on the blurb of specialist books and the lips of computer salesmen. Our target is less ambitious – to indicate how you, saddled as you are with myriad other duties, problems, crises and decisions, can monitor what is going on around you and to warn you, through our terrifying illustrations, of what can come to pass despite unblinking awareness.

The Buyer in a manufacturing company is one of the few people who can ruin it single-handed. He may be spending as much as half the firm's income. If goods arrive in the wrong quantities at the wrong times, the factory comes to a halt. If he consistently buys expensively or excessively, the loss may be irrecoverable. Despite the need for a close rapport between the Buyer and financial management, his responsibility has to be to the Production Manager. Any other method of reporting will make it difficult to run the plant efficiently, and give the Production Manager a valid excuse for any failure to perform.

The Buyer needs three types of budget to guide him. The first tells him how much he can spend in any period; the second lays down how much he can promise to pay trade creditors in any period; and the third, what is the planned material content of any job. If, to maintain the flow of goods inwards, he has to operate outside the budgets, he must report that at once. You must create a culture in which shortages stopping production are entirely the Buyer's responsibility.

Even the most experienced Buyer likes to see material safely on the shelves some time ahead of it being issued to the shop. It is a balancing act worthy of the exponent on the high wire to achieve a compromise between the Just-in-Time accountants and the realist Buyer, and there is no safety net. A few hours' waiting time may cost less than financing three weeks' excess inventory but, when you do run out of materials, the shut-down never lasts just a few hours and the cost of panic supplies will merely add to your discomfiture.

Except perhaps where you have a separate Sub-Contracts Manager, whom we will come to shortly, the Buyer should be responsible for buying everything, including office supplies – no, especially office supplies. The daily press used to be full of tales about smooth salesmen who had loaded susceptible secretaries with ten years' supply of carbon paper. No more: these days it is the Chief Accountant who falls for each miracle copying machine or laser printer, having already bought computer paper into the 22nd century. As he is senior, and a man, the firm pays up and it doesn't get in the papers. Even taking purchasing away from the Buyer for what looks like a valid reason can land you in trouble.

* Well over half the cost of elastic thread is incurred in buying latex. It seemed sensible for Globe, which manufactured in both America and England, to combine its purchasing power, and for the larger parent company to do the dealing. This was unfortunately to ignore the deep differences between the two operations. The American parent sold in its domestic market and only in US dollars, a currency in which it paid its workers and could buy

forward its latex. Protected by tariffs, it could forecast its monthly demand with reasonable certainty.

* The British operation had an unprotected home market where imports from Italy already dictated price and volume. Some 80% of its production went to about forty countries, many of which paid in their own currencies. Apart from its home market, almost none of its sales were in pounds sterling or US dollars, the currencies in which all its costs were incurred. In 1980, apart from unstable currencies, world demand was unpredictable, so that the British factory had constantly to vary both its product and its production rate to meet changing market conditions.

* After the parent had contracted on the subsidiary's behalf to buy latex for a year ahead at a peak price in a hardening dollar, the English company started inevitably to incur heavy losses, for which the local management was equally inevitably blamed. 35 tonnes of latex a week is 35,000 kilos, and one kilo of thread, unstretched, can be 70 kilometres long. It is commonly stretched by 60% in the end-product (or it wouldn't keep your pants up), pushing us to over 110 kilometres per kilo. My calculator doesn't have enough zeros to tell me how long 35 tonnes would be. Just accept that's a lot of thread. If you find yourself paying 15% too much for the latex, and then losing 20% on the currency, it's also a lot of bread.

* In this case the lesson was well and quickly learned. The English subsidiary subsequently made impressive super-profits on its latex buying.

A Buyer needs rules, and not merely so that you can see they are being obeyed. Every order should be on a numbered form, which must incorporate whatever conditions you wish to impose on your supplier, including a rejection of that shadowy smudge on the back of his form of acceptance which rebuts his every liability for anything. He needs to specify payment terms and to pick up any cash discounts which are worth having. If you require time to be of the essence of the contract, the order must say so; where it isn't, you need the right to reject excessive or early deliveries. Even the most reliable supplier needs the jolt of being asked to requote from time to time, in open competition. This applies also to auditors and insurance brokers, even if they do happen to have Wimbledon tickets to spare, or seats for the Calcutta Cup.

We noted way back that no invoice should be passed for payment unless it corresponds with a numbered purchase order. Nothing – but absolutely nothing or, in plainer language, zero – should be accepted into the plant without similar cross-referencing to the order, to ensure that the right quantity of the right goods has been delivered at the right time. Where the nature of your work involves Release procedures, as in aviation or military equipment, the Release Note is also an essential part of the package.

In an ideal society, there would be sequentially numbered orders to cover leased equipment, consulting services, stationery and charge accounts at those local hostelries to which customers and others are taken to revive their spirits. In this imperfect scheme of things, these are the areas where the Buyer gets by-passed. At least see that some discipline has been instilled into the Maintenance Department which, needing a spare part urgently, will order it from any source without enquiring about the cost or telling the Buyer. The fatal letters 'TBA' in the price column are a licence to thieve and should be proscribed. Any verbal order should be followed up by a fax with an order number and at least an indicative price.

Unless you are the seller, do not let anyone agree to an automatic escalation clause in a contract. Where there are, or used to be, rings, you might find yourself trapped. With stainless steel, for example, you knew that you would be caught for nickel surcharges, even though commodity reports told you the price was dropping daily on the forward market. Equally, if you are giving a supplier a long run, his methods and recovery of fixed costs should be leading to cost reductions; if he shares them with you, you might be able to hold a competitor at bay a little longer, or increase your own profit.

As the top man, you are going to have to sort out cases in which a director is said to have placed a verbal order, or has actually done so, without going through the Buyer, and, under company regulations, without authority. The dilemma is that, to the third party, a director may well have the authority to commit a company contractually. To prevent yourself falling into a trap, we introduce our Eighth Commandment – Never place an outside order for anything yourself; and its rider – Don't let your directors place orders either. In our first example, nobody thought they had made a commitment and everyone thought they were acting for the best.

* In 1979 Bridport-Gundry was looking into computerisation. I failed to associate this grope towards efficiency with a luxurious car parked from time to time outside the Pearsall offices in Taunton or The Court in Bridport (a lovely name for a Head Office but after 300 years in the same spot you're allowed a modicum of affectation). Lateral thinking connected the two events when I saw an 'interim' invoice for consultancy services in the sum of £12,000.

* The Financial Director explained that he had understood the consultant's work to be of a preliminary nature prior to quotation. The Buyer knew nothing about it. I don't think I ever discovered what the Managing Director thought. However, once the connection had been made, the extravagantly-wheeled consultant was no more to be seen; nor, it transpired, were the other actors in the drama before very long.

We will note, when we talk later about consultancy, that you must agree a specification before placing an order. Sometimes you can wriggle out of these embarrassing commitments, and other times you cannot. In either case it becomes rather sordid and wastes management time.

A director who also is at pains to demonstrate to the world his standing and decisiveness can prove a costly indulgence. As Chairman, give me indecision any day. This example also comes from Bridport.

* A director unwisely accepted an invitation to visit a netmaker in Taiwan at the latter's expense, travelling first class, if my recollection is not at fault. Having every reason, rightly, to know that an order for fish netting of the type manufactured by his host was imminent from West Africa, he was able to repay the hospitality he had enjoyed by placing the business there and then.

* Now we know, those of us who have read this far, that you do not place full credence in West African orders until you have also seen an Import Licence and a Letter of Credit which has been confirmed some distance from those steamy shores. These essentials failed to appear, although the netting did, inside Southampton Docks but outside the EC quota, incurring demurrage for some months while a subterfuge was developed, marginally within the law, enabling it to be resold.

* How grateful we should be that the memory expunges our most painful experiences, to the extent that I no longer recall what this act of generosity to our oriental friend cost us. When a replay threatened to take place some time later, this time involving the same director and a Dutch manufacturer, I was quicker off the mark. As I hope I remarked at the time, few of us are smart enough to learn from the mistakes of others but we really should make an effort to learn from our own.

Sometimes, when you take a look at the mechanics of buying, releasing, goods inward, inspection, invoicing and so on, you wonder if all this complication is the result of a deep plot by the paper manufacturers, or the Enemies of the Earth, pulping every last tree in what used to be called rain forests. Perhaps Accounts were right to hoard all that paper. You can cut down the documentation with good programming, but you can't cut it out. However tight your systems, mistakes happen.

> * Avimo made stainless steel quick release couplings for the supply of demineralised water to aircraft. When one came back with rust on it, we were able to trace it to our convenor who, after scrapping the correct material, had selected the replacement from the locker of his lathe, to avoid a loss of face and bonus.

Make or buy decisions are usually made by planners before production is launched, either to save money or because the factory has insufficient resource. From time to time production falls behind and some of the work is sub-contracted at short notice, and excess cost, to try to retrieve the programme. Then there are the times when the planners missed something out, forgot to call up special tooling or just had a bad day. Few planning errors are as felicitous as that of the officer in Delhi who laid down the spirits allocation for the British 14th Army in 1942, and put the decimal point in the wrong place.

All the best Sub-Contract Managers I have known started their management career as planners. In engineering, they end up with a ring of suppliers over a fifty mile radius. If at times they seem over-protective, even secretive about these smaller firms, the pay-off is that their protégés achieve miracles when you are in deep trouble.

Depending on the size of your operation, the Sub-Contracts Manager may report direct to the Production Manager and not through the Buyer. Especially where the sub-contractor is using free-issue material, the liaison between the two procurement activities must be close. You need to appreciate the essential differences between the two jobs if only to understand why the Buyer is normally in his office and the Sub-Contracts Manager seldom.

Where raw materials or proprietary items fail to turn up as scheduled, the Buyer has a chance of recovering the position from another supplier and anyway, the production cycle may allow time for recovery. He communicates with suppliers mainly by letter, phone and fax. Work done by sub-contractors – machining, processing or the manufacture of sub-assemblies – is usually dovetailed into in-house production, much of it arriving towards the end of manufacture. If a sub-contractor lets you down, the project often grinds to a halt. To prevent this, the Sub-Contracts Manager regularly visits his suppliers, monitoring progress. There will be few whose assurances he can accept over the phone.

The firm may be spending a lot of money on sub-contracting. All the points we noted about the Buyer's relationships with Finance apply to the Sub-Contracts Manager. You can help him by checking that his suppliers, especially the smaller ones, are paid promptly. If Accounts string them out, you will either receive poorer service next time round, or they will put up their prices. For every one who complains to you about slow payment, there will be nine others out there taking it out on the firm in other ways.

However smoothly your procurement seems to be running, you should take a personal interest in any development contract being placed outside, or one which requires special tooling, particularly if you are hoping for a long production run. It is normal for the supplier to charge you his non-recurring costs while trying to retain ownership of the design or the tools. If you submit to these terms, you will be landed with a price increase as soon as the project is launched, nicely calculated to make it too expensive, as it will be too late, to start again with someone else. I don't know that Norman could have handled this particular problem better, but the outcome helped put more grease on a slope which was already slippery enough.

* Buying in the aircraft industry has its special complications. The Norman management style, which had worked well in a team of 17 people, was less appropriate as the firm grew. A department store calls for more sophistication than a mom-and-pop corner shop.

* We chose Fairey Hydraulics as the supplier of the Fieldmaster undercarriage. Two of us knew the company well, and most of its engineers; after all, one of us had been its Chairman. The contract was pretty tough but we were friends, weren't we? They duly developed, tested and tooled the gear, retaining ownership of the design and tooling. Perhaps their service might have been better when it came to the drop tests, but they were also doing a military aircraft for Shorts, and the butter lay thicker on that side of the bread.

* When we came to order the second batch, the price per ship set increased beyond what the project could afford. After scratching around, we were obliged to go to a Yugoslav firm, which involved a rerun of the design and certification procedures. That didn't bring the Norman Aeroplane Company down, but, as I said, the slope became a mite more slippery.

You have constant checks from the management accounts and in your factory walkabouts to tell you how the Buyer and Sub-Contracts Manager are performing. Is production on time and within budgeted material cost? How are trade creditors against budget? Can you see any empty racking in the raw material stores? What is the queue like in Goods Inwards? As soon as the Production Manager knows what indicators you are watching, he watches them too. In the end, we all prefer a quiet life.

These two fellows in procurement are in the front line when it comes to temptation. Suppliers will try to bribe them and they will have their favourites. You mustn't be too prissy about it, but at the same time you must be watchful. It's not a good sign when they start taking more exotic holidays than you can afford, or the pink paper they read is not the *Financial Times*. But when they are taken out to lunch, you don't honestly expect the customer to be treated.

Remember, they do a difficult job, and they need a bit of magic. Those bottles which you see furtively carried into the buying department at Christmas will have vanished before you can put your nose round the door. You may, if you're in luck, be offered a diary or a calendar.

CHAPTER 9

Inventory and Storekeeping

'In Persia the daughters of Eve are reckoned in the inventory of their goods and chattels; and it is usual, when a man sells a bale of silk, to toss half a dozen women into the bargain.'

The Spectator

* It is rather late in the day to settle which of those two Old Carthusians, Mr Addison or Sir Richard Steele, penned the lines quoted above, lines which illustrate that giving a customer green stamps or the company of a female is no new phenomenon, although six for one bale seems over-generous. Operating two generations later than most of our sources of quotation, the fecund scribblers still had to tread a wary path between interests as bitterly opposed as those which had earlier taken up arms against each other – Whig and Tory, Protestant and Catholic, Stuart and Hanoverian – until Queen Anne's death allowed things to simmer down in 1714.

* Addison tended to write the heavy stuff. He is accused of reinforcing the prejudices of his readers, of insincerity even, and in the next breath is hailed, with his schoolfellow, as the father of modern journalism. We won't pursue that line of thought. Among other attainments, he was a Member of Parliament for 12 years, Chief Secretary in Dublin, a Secretary of State and bridegroom of the Countess of Warwick.

* Steele founded the *Tatler* as well as the *Spectator*. His high moral tone was at variance with his lubricious habits but he was livelier, less of a prig, than Addison. A poem on the funeral of Queen Mary in 1694 was enough to accelerate his promotion from cadet to captain in the Life Guards. Governor of the Royal Stables and supervisor of the Theatre Royal, he too was a parliamentarian. A Dubliner by birth, it was another such, the Dean himself, whose vitriolic pen had him temporarily removed from the Commons in 1714.

* On balance, I think Steele wrote the bit about inventory and free gifts.

What the Buyer buys and the Sub-Contracts Manager contracts for arrive in the factory and go into inventory: briefly, it is to be hoped, but this is an area where hope and practice seldom meet. With a new product, the person who tells them what to buy, and when, is the Planner, who gets a chapter to himself later on. The person who indicates what the Planner calls up should be the Estimator. He decides what the job will cost if you do it a certain way, which should be the basis on which orders are accepted. In this Vale of Woes, the Estimator may work out the price by one method, the Planner decide to manufacture by another and the Buyer pay insufficient attention to either of them.

Strangely, things usually work out, despite the designer calling up unobtainable materials and the Planner assuming that your best fitter will be available to put together every sub-assembly. There are two special hazards to guard against where estimators are concerned: wasting time on frivolous quotations, where all you are doing is providing a check for somebody's in-house cost or providing an anvil on which the current supplier can be hammered; and being side-tracked into weeks of costing work-in-progress for an audit to the neglect of current business.

Whatever your reporting chain, the Buyer and Head Storeman have to work closely together. The Buyer has a daily interest in any quarantine area which holds goods inwards which have not passed inspection or do not conform with the order requirement. Unless the supplier is contacted, the goods can moulder until production comes to a halt or the company secretary tells you he has received a writ.

The Buyer needs constantly to know what redundant stock is available for allocation to fresh purchase orders. Exact matches are easy. The real savings come when someone arranges a marriage which the computer hasn't been programmed to think about, cutting oversize bar down perhaps or substituting a suitable but more expensive material which happens to be in surplus. There will be times when a pair of eyes knows better than the computer. No storeman will ever tell you he has a negative stock holding. Where storeman and computer disagree, place your money on the storeman.

A good storeman knows what is perishable and what is 'lifed' – to be kept under special conditions or used within a specific time. Even good storemen become harassed or have moments of idleness. It is easier to load bins from the front but if they are racked on sloping rollers, they have to be loaded from the back so that the oldest inventory is used first. Some factory inspectors are paranoic about varnishes and paints. It is no use with these items relying on the storeman's common sense: reconcile yourself to providing a fire-proof paint store where they can be held alongside solvents, acids and other nasties.

However vigilant your staff, things will be stolen, sometimes involving expertise in logistics which the miscreants might more profitably have sold elsewhere. The damage caused by pilferage may far outweigh the value of the goods stolen. We have already noted that broken batches increase cost. It only makes it worse when the thief is stupid as well as dishonest.

* A large prism polished to two fringes of light is a thing of beauty, costly to make, too delicate to handle without gloves because the sweat from your skin will etch the surface: much too lovely, you would think, to sell for the price of a drink as a paperweight in a pub. That is what one of Avimo's most skilled and long-serving operatives decided to do.

Your loss is heavier when a bunch of workers on the scam decides to maximise its takings by systematic stealing. If they organise things carefully, it can be difficult to detect.

* In the winding section at Brownell in 1987, the plant manager noticed some twine being wound on tubes – quite normal – and being placed in a cardboard box which, unusually, was unlabelled. Not recognising the specific product or seeing any works order, he made an unobtrusive mark on the box and went about his business. When he returned to inspect the box later, it was gone; not in tubing, nor in intermediate stocks, nor in the stores, nor in despatch. Nothing had been booked out and there was no documentation.

* He soon discovered that the box, full of thread, had been routed through Goods Inwards, the domain of the senior union representative, for delivery to a trucker who regularly brought yarn to the factory on beams. If the union man had reported back for work next day, instead of falling prey to a retrospective and disabling sickness, we might have found out how long this trade had been going on.

* The amount of twine involved was probably about 200 lbs a week, and some of that would have been scrap anyway. The sale price was almost certainly less than the cost of the tubing labour. But the real hurt came when we looked into the additional waste caused by early doffing. Twisting spindles run out of yarn at different times because bobbins never hold precisely the same length of yarn. A good operator, watching perhaps 120 spindles, optimises the return by keeping a reducing number of spindles running, postponing doffing until a point when those bobbins

which have not run out do not carry excessive unused yarn. Once employees start converting and selling waste on the side, they doff early to provide excessive lengths of 'waste' to rewind. It had not helped that the supervisor was in on the act.

Another cost of pilferage, apart from the value of the goods and the inefficiencies caused by broken batches, is the loss of the skilled workers whom you have to dismiss. If your scrap is valuable, store it in a secure area. Remember that, with crooks about, goods can go outward through Goods Inward.

Good supervision and tight systems make pilfering more difficult but seldom stop it entirely. Unstemmed, it can bring down not just the dishonest employee but the entire firm, as those of us selling to shipbuilders in Britain witnessed in the late 1960s.

* Avimo supplied the engine room annunciators for the QE II, and I had to visit the Clydebank yard regularly. Every night the carpeting disappeared from lounges, saloons, cabins and corridors, along with everything which was portable and much which would have appeared not to be. The short-term advantages to the stout citizens of that deprived region in superior floor coverings and so on might better have been weighed against the incipient collapse of its major employer.

Stores become congested. When anyone suggests scrapping surplus or redundant items, you may find yourself moving into a dark abyss. We had, in Avimo, a Head Storeman whose nickname, Hammer, should have alerted us to his Cromwellian tendencies – to Thomas, the Malleus Monachorum, rather than his kinsman Oliver. Happily the ruthlessness of our Malleus did not involve his literally losing his head – the Earldom of Essex was indeed a poisoned chalice – but his crimes, heinous as they were, did not go so far as finding me an ugly bride, the act of *lèse-majesté* which did for his namesake. Three instructive happenings spring to my mind – indeed they have never left it despite the passage of nearly three decades.

> * Because we had been jobbing engineers with many government contracts, Avimo amassed many jigs and fixtures which are bulky, heavy and space-consuming. We made a close analysis of what was redundant; and what belonged to third parties (who paid us for storage) or, if our property, was likely to be used again. The tools were placed into separate piles and Hammer sent away the wrong pile on the lorries of the scrap merchant.

> * By all the rules which govern these things, his error should have proved a blessing but on this occasion Sod's Law failed to operate. Our original selection had been largely correct. It was a tricky question whether to stop charging government for the storage of tools which no longer existed (except transmogrified as a mudguard of a Morris Minor or the armour-plating of a destroyer) and so alert them to our default; or to continue to render invoices and hope for the best.

The second incident concerned the scrapping of castings. This time Hammer didn't consult anyone. As I was personally embarrassed, I withdrew his right ever to make any decision again without talking to me first. This is known as 'stable-door management'.

> * Time has obscured the reasons why I became involved in negotiating the details of a new sighting system for a shoulder-held missile with Short's. I agreed a price and delivery for prototypes secure in the knowledge that we had forty precision dyecastings from a previous order which would do nicely to house the optics. Hammer, however, was too quick for me. When we went to the bin, he had just scrapped them.

Hammer was the most well-meaning and conscientious of men. I eventually discovered, from a third fiasco, that a Head Storeman also needs common sense. As it happened it didn't cause us too much damage, although I was to observe a parallel mistake elsewhere which helped to ruin a large and well-known firm. I like to think this was Hammer's finest hour but that is unfair. With so many incidents to choose from, we must not show favouritism.

* The British government, faced with the choice of a new fighter, picked the English Electric Lightning rather than the Fairey Delta. It thus handed the Mirage design in its entirety over to the French whose engineers crawled nightly over the Delta prototype in its hangar on the Bay of Biscay where it did its supersonic trials to allow the inhabitants of British coastal towns to sleep more easily of nights. Avimo made the lifting gear for the Lightning, of which the key component was a specially-extruded aluminium beam to support the weight of the plane. These beams were too long to store on standard racks and so Hammer cut them in half.

* At much the same time I noticed what seemed to be an excessive number of DC-9 white-tails on the apron at Burbank, aircraft apparently completed but not yet done out in the customer's livery. The Head Buyer at Douglas showed no interest in what I wanted to sell him, not even the customary good-mannered enquiry of someone who has come a fair distance to see you. He was however desperate to find some non-standard flexible hose which ran the length of the aircraft, without which none of the DC-9's could be certificated or delivered. Price was no problem, he told me. Douglas was running out of cash despite having customers for every plane. I confess I didn't take him too seriously. People do tend to exaggerate.

* Hammer's counterpart, confronted also with an item too long for his racks, had solved his problem in the same way. Soon after MacDonnell, a profitable maker of military aircraft, took over Douglas, which was said to have 'severe liquidity problems'. It was broke.

The Head Storeman comes into his own at stocktaking, whether you wish to take an optimistic view (hoodwink the auditors) or tell things as they are. Stocktaking needs prior planning if you are not to snarl up the factory when it should be producing. If your Head Storeman can get stock taken over a weekend, he is a hero. If he also keeps all his drills and cutters sharp, he is a man to beatify.

It is wise to walk through stores with the Head Storeman when you have the time. As usual, don't make instant criticisms unless you find a bonded area insecure or pallets stacked in the alleys: the next visitor might come from the Civil Aviation Authority or the Factory Inspectorate. A well-kept store looks tidy. Redundant or slow-moving stocks should be segregated and it is often instructive to have a look at them.

Like company chauffeurs, storemen see and hear more than their superiors imagine, information they are happy to impart to a sympathetic listener. Unfortunately the snippets you pick up tend to be bad news, but it would have got progressively worse if they hadn't told you. I chanced on something which helped to put paid to Fairey early in 1977.

* At the end of 1976, the Fairey Group seemed to be in reasonable shape. Our exports had risen by a factor of thirty times in seven years. We had developed products and markets for a number of disparate factories which had been built up around the aircraft company forcibly incorporated into Westlands. We had achieved a half-yearly profit to 30 September of £2.165m., against £1.351m. the previous year, and that after sliding an arbitrary £500,000 into reserves. Although the Managing Director told the auditor he had 'profit coming out of his ears', my Interim Statement introduced a note of caution. To those who count cash more important than profits, an 'unplanned build-up of stock in some divisions' should have sounded a grim warning. As we have already learned, cash is all that really matters.

* In Belgium we had won the lead role in building the F16 fighter for the European four-nation consortium, although the promised medium-term loan to finance the massive contract had not been

concluded. Because the F16 was running late, we were keeping staff we were unable to lay off busy by building too many Islander and Trislander aircraft for which we had an optimistic sales forecast but too few orders. That cost however was budgeted. What we couldn't carry was any unbudgeted expenditure elsewhere in the Group.

* Early in 1977 I was waiting at Fairey's factory on Ringway airport for my Aztec to take me home and chanced to walk into the store. I was surprised to find it stuffed with components for the medium girder bridge which, it soon transpired, had been built in anticipation of a massive order from Venezuela. The commitment had already reached £4 million without Group approval. By the Summer, with the inertia these things develop, the cash deficit of Fairey Engineering against budget had reached £5 million.

You shouldn't have to rely on chance visits to throw up potentially fatal unbudgeted expenditure. If Fairey's stock control, or central financial control, had been stronger, I would have visited an empty store. If ... Building massive stocks for a single customer is something the Chairman should not learn about by accident. He can't complain if nobody told him. Naturally, if the deal comes off, there will be many about you who will modestly take the credit. If it doesn't, watch your back. The hands which recently patted it in congratulation may also hold daggers. And, as it happened, the Venezuelan contract did come off, when it was too late to recover the situation.

You learn, when you smell things are going badly wrong, to by-pass them all – accountants, estimators, planners, buyers, sub-contracts managers, production managers, storemen – and go back to first principles yourself. The sooner you can demonstrate the depth of the nightsoil, the more vigorous the shovelling will be. For all that, we were almost too late with Brownell and the Cut-and-Shape contract.

* Brownell had undertaken to deliver 800 cut and shaped

camouflage nets each month for three years at a price which allowed $11 for material and $24 for labour. The cost of labour in Connecticut at that time, if you could find any, was $9 an hour, including fringes. After adding overheads on a miserly basis, that gave an hour to make each net; which is what the estimate said too.

* The company's cash was looking bad and the inventory rising although the management thought things were under control. Material purchases were already excessive. Walking round the shop, nobody, not even the star performer, was making a net in an hour. You could cut the labour by increasing the material and allowing more scrap; even then, it would take 90 minutes and push materials over budget. Whatever way they turned, it was a loss-making contract which, in that plant with that cost of labour, would always make losses. If the local management can't see it, it's because they've been hypnotised by the size of the order – what is known as the 'wood and tree syndrome'. The thing you have to realise is that you stand to lose a lot more on a $7.5m contract at the wrong price than on one worth $750. The sooner you bail out the better.

The message then, as ever, is to keep your eyes open and ask questions: that storekeeping is one of the important functions and storemen people to talk to. Inventory costs money and when you run out of money, the bank sends in a receiver. We don't want that, do we?

CHAPTER 10

Plant and Machinery

'Man is a tool-using animal.'
                    Carlyle

* And so, these days, is woman, although old Thomas thought of females more as targets for tea-cups than, if Frank Harris is to be believed, for the gratification of carnal lusts. But is Frank Harris ever to be believed?

* By the 19th century, Disraeli apart, writers stuck to writing and politicians to politicising. We remember Carlyle these days only for his History of the French Revolution. He lent the manuscript of the first volume to John Stuart Mill who carelessly allowed it to be burnt. With no carbon paper, copier or floppy disk, the historian had to refill his inkwell and start again. History does not record what missile he directed at Mill, or why he turned down the baronetcy which Disraeli offered him in 1874.

* Compare Carlyle with his 17th-century counterpart, Edward Hyde, who gave the profits from The True Historical Narrative of the Rebellion and Civil Wars in England to pay for the Clarendon Buildings where his name lives on, as it does in the Clarendon Press. Hyde was not a man to turn down honours, becoming Chancellor of the University of Oxford, Lord Chancellor, an earl and grandfather to two queens of England, among other things.

* As we have already noticed, no script-writer today would dare to contrive a drama as heightened by coincidence and volte-face as that played out in these islands between 1625 and 1689, the same characters constantly entering and leaving the stage left and right, and quite a few exiting through the trapdoor.

Machinery, like inventory, costs money. Inventory usually changes itself back into cash within days or weeks. A machine may take years to pay for itself. Let us then start with our Ninth Commandment – Do not tie up your working capital in fixed assets.

Manufacturing on obsolete or unreliable plant, even if you survive, will prove more costly than replacing and modernising it. When a machine breaks down, you have not just the cost of the repair but the knock-on effect through the whole production process. You can no longer expect to turn out a repetitive item on equipment which calls for the repeated application of skill. The cost becomes prohibitive and the trained labour is no longer about. It's hard enough these days finding a centre-lathe turner for the toolroom or model shop.

Keep in mind that while you have been climbing the ladder, the world has been changing, and nowhere more so than in production machinery. The shop floor where you were apprenticed or which you once supervised is a now museum piece, something for the industrial archaeologist. The British machine-tool industry destroyed itself by staying with radial drills and shapers in a world committed to automation and computer control. The firms which stayed loyal to Herberts, Asquiths and the rest went down the chute with them. This is one area where it will be damaging to rely on your experience unless you appreciate how dated it has become.

Buying the wrong machine can be a multiple disaster: you continue inefficient working and you probably can no longer afford to buy what you really need. If the purchase is of anything other than a standard twister, dyeing machine or whatever, make sure that the equipment you choose has been seen by one of your own staff actually producing your product out of your material, and preferably in your own factory. The safest bet is to install the machine on sale-or-return, even if you have to pay a deposit or give a bank guarantee. Let me tell you about a typical problem.

* The first operation on much of the material which goes into a pressure dyeing machine is done on a CNC puncher-nibbler. After years of reliable service from a German machine, Longclose decided to move with the times and spend £250,000 or so on a new Swedish product which has a larger table, more versatile tooling and other desirable features. The initial trials on a similar machine in another factory indicated that the clamping of the stainless steel plate to the table was inadequate. We therefore negotiated installation in our own factory of the machine on a six months' trial.

* When the six months had elapsed, the clamps were still unsatisfactory and the punch tended to pick up the material from the table on the first insertion. We had also learned that our CAD/CAM system, which had been adequate for the simpler German machine, was unable to cope with nesting on its more complex replacement. Although we were able to delay paying for the machine well beyond the initial trial period, our eventual cost before everything worked as planned was much higher than we had budgeted.

Visits by production managers, planners and engineers to the major trade shows where the world demonstrates the latest machinery actually operating are important. Happily they cost too much to come around too often. If you are going too, as you should, make sure someone books you a room well in advance. A boxroom or cupboard in Paris, Birmingham, Milan, Hanover, Greenville or Atlantic City is scant reward for ten hours of pain, tramping hard exhibition halls and refusing proferred stimulants.

If there is no major exhibition pending, always arrange for someone to inspect a planned purchase in a working environment. Even a direct competitor may be happy to show you how he has upstaged you, just as we are all delighted to boast about some gimmick on our new car.

You should encourage your Production Manager to keep a shopping list for machine-tools. The annual budget will make him sort out his priorities and also address his mind to the allocation of enough cash for the inevitable purchases of minor items and tooling. During the budgetary process, it is wise to keep production machines apart from computers, copiers, company cars and other assorted toys, which the financial people understand and tend to accord a higher priority.

Even when it is in the budget, each major machine acquisition should be justified in detail, setting out not merely the bare cost but also other expenditure like special tooling, new foundations, training and so on. It is almost impossible to prepare convincing financial justification for replacement plant, apart from knowing that if you don't replace it, you will eventually go bust, which is justification of a sort, I suppose. Any other major new acquisition should be measured against your policy for return on capital on new investment. If that looks worse than 25%, or less than 10% above current inflation, think again.

Upgrading plant in a factory is like cutting the legs of a kitchen chair to make them level: you are bound to end up with some wobble. Too much capacity is better than too little. As with a new motorway, an advanced and very productive machine-tool creates its own traffic. Like highway planners worldwide, we find it difficult to provide for the demands elsewhere our major investment is going to generate. So you end up squeezing the toothpaste down the tube, adding capacity down the line until the monster which started it all is running at full efficiency; or, like the highway engineers, throw your hands in the air and accept the inevitability of jams.

When a decision has been made in principle to go for a certain type of machine, let the production team do the sifting and selection. They are the people who are going to have to live with it. Asking a Board to decide between alternatives is to seek from it a decision which it is unqualified to make. Even if the Financial Director knows a slotter from a shaper or a water-jet from a fly-shot, his inclination will be to choose on price rather than value, which is silly: or keep the money in the bank, which may be even sillier.

There are a number of traps, when it comes to buying machinery, in which I have unwittingly placed a limb and in consequence suffered lacerations, or worse. Bear with me while we run through them. There are lessons to be learned.

If you plan an overall improvement of your production facilities, start at the bottom of the pyramid rather than halfway up the sides, or at the apex. There is nearly always one initial process through which materials pass before wending their way through the factory, like the punching and nibbling for pressure vessels: carding for spinning, where the fibres are teased from a fluffy mess into a substance looking like filamented rope: the primary melt furnace in casting: or auto-insertion in electronics, whereby components in pin-through technology are located on boards by computer-controlled robots. You know the gate through which most of your materials have to pass. Before beefing up capacity elsewhere, make sure it is wide enough.

My first industrial management job was in 1958, when I quickly learned two lessons. The first was how not to invest in machinery.

---

* Avimo was then still equipped with machine-tools acquired during the war, one of which had spent time in the Mersey when the vessel carrying it had been sunk. The capstan represented automation among banks of centre lathes and the die-sinker a sole attempt to take the skill out of milling.

* For most jobs, we had first to face a casting, providing the location from which subsequent milling, turning and drilling could be measured. Only one job, the production of shafts on sub-contract for food mixers, called for external grinding, and I suspect a linisher would have produced an acceptable finish. As soon as we had cobbled together enough cash, we gave the General Manager authority to buy the first new machine-tool the shop had seen since 1945. There was great excitement on the shop floor and much speculation. He spent the money on a centreless grinder.

* From then on, you couldn't detect any cutter mark on the shafts for the food mixers. We soon lost the contract anyway and, as a last-operation machine, it wasn't one which you could load with sub-contract work. It was still idle when I left the company in 1971 – in pristine condition, a lovely machine, but idle.

The second lesson was that sacking a General Manager is an unpleasant job.

When any process which is essential to the product depends on the constant availability of just one machine, make sure life will go on if that machine stops. If the critical plant has by its nature a tendency to self-destruction, duplicate the facilities before disaster strikes. We failed to do that in John Williams.

* The automated foundry had a single shake-out, the device which rattles like a cake-walk to separate the sand into which the molten iron is poured from the casting which the iron becomes when it cools. The shake-out used to shake itself to a mechanical breakdown every ten days or so, stopping the entire line while it was repaired. This single factor reduced the efficiency of the foundry by $4\frac{1}{2}\%$ and it was the consequent loss which made the company an easy target for takeover on the second attempt.

When a new process is being introduced, do not overlook the

need to enthuse those who have to make it work, and to train them properly. We are going to talk about trades unions later; let us just note here that, in the early 1960s, Ned Lud was still alive and well and living in Taunton.

* With a new Production Manager, Avimo was eventually able to afford two early NC milling machines, which were ideal for our staple load of precision aluminium box-making. The Shop Superintendent couldn't understand how the tool was located so accurately when the holes in the paper fed through the tape reader had been punched with such evident imprecision. It might have been easier for a Victorian familiar with the operation of a barrel organ or a dobbie to come to terms with the microchip.

* The essence of numerical control is that the job is pre-planned. Our union demanded that these new machines should be manned only by skilled millers. If you're a skilled miller, you want to give the machine instructions, even if that involves overriding the programme. For some weeks cutters were driven into aluminium walls and fragments of metal flew like shrapnel around the shop at heights calculated to cause injury where most men, and some of their wives, would least wish it. It was this factor finally which drove the skilled men back to their vertical mills and allowed us to train youngsters to operate the NC machines properly.

Some requisitions for new plant have to be dealt with between Board meetings. Make sure that any such are reported to the next Board or it will become a habit. The general rules about preparation for a Board meeting apply particularly to machine procurement. It is unwise to allow any paper to be discussed which is produced only on the day of the meeting. It is still more unwise to allow any matter of substance to be raised under Any Other Business. The more dubious the proposition, the closer to lunch will it emerge.

* I joined the Board of Stone-Platt Industries in 1972, a bare two

years from daily treading an engineering shop floor. Shortly afterwards, we met in the huge Oldham factory where Platt manufactured textile machinery and the variable drive gearboxes in which it led the world. At lunchtime on these visits – progresses might be a more appropriate word – the Main Board used to mingle with the local managers. The meeting was running late. The Managing Director slipped away to make our apologies and I remember the hubbub through the partition as we waited for our distinguished Chairman to bring our deliberations to a close.

* Then, under Any Other Business, a proposal was tabled to invest some £47,000 on overhead cranes in Oldham for the movement of cards. Carding machines are heavy and awkward brutes, but you don't make that many of them and they can be shifted on dollies equally well. I, a newcomer, objected to the expenditure but was howled down. We joined the natives, who were pleased to know their capital requisition had been approved.

* Later that day we admired the skill of operators making the housings for the variable drive gear boxes, doing in 17 operations what modern plant would have done in two. On the job cards there were no less than five interim inspection stages (which automation would have made unnecessary). The work-in-progress was double what it should have been and the labour cost excessive.

There were, as we shall see, various reasons why Stone-Platt went into receivership. I had cause to remember that day in Oldham on three subsequent occasions. The first was when the Chairman took me aside in his London club to tell me it wasn't done for new directors to shout the odds at Board meetings. The second was after we had decided to close Oldham; the factory manager who had originated the crane application told me the cranes had been installed but never used. The third, and saddest perhaps, was when I had to authorise some replacement variable drive boxes on the thread extruders at Globe and the plant engineer insisted that we didn't buy as previously from Oldham because a new German product was cheaper, lighter and no worse than that made by Platt.

Before making a major purchase, check up on the supplier's reputation for after-sales service. There are exceptions but firms can usually be judged by their country of origin. The British belatedly brought out some good automated metal-working tools but their product support remained inept. The Swedes don't support their machines too well either. The Germans make good kit but charge too much for spares. The Swiss tend to wriggle out of warranty claims. French and Spanish machines are often unreliable and they will wriggle out of anything. The Japanese ... oh, well – none of us is perfect. Are you in the market for a second-hand Russian guillotine, by any chance?

Whether or not you buy the recommended spares package with the machine, it will need special tooling and adequate ancillary equipment. The primary object in installing a new machine is to reduce cost, and that means cutting out labour. If you are buying a twister, for example, speed is less important than the time between doffs. What matters is the size of the package, so that the machine can run for hours with no human intervention. If it has a 2 kilo package and 240 ends, it will need 240 bobbins running, 240 when you doff, 240 in transit, 240 on the next operation and as many again for those which will be lost, stolen or broken. We overlooked these fundamentals when we bought some American twisters for Halls Barton.

* Bridport-Gundry bought Halls, Barton mainly to secure its own source of extrusion and twine making. We carefully prepared its specification for some new twisters which could be met by the conversion of second-hand Collins machines in New England. Their speed of operation and the quality of the twine were great. The plant manager came back from the pre-delivery inspection full of praise.

* When we installed the machines in England, we found they

needed doffing every ten minutes, with a consequent crippling on-cost in bobbins and labour. We were landed with the white elephants long after the plant manager decided to seek his fortune elsewhere.

There is nothing wrong with buying second-hand machines, especially if they have been reconditioned by the maker. Any engineer will spot the obvious defects – scarred slides, sloppy bearings, excessive backlash and so on. As usual I was party to a major miscalculation which cost more than just renewing the odd tired gearbox.

* We decided to close Fairey, Canada in 1970 because it was losing money with no prospect of things improving. The maps which required major aircraft facilities in Prestwick, Shannon, Gander and Halifax had been redrawn by the jet engine. Nobody would offer us a half-way respectable price for some excellent NC tools in the back of beyond and, wanting the same machines in Belgium, we shipped them across.

* We knew we would have to change the motors. (Connect 60-cycle motors to a 50-cycle supply and you lose one sixth of the speed: oddly, you don't have to change motors sending machines the other way even though they will be running 20% fast.) What we didn't think through was that every relay and other electronic component on the machines would also need replacing.

We have room only for a few more generalisations before a summary. Plant managers are compulsive re-arrangers: at least check the cost of their plans in dislocation and down-time before they turn the shop upside down yet again. They are also jackdaws: make a real effort to throw out the old when you install the new. Don't rely only on the statutory inspections when you consider replacement of cranes, boilers and hoists. If you have the ability to manufacture non-standard machines in-house, check up on cost from time to time by going outside for a quotation. Insist on a post-acquisition audit for all major purchases: that will tell you for the first time what the real cost was – the inward freight, the duty, the reinforced foundations, the new run for power, the special tooling, the training, the maintenance labour on installation, the spares holding, the increase in depreciation; and after all that, the true return on capital. And the summary:

*   machine acquisition is a key part of budgeting

*   encourage the Production Manager to say what he needs and why

*   keep your team and yourself up-to-date in machinery and technology

*   find out what plant your competitors are using

*   let people visit major exhibitions and go with them if you can

*   try to see a new machine making your product with your materials before you finally commit yourself

*   remember to budget for the additional costs which are part of any major buy

*   bring every major purchase to the Board with financial justification

*   start re-equipping at the base of the pyramid

*   throw out the rubbish

*   use the post-acquisition audit to avoid mistakes in future and not to allocate blame for the past

*   and our Tenth Commandment – Never commit any resources to plant or machinery without understanding why.

To restate the obvious, in manufacturing we exist by adding value to materials through labour. Because materials cost much the same everywhere, we prosper to the extent that we economise on labour. We do that by constantly updating our machinery and improving our manufacturing methods.

How boring! We all know that. What if your Board or your owners want to boost cash in the short term by unreasonably restricting capital expenditure? Place a copy of this volume, suitably tagged, at each place around the Board table, and send one to each major shareholder. If that fails, emulate the rat. Join another ship. You may be mortified to watch the time it takes for the vessel you left to sink, or regret you weren't there when the pirates came aboard and set a wiser course. But life's too short to hang around waiting. There's nothing more soul-destroying than working for a stupid employer.

CHAPTER 11

More about Plant and Machinery

'I have known some such ill computers, as to imagine the many millions in stocks so much real wealth.'

Swift

'The chief end of language, in communication, being to be understood, words serve not for that end, when any word does not excite in the hearers the same idea which it stands for in the mind of the speaker.'

Locke

* Swift has already been accorded a short note in Chapter 3. His Dublin birth, seven months after the death of his 'blow-in' father, never made him an Irishman and he spent much of his career in England, a friend of Pope, Arbuthnot, Boswell, Addison and Grey, among others. Yet no Irish patriot wrote more powerfully or effectively on the iniquities of English rule.

* While Swift's clerical grandfather was devising weapons of war to help the king, John Locke senior was laying down his arms and his parliamentary commission at Roundway Down in July 1643. John Locke junior went to school with Dryden and was a student at Oxford during the Commonwealth and Protectorate. His personal experience of a society based on dogma and autocracy was to make him for us the least dated of philosophers. The original draft of the constitution of Carolina, a model of religious tolerance, is in his hand. He was to suffer loss of place, exile, promise of pardon and eventually royal patronage as the drama of the Restoration, the Monmouth rebellion and the Glorious Revolution unfolded.

* William III had the virtue of recognising and respecting intellect. When Locke argued against a proposed devaluation of the currency in 1691, the King took his advice to good effect. And, to link in with Ireland, it was Locke who urged in 1696 the development of the linen trade if the ban on the export of Irish cloth was to be retained.

* How sapient those sages were: computers which overvalue your stocks and communication systems which cannot accommodate different protocols. Has nothing changed in three centuries?

We looked in the last chapter at production plant and machinery – essentially the kit which ends up on the factory floor. Thirty years ago, that was all a senior manager had to worry about, given a few drawing boards and calculators, the odd slide rule or log tables, typewriters, desks or filing cabinets. Computers and copiers were esoteric innovations, telephones and telexes things you hired from the Post Office. The only Management Information System for many firms lay in a Kardex system or between two ears beneath a bowler hat.

Today, not only are you expected to finance a Management Information System (or MIS) and networking, you also have to understand how they function, what are the choices and where are the pitfalls. If you don't, you run the risk of ending up in the industrial graveyard, along with those old shapers and centre lathes we were talking about. Much of the stuff you are paying for will consist of software, which you can't even see, has no resale value and, if you choose wrong, will cause endless inefficiency and loss. Even the hardware becomes almost unsaleable the moment you have taken delivery, which is why the suppliers like to tie you up with long leases.

You don't need to keep abreast with the technology: even the experts, the whiz-kids and computer buffs, have trouble doing that. On the other hand, just as you know that a lathe is for turning wood or metal, or what a draw-frame does, so you have to learn what computers and networking are capable of doing, and then, much more important, what they can't do. Armed with this knowledge you may at least attempt to walk through a jungle in which ravenous wild beasts, disguised as computer salesmen, software consultants and systems analysts, lie in wait.

To discover what we can get from a MIS, we will look at two different types of operation, of which the one providing a service ought to be the less complicated because it buys no raw material, adds no value to labour and carries no work in progress. Manufacturers face greater complications. Let us first see what our options are and, to keep it simple, assume we are in the business of designing and manufacturing an engineering product from a single factory.

All business is more difficult because we have to start from where we are rather than from where we would like to be. That is especially true of a MIS, where the speed of innovation combined with changing demand means that nobody ever enjoys a perfectly conceived or integrated system; or, to put it in simpler terms, you never begin with a clean sheet. In most factories, the MIS will have developed like the 19th-century railways: bits of track here and there being gradually joined up or replaced, a variety of incompatible equipment, different gauges, competing and overlapping services, empires to be protected, inefficiencies to be defended.

So it is with the growth of a MIS. The payroll was probably the first thing to go on a computer, with other accounting functions following piecemeal. In parallel, planners and buyers, designers and stock controllers may have laid their little bits of track, some of them using insubstantial software houses which duly failed, leaving nobody to support that part of the system. Data, you will find, can only be transferred from one section to another by keying the information in afresh. It often seems that the earlier the firm decided to adopt the new technology, the greater is the confusion.

For a manufacturer, the ideal MIS often starts in the design office, with Computer Aided Design (CAD). An increasing library of modules saves the designer's time and the resulting drawing, with its associated parts lists, instructs both the Buyer and the Planner through their parallel systems. Whether you have a Reduced Instruction Set Computer (RISC) with a large capacity, or a micro, in either case backed up by personal computers (PCs), it is essential that they all use the same non-proprietary language, so that information can be transferred by disk or cable without the labour of having to enter data by hand.

The planning system, instructed by design and sales, raises the works orders and the data is passed to the Computer Aided Manufacture (CAM) section. Turning and milling, bending and rolling operations are straightforward but punching and nibbling, where the outline of a component is cut from a sheet of metal, calls for nesting (choosing a variety of shapes so as to minimise waste in the form of offcuts). We have generated a lot of paper by now, but at least somebody should be able to start cutting metal.

The shop floor will have been trained only to undertake tasks nominated by the computer. The parts flow from the stores, the labour is allocated and information passes back to Accounts and Cost Control in a perfect and uninterrupted stream. We have come to Accounts late in the day, you may feel, and mentioned Sales only in passing. It is almost certain that the

Sales department will have installed its own sub-system, ancillary to the main network, although it needs access both to pass orders to Planning and to monitor capacity and progress. Accounts, which embraces costing, must be able to accept data from everyone else, and in a perfect world the computerisation of accounts follows rather than precedes the same process elsewhere in the organisation. It's that old adage about building from the base up and not from the apex down.

Much simplified, this is the structure you hope to achieve. The greatest danger is that too much reliance on computerisation can stifle initiative and gum up the works. On the shop floor, inflexibility can turn into morbidity and a necessary component can be missing because it had not been allocated a code in the purchasing department. Next in order of menace is the delusion that, because information is for the most part in the form of figures, financial people should dictate the structure of the entire MIS. Having avoided that error, you may find that your MIS team has forgotten that it exists as a service to others, not to build an empire, erect a wall of technical arrogance around it and divert most of its time to repelling boarders. When you look closely you will discover that some of the sub-systems can't communicate with each other or the centre; the genius who wrote the special software wasn't using UNIX or DOS and has disappeared; the nesting system in its search for efficiency produces piece parts you don't need until next year; and the Financial Director has decided to go his own way regardless of what Production is up to. You have been warned!

So much for the theoretical structure of a MIS for a manufacturer. Of course, a service operation, without any manufacture or work-in-progress, is much simpler. To test that hypothesis we can look at a working example – Langdons, a medium-sized haulier on the spot market, which makes a living picking up its customers' goods and delivering them as instructed. Get the order, do the job and get paid. Not many complications for the boss to think about in this one, you might think. Let's see.

The process starts in the Traffic Office with an enquiry, almost always by telephone although occasionally over the fax. One of the traffic operators will log it into the main computer which gives it a number. Unless there is an agreed rate structure, the customer will need an instant quotation, based on distance, the number of pallets, the weight, the temperature at which the goods are to be carried, the ferries to be paid, the number of drops (at different destinations) and the cube (the volume of the material). If the enquiry is for less than a full load, can it be consolidated with another order? If not, is there a suitable vehicle available, and in the right place? Can we anticipate a return load from another customer, which will affect the cost? Is the enquirer credit-worthy? All these things have to be evaluated while the customer is on the phone, which calls for a combination of knowledge, intelligence and accessible information.

The distance is easy – if in doubt, just key in the place names and the mileage comes up, on the screen, with the recommended route. No time to ask if there are any hold-ups today like major roadworks, although there is a programme to tell you that too. No problems about credit either: key in the caller's name and the status of the account appears. Is a vehicle available? Well, any operator knows the general state of traffic at any given moment, but a refrigerated trailer with 26-pallet capacity in the right place, and the driver with unexpired hours? A quick check on today's and tomorrow's loading schedules gives that information. So the price is quoted, the job confirmed. The MIS changes the status from enquiry to order.

We pause here a second. In under a minute the operator has used three programmes. One of them, the computer map, is free-standing. The second, giving him the credit status of the customer, originates from the credit controller, to whose information he has access, but over which he has no power to input. The third, giving the commitment of drivers, tractors and trailers with their location, is something he and his six colleagues constantly create, and it is the foundation on which this particular information system is built. By logging in the enquiry, he has started a new information trail, affecting the customer, the driver and the equipment; accounts and credit control; the workshops; and possibly a warehouse.

The job is carried out and the Proof of Delivery (POD) returned by the driver, followed in due course by his tachograph and his temperature recording log. If there is no direct debit, the POD automatically generates the invoice. But Accounts want more information than that. Is the driver an employee, a self-employed driver driving exclusively under contract for the firm, a sub-contractor hauling a company trailer, or a 'subbie', someone from another firm helping out when there are too many orders? What were the hours, what was the overtime, what were the allowances for being away from home? This information, apart from special items like ferry costs, will come off the time sheets, subject to random checking against the tachograph, and that too is entered in the system. And what about the pallets? How many did the driver pick up and how many did he win or lose? The customer will want a credit if some are missing, and the driver will have to be debited.

Pallet control needs analysis of every journey and the reconciliation of monthly totals with both customers and drivers. That's a specialised job and so we can treat it like the map computer, and merely enter totals in monetary terms each month into the main system. Anything else? Well, yes. Did we hold the goods in a warehouse at any stage, consolidate with another load or 'pick' them for this particular delivery? If so we need the warehousing cost, the handling charge and, where appropriate, to adjust the inventory for which we will be held responsible, and re-order where appropriate. Those costs need to go into the system too. The record of warehoused inventory needs a control of its own, with its own sub-system, to which certain customers will demand limited access.

We've taken care of the driver already – or have we? What about the cost of his fuel, the charge for the trailer if he is not an employee and all the other payments associated with the job? To make it easy, we'll assume this load was hauled by an owner-driver, using his own tractor. Under his contract, he pays a percentage commission to the firm for finding the work, providing the trailer, collecting the cash and carrying the administration. Now what we have to ensure is that the appropriate expenses, including fuel, are debited to his account, along with the credit for the work. After all this, was the job worth doing? Did the traffic operator obtain a good price? We need the facility to look at each individual costing, and then to monitor in detail each driver's monthly earnings and expenses.

That takes us into another area. To arrive at accurate costs, the firm needs to watch, as does the driver, his mileage per gallon, tyre wear, and his other expenses, both routine like insurance or exceptional like repairs. Hubometers on the trailers will tell us their overall mileage and, most of the time, the mileometer in the cab gives the same information. The MIS will throw up any exceptional statistics, indicating inefficiency or ill-usage, and warn us when the mandatory inspections of the equipment are due. The traffic operators, the fellows (and woman) we started with, need to know about these inspections too, to ensure that the equipment is off the road and back at the garage in time.

Fuel – no problems there, you might suppose. You would be wrong. On site, access to the automated pumps is open to all company drivers, to visiting drivers who use Langdons' truck-stop and to members of the Keyfuels service. The unmanned system delivers diesel 24 hours a day, with demand controlled by coded cards. Someone needs to extract the log regularly and feed it into the costing system. In addition, Langdons' drivers buy a lot of fuel on the road, anywhere between Aberdeen and Cadiz, which could be a serious problem were it not for the fact that the computer detects aberrations, when what is charged as fuel goes not into a tank but into a wallet. The same is true of the abuse of mobile telephones, the lifeline of the traffic operator and the driver alike.

Already this apparently straightforward business has generated a complex integrated booking, charging, costing, accounting, credit-control and monitoring system, with a number of sub-systems to deal with geography, pallets, consumables (diesel and tyres), warehousing and so on. We haven't got round to the garage yet, with its stock of spares, its repair and overhaul statistics, its test records and individual cost information for each vehicle and trailer. That is another sub-system to be fed into the centre. Then there is the truck-stop on site, with its restaurant, bar, snooker room, bedrooms and shop, the separate cold store in Bristol, the licensees on the site, and other exotica; to which you can add the need of the Sales Director to have instant access to each customer's record, how many loads in the past week or month, where from and to, at what rate.

The turnover of Langdons is about to move into eight figures. It is just managing with a micro and will shortly have to upgrade to a RISC. I haven't counted the PCs (although I assure you they are within the various licences for software), but everyone seems to have an individual work station. Each screen has access to common data and each sub-system can communicate with the others or the micro by cable or disk. Naturally the Systems Manager has tweaked most of the proprietary software to make it compatible with the firm's needs, writing programmes to cover things like telephone cost monitoring or pallet control when standard packages were not quite appropriate. And still things go wrong.

* In the summer of 1992, we were concerned about the account of a customer who was big in toilet rolls, which was always being settled late. Eventually we received a series of post-dated cheques on a weekly basis, and agreed to continue to do the haulage and warehousing, although at a reducing tempo. With the cheques and quite a lot of material in store, we felt reasonably comfortable.

* The credit controller had a bad back and was away for some weeks. The head of the traffic office was on holiday, and failed to see the instruction to cut down on the work. The warehouseman allowed almost all the inventory to be moved out. The traffic operator, short of outward work from Plymouth in the holiday period, allowed the volume to double. The director monitoring the situation had to rely on a screen into which information was no longer being fed on a daily basis.

* When the first cheque bounced and the receiver went in, the property on which we had a lien was insignificant, the customer's factory was empty of stock and our debt had doubled.

And a story about letting junior staff input to computers.

* The person in charge of the accounts payable ledger needs to be steady rather than brilliant; dynamic, and your suppliers get paid too quickly, unintelligent and they get paid too much. The woman at Langdons, having allowed someone else to use her work station, borrowed that of the Financial Manager, having first been given his entry code. In any system, people should be barred from those functions which they do not need. This poor soul, calling in the menu for 'archive information', was given access to 'create new archive', put the cursor in the wrong place and compounded her error by overriding the warning which followed. The entire management information system was shut down for a day.

That brief look at Langdons covers the simpler case. A company which designs and manufactures its own products, and then sells them around the world in many currencies, presents greater complexity, not least because, as we have already said, we all have to start from where we are, not from where we would like to be.

What else do you need to know, when your colleagues descend on you with ambitious plans to improve efficiency and reduce cost by spending a lot of money on hardware, and as much again on software? If the approach originates from your MIS group, by whatever name, have it independently checked. Like all boffins, these people have a tendency to conceal their past mistakes and perpetuate their errors, largely because the people who blame them fail to understand how rapidly the relevant technology has developed and they develop a protective shell. Even though the system they extol depends on an obsolete mainframe which is buttressed by myriad PCs, they may feel they are more secure in adding to it rather than replacing it in sensible stages.

If anyone suggests that you summarily scrap the old system in favour of something new, say no.

> * A.T. and E. was a good medium-sized telecommunications firm with headquarters at Bridgnorth. Avimo manufactured its electromechanical instruments and I visited it regularly, until it scrapped its old production system at the behest of its accountants and computerised its entire operation. In fact, I went there for three months after the changeover, by which time it had run out of cash due to non-delivery of product, and was taken over by Plessey.

Remember that you are going to end up with systems and sub-systems, whatever you may think. If you stick to DOS or UNIX, they will be able to communicate with each other, by cable or disk. If you don't, you will at best be at the mercy of a software house and at worst may have a pile of expensive junk on your hands.

> * I am, as I write, helping a fine old firm which expanded too much

at the wrong time, with bank encouragement. It is still trying to find a buyer at any price for almost new hardware which cost over £120,000 based on a proprietary operating system which quickly turned out to be inappropriate for its continuing operations. It also had to buy out the maintenance contract to a software house.

Remember that Management Information Systems do not think, but they should take the drudgery out of routine operations and eliminate human error. Too rigidly imposed, they stifle initiative or, as with the proposed paperless dealing system on which the London Stock Exchange wasted some £300 million, they become so complex that they never get off the ground.

At the same time, you need to understand what these business machines can do, which is why we have indulged ourselves with a closer examination of the detail than usual. As the person responsible for the final decisions, you must do better than merely accept the advice of your Financial Director, a consultant or a committee of experts. Management Information Systems and computers cost a great deal of money when you buy them and even more when they fail to perform. Let us then recapitulate:

do not stray from a common computer language

do not try to computerise everything just for the sake of it

recognise the cost-effectiveness of sub-systems on PCs

restrict access

stay with off-the-shelf software as far as you can

try to resist having an accounts-based MIS if you intend to make a living out of haulage, manufacturing or anything other than auditing

ensure that computer rigidity does not stifle initiative

let your MIS Manager be your servant, not your master.

Having acquired the perfect MIS, you need to ensure that the information is efficiently and economically distributed. I have to assume we all understand copiers and faxes, conference call facilities, voice mail, word processors, bubble-jet and laser printers, electronic mail (where you cut out the paper) and all the other gadgets. If you have an operation which needs a corporate telecommunication network, at least obtain proposals from more than one source.

We closed the last chapter by reminding ourselves that in manufacturing we exist by adding value to labour. An MIS helps us to do that too, although in the end the savings in labour too often turn out to be illusory; but the alternative is industrial perdition. On which thought we can move on to Planning and Production Control.

CHAPTER 12

Planning and Production Control

*'Let us, since life can little more supply
Than just to look about us and to die,
Expatiate free o'er all this scene of man;
A mighty maze! but not without a plan.'*

Pope

* We can expect a man who stood four feet six inches in his bare feet to have been down-to-earth and Pope's reference to planning indeed shows industrial realism. The shop floor becomes a mighty maze without it.

* Born in that final tempestuous year when a papist king ruled, Pope was as gregarious as those who had scribbled away through the Civil War, the Protectorate and the Restoration. Addison, Swift, Gay, Arbuthnot, Congreve and Bolingbroke were among his friends and his appetite for making enemies was insatiable. In those cultured times, no literary criticism was rated unless it contained personal abuse, and Pope's pen was as sharp as his wit. A midget who wears a corset and three pairs of stockings to pad out his legs cannot be criticised for being thin-skinned.

* Who today would, as Pope did, refuse a doctorate on a visit to

Oxford merely because his companion cannot have one too? (The companion, Arbuthnot, had been offered a Doctorship of Divinity, but the offer was withdrawn in the face of clerical objection.) Pope was also ahead of his times, if not avant-garde, in sustaining injury in a car crash in 1726: well, a coach really, but the forerunner of things to come. The history teachers all tell us about the fortunes lost in the South Sea Bubble, ignoring the winners. Pope did rather well out of it and would have done better if he had listened more closely to Steele and got out at the top.

In any firm, memos are likely to circulate (cc. anyone who can exert pressure or allocate blame) attacking the Production Manager for late delivery, excessive costs or inefficient use of working capital. These evils normally stem from unrealistic commitments by salesmen, poor estimating or failures in production planning and control. Beating the whipping boy is less likely to improve things than finding out where the problems lie. To do that, you need to understand what planning entails. Then you can ask sensible questions and occasionally make a sound decision.

There are four different types of production planning – for continuous manufacture of a single product; for batch production of similar products; for production of one type of product but in many permutations; and for one-offs. These distinctions may become clearer when we have looked at examples, all taken from the textile industry. As we run through each in turn, we can pick out the things to keep an eye on.

Making elastic thread by extrusion is an example of continuous manufacture of a single product. The latex goes from its storage tank to a box of packed elastic ribbons without any intervening manual operation. The capital investment is heavy and only justified if the machines are planned to run 168 hours a week with a minimum of changeovers (from one size or colour to another) or breakdowns (to clean the nozzles and acid tanks). The productivity of labour is not a worry because the machines dictate the tempo. Naturally you have to monitor the scrap rate, but that applies to all manufacture.

The Planner can explain this kind of continuous process to a computer quite easily. Incoming orders are consolidated and entered as a demand on the system, to be matched with finished stocks and production. Sales, materials, costs, wages, production schedules, machine loading, unallocated inventory, despatch and accounts are integrated in a single programme. Every day the Commercial Manager knows what capacity he has to sell; every week the machine spits out efficiency, scrap percentages, production volume, profit, inventory and other detailed financial statistics.

So long as the figures look right, you know production control is on top. Even the Production Manager need do no more than give the helm the occasional nudge. A director has the luxury of having time to think about currency fluctuations, power cuts, the unreasonableness of his customers and dock strikes – until someone with lower costs, cheaper labour, the same product and an acceptable brand image appears on the scene and drives him out of business.

Batch production makes things more complicated for the Production Controller although here again the computer should remove much of the drudgery and some of the uncertainty. In this environment, customers are asking for delivery in enough variations to stop him consolidating orders into continuous production of the same product except, perhaps, to an intermediate stage in the process. The variations may be to the product specification, or to conform with a delivery schedule, or in size, colour, packaging and so on. Aside from intermediate stocks, the Planner has to take ticklish decisions about commitment to unallocated finished goods. Nobody thanks him when he guesses right and everybody is on his back when he gets it wrong.

Our old friends, James Pearsall, had two batch production

businesses, one making surgical sutures and the other continuous filament industrial sewing threads, which are used in car seats, mattresses, shoes, anoraks and so on. Up to the grey, or undyed and untreated state, planning thread production is quite straightforward. However anyone can manufacture grey thread, given the right machines. A sixth-former could write that production control programme, but couldn't keep himself in bubble-gum on the margins if you only sold grey thread.

The Planner's problems come with the permutations demanded by the customers. The first is colour. A colour-match computer in an automated dye-house (using Longclose machines of course) removes human guesswork, but the shades shift after bonding, a process which protects the thread against the 320°C generated by needles on automated sewing. Then you have the type of package, the specific weight or length on a king-cone, a cheese, a tube or whatever, with the customer's labels within the shrink-wrap. Export orders give you time to plan. Home customers want immediate service.

What the computer won't tell you is when to re-dye or rewind slow-moving stock; or to what extent you dare ship thread which is off-shade to a customer who has specified, but doesn't need, something more precise; or when fashions are going to change, leaving you with shelves of tan shoe braids you couldn't make enough of a few weeks ago. And there are Acts of God, which no man can anticipate.

* Pearsalls manufactured an own-branded continuous filament thread for an international textile giant. (There's nothing unusual about own-branding, although the advertising of the petrol majors assumes the public is pretty stupid, claiming distinctive qualities for interchanged and interchangeable product.) The one thing particular to this customer was its world-wide standard corporate colour card.

* Pearsalls was dismayed to have heavy returns for mismatch from

some of the customer's overseas subsidiaries. It took weeks to establish that two of the foreign colour cards had faded, and no longer tallied with that used by the UK parent. We also discovered that one of our final inspectors was partially colour-blind, but we kept quiet about that.

Here too the figures should tell you whether your planning is in good shape, although the complication of intermediate stocks and work in progress will make any weekly figures unreliable. Remember, before you start shouting at anyone, that a production planner is like a lone air traffic controller keeping Heathrow fully operational in a fog. If you sense trouble, home in on the key decision areas – intermediate stock levels: the demands salesmen are putting on the system in terms of batch sizes or delivery: any areas of queuing through plant breakdown or shortage: the quantity of packed and stacked inventory. And don't forget to have a quiet word with the Head Storeman when you can spare a moment.

Now for batch production, which is more common in engineering than in textiles, but for consistency, let us stay with the rag trade. Here the factory will be using its resources to make a variety of products of a similar type but to differing specifications and often in uneconomic quantities. As ever, customer or stock orders will be fed into the control system as a demand on the works. With any luck, the computer will tell you what is already in stock, and raise purchase requisitions for what isn't. In theory, it should also tell the Planner his available capacity so that all he has to do is press the button and the machine spews out job cards. That's what should follow. What usually happens is rather different.

Crewkerne Textiles makes narrow fabrics, what we call webbing but as some Americans call netting webbing, we have to use a degree of circumlocution. The one product which it could turn out in volume would be car seatbelts in black, but the margins there are so tight it would lose money. So the Planner has to live with many materials – linen, hemp, cotton, nylon, polyester and the other synthetics, with occasional blends: a variety of sizes, lengths, strengths and widths: different constructions according to the end use – lifting slings, harnesses, safety belts, fashion goods, shields for divers' airlines, parachute webs, military webbing, and so on: specialist finishes – dyed, stretched, stitched, shrunk, heat-set, calendared, impregnated: and any inspection standard from cursory to aviation.

Some customers want a sample batch before placing the order, which, for the Planner, means as much work as the order itself. Even when there seems to be a decent quantity, the call-off will be protracted, making it uneconomic to put through everything at once and hold it in stock. Fashion customers especially have the divine right of arbitrarily delaying delivery if sales are slow and then making claims against you if you are delinquent.

This is territory where the computer can take the Production Controller only part of the way. When he is struggling, you must appreciate that the best he could ever achieve is 80% of his theoretical capacity. His looms are not interchangeable nor are the skills of his weavers. Run through the order backlog and see what kind of demand the salespeople have been placing on him. Look too at the samples that have been called for, and the cases where customers have arbitrarily delayed delivery. Before you start apportioning blame, at least find out where the fault lies.

Crewkerne Textiles suffered a lot of grief on one occasion because I caused resources to be committed without proper contractual cover.

* Conforming bandages are the loosely woven ones which are used for grazes and similar wounds. There were problems with the

selvage and texture unless they were made on shuttle looms, which are slow and expensive to operate. A major international medical supplier asked us to devise a method of making the bandage on the faster needle looms and, after a lot of sweat, we cracked the problem. The customer inspected the product and our method, expressed himself delighted, took samples away for test and placed the production orders in France.

* The price of conforming bandages hasn't fallen in the shops yet.

With a load like that at Crewkerne, the Planner is bound to end up with excess stocks at every stage from raw materials to finished goods. Especially with fashion items, shift them as fast as you can. Never mind the write-off you hoped to avoid this half-year: the longer you wait, the less you recover, most of the time.

Now for the one-off, the order you only allow people to book if the designers and planners have had a look at it first. Ideally, you accept it at a price 'to be agreed', but even the Ministry of Defence is wary of those words nowadays. When someone assures you that, although the price is poor, it is a prestige project, tell him he can have prestige in his next pay cheque. One-offs respond to production planning only insofar as it copies the method on which the estimator worked out the cost. You will waste time and run risks if you re-plan once you have the order, as you might for a repetition job. Again it was up to Brownell to demonstrate how not to do things.

* In 1987 a railroad company was having trouble with the roof of an old tunnel in New York City. Masonry fell on the tracks, on passing trains and on the down-and-outs who squatted there. Brownell, as a maker of nets, took on a fixed price contract to design, build and erect safety netting the whole length of the arch.

* Building regulations in Europe are tougher than in most American states. Over here, you have to guard against an overweight man with a bag of cement under each arm dropping his

trowel (into debris netting) before plunging fully laden into the safety net. If the installation doesn't satisfy him, a building inspector will shut down the site and keep it shut until he is satisfied about safety. Before bidding for the contract, Brownell neglected to talk to its English sister company, who knew what the problems would be, and also to take sag into account.

* As Newton and others have pointed out, gravity pulls things downwards. Having overlooked this law of physics, the Brownell nets were too small. After being remade and rehung, they sagged enough to be carried away by a passing train. The vagrants among whom the riggers had to work were not sympathetic to Brownell's problems; nor was their customer when it came to payment, the entire project having come to a standstill while Brownell tried to sort things out. If anyone had suggested to me that it was a prestige contract, I could not have been held responsible for my actions.

Although we have identified four basic types of production planning, in real life one-offs, samples, batches and broken batches, intermediate stocks and mass production all jostle for the Planner's resources at the same time. Engineering is worse than textiles: the skills required on a single job may be electronic, mechanical, optical, hydraulic or pneumatic; there are decisions on the scale of tooling, the manufacturing methods, the finishing processes and on make-or-buy besides the common problems of optimising batch sizes, specifying inspection procedures, keeping within allowed cost and delivering on time. So, when the figures look bad or you see plant idle, remind yourself that Planners and Production Engineers aren't doing it deliberately to raise your blood pressure. They have probably been forced into accepting costs or delivery dates which were never realistic; or, in a weak moment, have assumed that everything will run smoothly. As we know, it seldom does.

Broken batches are the Planner's nightmare. No scrap allowance can be accurately judged and it will be exceeded as often as it proves excessive. Materials will arrive in other than the precise lengths the Buyer ordered (without time to reject them and replace) and as a result you will find there is one less piece out of each bar than was planned. When casualties occur on the shop, it is simpler to press on with the reduced batch, leaving the wounded littered around the battlefield, even though that means the eventual delivery will be short or, if the customer insists on precise quantities, impossible. Rectification needs special skills and often cannot be done in time to catch up the rest of the batch anyway.

If you understand how hard it is to deal with broken batches, you may do some good by seeing that adequate scrap allowances are permitted, raw materials ordered correctly and enough resources allocated to rectification. A struggling firm which concentrates entirely on straightforward production and neglects rejects will only sink deeper in the mire.

* Early in 1988, as we have already noted, the John Williams foundry was itself foundering. Its Production Manager, with obsolete and run-down equipment, had as much chance of success as would a family banger entered at Le Mans. The motor industry demands its castings at the hour on the day specified. Absolute rejects in production are tossed back into the furnace but the majority of imperfect castings can be recovered from rejection in break-out, shake-out, annealing, fettling or final inspection. It is imperative that rectification takes place immediately if you want to avoid short deliveries and piles of half-finished, unsaleable scrap.

* At a critical board meeting – there was a crisis and some of us were being critical – we were assured the figures were not as bad as they looked because there were some £100,000 of castings in the system additional to the normal flow. If the Production Planner had managed to put through this increased volume, that was excellent. But what if he had done what I – the Good Lord forgive me – have done under similar pressure: kept up the daily schedules

by ignoring rectification and pushing through incomplete batches?

* The lubricant for most Boards is coffee and the age of some directors leads to frequent adjournments. During a natural break, I sought out the Production Controller and he told me what I had hoped not to hear.

* £100,000 in good stock would have led to one course of action: of doubtful stock to another, the difference being between solvency and possible insolvency. Within weeks the company was taken over and I hoped that the new owners would be willing to support the workforce with the resources which we had lacked and they deserved.

In the Williams case, the accountants had made the mistake of putting full value on incomplete items, merely adding the quantities of material, labour and overhead in the works, and coming up with a figure. That is the trap people fall into when they don't walk through the shop and use their eyes. It helps if you know what to look out for: the inspection quarantine areas are a good place to start.

You need to think out your inter-company trading policy because that is somewhere else the Planner can face problems not of his own making. The seller will tell you he is being screwed down on price to favour a sister company when he would do better selling to outsiders. At the same time, he expects a long-term commitment and to dump stock at the end of each accounting period. The buyer will say he could do much better shopping around, especially on service. However good the relationship at managerial level, inter-company trading suspends all normal supply principles, with each partner treating the other worse than he would an outsider. Too often the Planner has to pick up the pieces.

I once had a Group Managing Director who also expected each party in the Group to make a 30% margin on each constituent of the same product at every production stage, with up to four inter-company transactions. No Planner can compete with that and before long the company couldn't compete with its competitors either.

The simplest rule is to give the seller the right of first refusal of any order at a competitive price, after which the buyer can go outside the Group. If the managers have come to blows, meet them for lunch on neutral ground and do some head-banging. But, before they kiss and make up, establish who is to pay the bill. The last time I did this at Bridport, they walked out in great amity, and I picked up the check. Harmony in a Group is desirable, but not at any price.

You cannot run a manufacturing company without knowing in detail how its products are made – how plastics and metals and natural fibres become garments, engines and pop-up toasters. In a world which takes technology for granted, as though all material comforts descended into the shops in a western Cargo Cult, you have to know how things are planned and machined and processed and assembled. Then you will understand what a Production Planner has to achieve and you will be able to help him, competent to judge him and ready to sack him if he isn't up to it.

CHAPTER 13

People

*'We cannot all be masters, nor all masters
Cannot be truly followed.'*
Shakespeare

* As once before, I will not presume to add anything about Shakespeare, remembering how Shaw revealed his own mean nature venturing the comment 'I despise Shakespeare when I measure my mind against his'. If Shaw meant it, he was a conceited twit, and if he said it merely for effect, that proves the same thing. We should always beware those who affect more than a single Christian name or initials, even when we have no prejudices against Irishmen with messy beards and philandering drawing-room Socialists.

We keep reminding ourselves that manufacturers exist by using labour to add value to materials. The better the design and the more efficient the plant, the less the labour. The fewer people the better. As the old saw goes, costs walk on two feet.

A senior manager has to deal with two sorts of people having different aspirations, the workforce and his colleagues. Despite its etymological derivation, he is unlikely to have chosen the 'colleagues': indeed, in a re-run, he might prefer to have none of them around the place. We will pick up this topic in a later chapter, on Directors and Direction. For the moment, let us stay with the workforce.

We must eschew sentimentality. To prosper, we need the greatest output from the fewest bodies. The claptrap about the obscenity of unemployment and the sanctity of job creation is best left to politicians or gong-hunters. You do not have to like people to be a good manager, nor do they need to like you; but it pays to understand them. People in the mass anywhere are pretty objectionable, whether soccer spectators, tourists abroad or employees at the factory gate. In any mob, the instincts and behaviour of the stupid and brutal prevail. It is the rational, insecure, honest, loyal individual to whom you have to relate. To succeed in this, you must study what people are aware of wanting out of selling their labour, and what they may subconsciously want.

People know they want security of employment, especially older employees and married men with families and mortgages. Their security is linked to the firm's prosperity, how busy it is and how much new plant it can afford. Being much closer to the action than shareholders, you can't conceal bad news for long and it is much wiser to disseminate it yourself than let it trickle down through a twisting and distorted grapevine.

People also consciously want as much pay as they can lay their hands on, even if that in the long term damages the firm and so puts their security at risk. What matters is the basic wage. Overtime doesn't count, even when it has become a regular pattern (until you try to stop it, but that's something else). We will look at piece work and profit sharing later but neither of these will be taken into account when a worker is comparing the present wage with what is on offer down the road.

People are also aware of their working environment. Is it clean, light (or well-lit), tidy, in good repair and safe? What are the lavatories like? You should occasionally take a peep, or a pee, there yourself.

On the borderline of the conscious and the sub-conscious lies status, not squabbles about reserved car spaces or job titles but the respect with which each individual is treated. It is a truism to say that nobody should be on the payroll unless there is a job for someone. Turn that on its head. Everybody who works in the firm is actively needed if it is to operate efficiently. Get that across, to other managers and workers, and you will find it helps in many ways, including reduced absenteeism. You won't get it across unless you believe it to be true.

Another facet of status is opportunity. Good people are less likely to be footloose in a firm which offers further education and training, and advertises all jobs internally before looking outside. When the natives are getting restless, it is the able and enterprising who emigrate, the idle and less competent who stay behind.

People also like to work for a firm which enjoys a positive reputation with the outside world, reflecting credit on all its employees. Good publicity in the local press may not help your sales but it can do wonders for morale. Recognise that we live in a society which sees fit to venerate the royal family from the Queen to its remoter and often louche components, and indiscriminately to adulate the seedy stars of the soaps. I was more highly regarded by Avimo's workforce for turning out as a resident performer on a local television filler than for having steered the firm to survival from insolvency, the benefits of my public appearances lasting long after I chose to revert to faceless anonymity.

Part of your employees' psychology is based on their image of a 'boss'. He is seen to sit at a desk, dictate memos, call unnecessary meetings, gormandise at someone else's expense and drive a luxurious car which the company pays for. As you may do all of these things, you can only improve your image by showing that you also see customers, listen to problems, inspect factories, take decisions and generally make yourself useful about the place. The animosity will be less and the understanding greater in proportion that you see and are seen by your employees. But if you are uncomfortable on the shop floor, and listening to people there, stay away: nothing is so transparent as insincerity.

In the factory, try not to grandstand or by-pass those managers who have to keep things running when you have moved back to the office. If a complaint turns out to be unfounded or malicious, it is unwise to enter into further dialogue with the complainant. You should follow up sensible complaints and suggestions, protecting your sources wherever possible. As I often discovered, that isn't easy.

* The operator of a new twister in Bridport told me that one of its defects was that a plastic carrier sometimes flew off a spindle at an impetus imparted by a bobbin rotating at 6,000 revolutions a minute. His mate on the other shift had been struck on the trouser zip, the cloth being insufficiently absorbent to prevent bruising on the flaccid member below.

* I asked why the machine hadn't been modified or guarded. In time, the Personnel Officer protested because this was an accident which had not been reported to her, taking the victim to task. Thus the man who had not wished to publicise his injury was embarrassed and my credibility as someone in whom employees could confide was dented.

There is no right way of dealing with people, although there are lots of wrong ways. You cannot hope to be in constant touch with everyone but you can ensure that a route exists through which information can pass accurately and quickly. Many British companies are bad at this, partly because they have gone along with the union tradition which seeks to insulate workers from management. I can't see us following the Japanese into physical jerks for all or self-criticism sessions, but we can learn from their insistence on constantly briefing junior managers who can then tell their sections what is going on. It is dangerous to channel information through union officials unless you wish it to be distorted and your junior managers to be discredited.

Works newspapers or bulletins distributed to everyone are fine so long as you don't patronise your employees or include price-sensitive information which will upset the Stock Exchange: if there are to be leaks, hints or disclosures, brokers like to be the first to know. Your employee readers will have a pretty shrewd idea of how things are going, which makes it sensible to tell them no lies and as much of the truth as you dare. I am against putting wedding photographs and 'lost and found' among the company news, but that doesn't mean it is a bad idea if you have the right editor.

Especially if you are in dispute with the union, or labour relations are poor, post any publication to the home addresses of your employees. If it is distributed on the shop floor, it will either be contemptuously crumpled up and discarded, or read slowly in the firm's time. At home, wives and husbands will also look at it and may even comment objectively on its contents.

Junior managers who have been treated so that they seek security by throwing in their lot with the shop floor make effective communication between management and workers almost impossible. The impasse can even lead to closure, as Bridport-Gundry found with its Lolift factory in Ripon.

* Lolift manufactured intermediate bulk containers, those huge bags you see on lorries, each carrying up to a tonne of powder. It had gone into receivership as a result of the failure of its parent company. When we bought it from the receiver, we decided against making all the staff redundant, partly because I had done that once before, and lost many of the best workers, and partly out of misplaced altruism. After all, Ripon, that dreamy Cathedral City, was not a place where you would run into labour problems.

(The rules affecting the rights of employees on a receivership have since changed: in general terms, they are deemed to enjoy continuity of employment if retained by a buyer from the receiver, even if there is a break in their employment.)

* We soon found that Lolift's labour management had been dreadful. The supervisors and foremen identified themselves exclusively with the shop floor. Communication with the workforce had been through the Trade Union, to which all the junior managers also belonged.

* In 1986 the factory lost its biggest customer of bags for artificial fertilizers and the market for nitrates dropped away, affecting demand elsewhere. The business would only survive if we were able to abolish some of the crazy practices and anomalies which were making it uncompetitive. ACAS came in and, after a manful effort, conceded defeat. Even the full-time Union official eventually lost patience, after which the shop stewards relied for guidance on a nearby university lecturer, who was no doubt delighted to have this opportunity to put into practice the politics of confrontation.

* Unable to convince the workers of the extent of the crisis, we closed the factory. They continued to think this was just another move in a game of poker. We can console ourselves that the lecturer was the only one who didn't lose his job. Tenure in our British universities is a fine thing.

For all the legislation to the contrary, women are still not the same as men, either at work or in the home. Those in manual jobs tend to be unambitious and less available for training than their male counterparts. Those in management may seek to compensate for real or imagined prejudice against their sex by intolerance or assertiveness. You may well have noticed for yourself that men are less likely, when criticised or under pressure, to slam doors or burst into tears. You should also reflect, when these things happen, that for most women their career runs parallel with or ancillary to other responsibilities. They do not arrive home to find their slippers warmed by the fire, their supper on the table. There are times when you should hold your tongue.

Having a husband and wife on the same board need pose no problems so long as only one of them holds an executive position in the firm. A manager needs to escape from business at the end of the day if he is to think clearly, or at all, on the morrow. People who take the business home with them seldom perform well under stress and if the marital partner is in the firm too, they lose the relief which the home should provide and the detachment in a spouse which should help them to relax. A third party in the management will find life equally frustrating. A decision taken one day may be cancelled or varied after domestic discussion overnight. None of this makes for good management and I don't think it is much good for their family life either. So, if you find yourself becoming involved with a management team where both spouses are executively employed, cut your losses and seek your fortune elsewhere.

Everybody but the Anglo-Saxon white non-Catholic adult male is protected from supposed discrimination by some law or other. There are classes of skin pigmentation and religion against which you discriminate if you are not seen to favour them. In parts of the country you dare not advertise for someone with a specific skill because one of the favoured groups will take you to a Tribunal if not appointed, whether or not qualified for the job. (You should win, but every Tribunal costs around £1,000 with no recovery from the unsuccessful applicant.) That said, things are improving, although until public sector employers start judging people on what they do rather than what they are, the private sector will have to steer carefully around a hotch-potch of unfair and unwanted regulations.

You will already know that women are better at many jobs

than men and that, if a worker is capable of doing the job, it doesn't matter a hoot what colour his skin is, what church he goes to, if any, or what are the sexual characteristics or preferences. Our only concern is to convert labour into added value as efficiently as possible.

A strength of the United States economy has been the ability of its industry without fuss or cost to equate the size of a workforce to current demand. Freeing human resources for a more useful purpose is not looked upon as socially reprehensible. In contrast, we have destroyed our public sector education not by shortage of funds or the absence of public goodwill but by four decades of rising inefficiency due to the impossibility of ever firing any teacher, however incompetent, idle, subversive or stupid. To survive in industry, you have sometimes to increase your labour force, sometimes to reduce it. Let's look at how a reduction should be handled.

Before announcing dismissals, study the relevant facts – on notice to the government, redundancy entitlements, holiday pay, pensions and so on. If anyone is working out a period of notice, allow time off for interviews. If necessary bribe key workers in a run-down not to leave early. Dismiss the people who are least needed and beware voluntary redundancy, which may result in your losing the very people you most need to keep, they being the ones confident of finding other work. Do not accept the hallowed formula of 'last in, first out'.

With an individual, if he is going to be fired, fire him. Don't try to explain and don't let yourself become involved in an argument. Have previous written warnings handy even if you don't refer to them. Do the deed in private, and not in the workplace. If you cannot get the unfortunate employee out of your office in ten minutes, you've made a hash of it.

Never sack an individual on a Friday or the eve of a public holiday: the shock is best absorbed when the victim stays in the working environment for the following days. However generous or sympathetic you think you have been, don't expect any thanks or goodwill from those who go. If you have to dismiss people in a society accustomed to violence, look out for incendiary devices under your car or, in my case, the suggestion of a bomb on your light aircraft.

On top of paying enough to attract and keep good workers, you have to devise ways of rewarding effort or discouraging idleness. All incentive schemes have drawbacks. They are costly to administer; they lead to sterile disputes; and the impetus they give when first introduced is soon absorbed by the ratchet syndrome – we've got that under our belts: what comes next? Let's run down the list.

* Piecework is appropriate when a single operator performs a discrete process repetitively, like sewing a bag or machining a shaft. Once a time is agreed, it is hard to reduce it and in a union shop, a good worker has to obey the convention against making more than twice time. You may also find yourself paying bonuses on bad work because it can be hard to pick up scrap if there are subsequent operations on the same material.

* A group bonus, for those involved in a common and identifiable project, has the recommendation that the union will dislike it. Any gang controlling an entire operation with a shared bonus will prove smarter at achieving results with the least effort than a Production Planner dare dream. You can even let the group fix their own hours of attendance, in a continuous process, knowing that they will weed out the laggards for you and keep the plant turning.

* A shop bonus rarely has much effect because people hate the thought that their hard work is benefiting some idler or incompetent across the gangway.

* Full profit-sharing works so long as profits keep rising and the sums paid out are significant. A typical plan is to allocate 10% of the profit before tax as certified by the auditors to be paid out pro rata according to the gross pay of those employees serving while

the bonus was earned and still there when it is paid out. Everyone finds a lump sum acceptable just before Christmas or the annual holiday. In Avimo and Globe, the share of profits grew to such an extent that employees became the first to criticise waste and denounce slackers. Elsewhere, smaller and less constant payments have been gobbled up as the grudging dessert to an unsatisfactory meal.

* Handing out shares in a private company involves disclosing financial information you might prefer to keep to yourself, and you also need a system of buying the shares back when people leave. In a public company, bonus issues to employees are a real incentive even though most people immediately unload them on the market.

We have already heard of the tribulations of Lolift. It was inevitable that the management had lost control of piecework times, with catastrophic effects.

* After years of cutting up rolls of material for its intermediate bulk containers by hand, Lolift at last commissioned and installed automated measuring and cutting equipment. Unable to agree anything with the Union, the management continued to pay the operator of the automated machine, now a mere spectator, the same bonus per bag as he had received for doing the job manually. Before long those on this duty were earning more than the supervisors and double what other manual workers took home. The supervisors became even less effective than they had been, which was in itself an achievement, and the rest of the workers, already on inflated bonuses, introduced guerilla stoppages to achieve parity. We know where it all ended up.

And an example of what can happen in a Union shop when a good operator has been given too generous a time on piecework.

* Avimo made the nose-cone for the Firestreak infra-red homing

air-to-air missile. They look like the miniature greenhouses you see in suburban garden centres. In those days before molten glass was floated on a bed of tin, you had to grind both sides if you wanted it to be parallel. Chamfered sections were then mounted on an iron base, sealed with rubber and glued with epoxy resin. Stress calculations showed that the design would not stand up to its hostile environment, leaving the pods of a Lightning fighter flying faster than the speed of sound and catching up its equally speedy victim.

* Although there were supposed to be two suppliers, Avimo and Barr and Stroud, only one operator in either of them, a minister's son, had the knack of defying physics and assembling nose cones which worked. His output of 20 a week, which was what the stopwatch had dictated, was insufficient to enable the RAF to keep the red hordes at bay. Happily we were able to abandon piecework by making him a chargehand, whereupon he produced 120 units a week, and more with overtime. We also showed Barr and Stroud how he did it, which was good for the defence of the realm but otherwise not a sensible thing to do.

We can leave the question of incentives for senior managers until later. Most of them are no slouches when it comes to looking after themselves anyway. We're all greedy: the only difference is that not many of us are let loose in the tuck shop.

The key to efficient use of labour is to recognise that everyone on the payroll needs to be there and that each number is in fact an individual. Inevitably you will receive reports which treat people statistically, so many staff, so many directs and so on. Let's say it again: each one is a person. The Victorian Quakers and Freechurchmen, who thought that way and acted accordingly, built prosperous businesses which are still around. You don't have to quake or dissent to secure the same advantages.

Yes, I appreciate you are a senior manager nowadays. You've been around longer, or had a better education, or are cleverer, or more cunning, or luckier. We're not asking you to go slumming or even show some humility – merely to respect the integrity and individuality of others. You are paid more than your staff because you are meant to give more. If they were as good as you, they'd be doing your job. And that leads us to our Eleventh Commandment – Never expect your juniors to be as smart and dedicated as you are yourself. Those who best look after people in their businesses end up with the best businesses.

CHAPTER 14

Research and Development

*'I submit these mistakes, into which I may have fallen, to the
better consideration of others, who shall have made research
into this business with more felicity.'*

Holder

* My namesake, William, was born in 1616 and lived through the
momentous years of the Civil War, the Commonwealth, the
Restoration, the Monmouth Rebellion and the Glorious Revolution before he died in 1698. I don't know whether he and his wife
Susanna, née Wren, were blessed with issue but, ancestor or not,
I would give a great deal to have been around when he was, to have
seen what he saw.

* He attracted notice first by teaching a deaf-mute to speak. When
the condition recurred the victim was cured again by another,
which led to an unseemly squabble as to which instructor was
entitled to the credit. Suffice it to say that Holder was an eminent
musician as well as a lifelong authority on speech. A good man in
the box, as they used to say, he was no niggard with words, using
no less than 48 in his last published work, on Time: and that was
just the title.

* Holder managed to secure favour from the universities of both
Cambridge and Oxford, the cathedrals of Ely and St Paul's,

although the latter was not surprising, given the family connection. His father-in-law, also named Christopher, was Dean of Windsor and Wolverhampton, which doesn't have the same ring about it as Bath and Wells, or St Edmundsbury and Ipswich. Or Research and Development, come to that.

The letters 'R and D' tumble easily from the lips, mentally accepted as twin aspects of a single function. The manufacturer, using his own or his shareholders' cash, needs to differentiate between research, inventing something new or extending human knowledge: and development, improving something which already exists. As most artefacts are already around in one form or another, there are plenty of manufactures to develop without wasting our sustenance on research. Indeed, industrialists usually find investment in research a dubious proposition, best left to the pharmacists and nuclear physicists, or to professional academics who need a constant flow of publication with which to pad their curricula vitae.

What follows, then, is not for pill manufacturers; or academics, among whom I give the palm for a thesis 'Overcrowding in Prisons – A Way Out'. Reading on, I was disappointed to learn this was not about the exploits of George Blake or introducing a new filing system: merely that we should incarcerate less villains in the first place.

We must not however poke fun at worthy scholars, whose constraints are less rigorous than ours, whose deadlines less fatal, whose costs come so often from the public purse. As manufacturers, we must concentrate on spending our resources on taking something we already possess, or can copy, and then improving it, cheapening its production, or widening its application or its market. While we are about it, and very occasionally, something may by chance emerge, like Fleming's penicillin or Watson-Watt's radar, which is both original and commercially valuable.

You may recall the anecdote about the Firestreak nose-cones, and how a new process, the floating of molten glass on a tin bed, made it possible to automate the production of a product which was flat and parallel. A successful development like that is just as likely to be a process as a product. What lifted Avimo out of the ruck of glass grinders was the result of lateral thinking by someone in the drawing office.

* In 1965 the desktop computer gave designers a machine which was much more than a sophisticated calculator. A ray-trace is what happens to light as it passes through the lenses and prisms within an optical system. It took a skilled designer with a log-book six laborious weeks to do a ray-trace for a standard instrument, and the result was seldom free of error. With the computer, it took minutes, and no mistakes.

* The specification of a military instrument laid down the precise particulars of each lens or prism as to molt, curvature, focal length or light transmission, so that the final assembly achieved a desired result in terms of magnification, field of view and so on. There are very many satisfactory optical solutions to any problem, involving variations in glass type, curvature of lenses and other refinements. By loading a data base with the tools and glass we held in stock, we were able to redesign the optics of any instrument at will. If glass components had been scrapped, or were on long delivery, we could replace them with something else from stock and revise the system so that it used only what was readily available. We had to tread carefully with interchangeable parts, like eyepieces, but for the rest, so long as a sealed instrument met the final test specification, nobody was ever the wiser.

* For years we confounded competitors and delighted customers by the reliability of our deliveries. The secret got out eventually but by that time we could afford to develop new products as well as new processes.

Once a development programme has been costed and agreed,

there has to be a regular mechanism for monitoring progress. I detest meetings and committees, which turn into expensive paper-chasing coffee breaks, substitutes for thinking and working. Yet something formal has to be in place or the project will merely drift on, gobbling time and money. The average development takes twice as long as you plan, and costs twice as much. You must at least know what is happening. Unchecked, someone will also start rewriting the design objectives, and then you really are in trouble. As production approaches, ensure that a planner joins the team to provide what will be needed in the way of tooling and test equipment in parallel with the launch of the manufacturing programme.

You must be ready to stop a development project the moment its original justification ceases to be valid. A competitor may have got there first, or you discover that the concept is flawed, or you have allowed your heart to rule your head. As usual, I have lost my own and other people's money by failing to kill unwise projects, throwing good money after bad and wasting a design resource.

As an example of being beaten to the punch, I reacted wrongly when a competitor brought out a pressure head for commercial aircraft which was lighter and slimmer than ours.

* I felt miffed that our old customer de Havilland hadn't warned us before switching to a product developed in America and was anxious not to lose the Fokker business too, having recently captured it from another American supplier. A pressure head, which records forward air pressure in flight and sometimes also static pressure, may be mast-mounted: you see them poking out from the fuselage as you mount the forward steps. The design has to allow for pilots wrongly switching on the internal heaters on the ground. In the air, the heat is needed to de-ice the mast and keep the orifices open.

* The secret of our competitor's miniaturisation lay in the use of

thermostatically-compensating sheathed nickel wire, which he had access to and we didn't. We thought that normal heating wire moulded in mastic would achieve the same result. So it did, in the wind tunnel and the laboratory, but not on the aircraft. In the end Fokker were lucky not to lose an F28 and we not to lose the F27 business we already had.

The second case where we ran into trouble was with a fundamentally flawed concept.

* Fairey Stainless made beer barrels out of stainless steel under licence from Firestone; the procedure for rolling truck wheels and beer kegs is similar. Our British competitors made barrels out of aluminium, which is lighter, cheaper and more easily recovered as scrap. Because aluminium, unlike stainless steel, is not compatible with beer, their barrels had to be lined with epoxy resin. When the resin cracked, the beer was tainted, although, with keg beer, not many people could tell the difference.

* We decided to line an aluminium keg with a thin gauge of stainless steel, to produce a light, relatively cheap and hygienic product. The prototypes were fine and our customers liked the concept. A keg has a vertical insertion, to introduce gas and draw off beer. If we had recalled the diagram in our physics text books illustrating the classic construction of an electrical cell, we would have avoided all sorts of grief.

The third example – would there had only been three – occurred because I allowed my commercial judgement to be swayed by outdated personal experience of the problem.

* A manufacturer of guns mounted one on an armoured vehicle chassis so that it could be fired in either register, the lower against tanks and the upper against aircraft. I had seen the effectiveness of anti-aircraft guns against tanks in the Far East, and suffered the embarrassment of trying to use a field gun as a howitzer, by burying the trail. The market seemed right. There was the usual

crop of post-colonial squabbles in the world, with presidents and chiefs of police trying to wipe each other out. It was the time when two such vehicles in Tripoli would have seen off Gaddafi – as indeed would the few British soldiers training the King's men in anti-tank warfare, given word from the Foreign Office. (It was requested, but refused.)

* We were already using infra-red homing weapons against tanks and aircraft. A white-light sight using an analogue computer with variable magnification to operate with artillery in either mode was a clever idea, but already out of date. I should at least have made the customer pick up the development cost, which in the end we had to write off.

Ideally, the size of your development department needs to be smaller than its constant demand. The devil, you may recall, finds work for idle hands, like starting unauthorised projects, or doing work on spec for customers to save a salesman's face. As with our other counsels of perfection, there will be more exception than compliance. You have to respond to serious enquiries from good customers, which often involves doing initial design work on spec. Some of the team will be specialists, who have to be retained even when the workload drops: they'll have plenty to do before long and they're hard to replace. And so on. Your Chief Designer, however limited his innovative flair, will be endlessly inventive in protecting and enlarging his establishment.

Whatever the controls, some of your design resource will be wasted. When you have spare capacity available to be diverted to useful routine work like value engineering, a salesperson will creep in with a new idea which is more exciting than taking 8% out of the metal content of a casting. Who wants hours of stress calculations and tool redesign when the scent of true discovery is in the air?

You need constantly to be on alert for slippage in a

development project. The first decision is whether to kill it or not. If you give it a reprieve, view any 'recovery' scheme with a jaundiced eye. Those who have allowed it to slip are unlikely to pull anything back, whatever extra resource they secure. Outside bodies – research institutes, universities, design houses – can help but only if someone specifies precisely what services they are to provide, when and for how much: which, in development, is a rash burden to assume. If you decide to draft in extra people, the best qualified will be found among your own planning and test engineers. It often takes longer explaining the problem to a third party than solving it in-house.

Unless you wish shortly to tramp the streets, you never allow a development project to begin without clearly identifying your customer or market. This involves also planning backwards from the date when the product is to be launched. If insufficient time has been allowed, leave the project alone, or postpone the launch date. It is hard enough estimating how long things under your control will take – the basic design, detailed drawing, prototyping, tooling, writing software or as the case may be; it becomes impossible when your product has to be wedded into a larger project managed by someone else, or if field trials are a prerequisite to any sales.

A field trial ensures that the device works in the environment for which it was designed, as that F28 pressure head did not, or the Call Logging Indicator which turned out not to like non-rotary dials. Although the trials are central for you, they may be peripheral for your customer, who has bigger things to worry about. Then the trial may be aborted because somebody else's gear failed to work, or, more often, because your product was wrongly specified in the first place and needs modification. You know in advance that these things happen, but it doesn't make life easier.

Technical products need maintenance and instruction manuals, often approved by the customer. Writing them calls for a combination of skill and knowledge hard to supplement at short notice, which is why you hang on to technical writers even when they are not busy. Few things are more frustrating than having a product held for delivery because the manuals aren't ready.

An efficiently run development project involves regular co-operation between designer, planner, test engineer and salesman, with financial supervision and progress reported against fixed benchmarks. The physical location of the model shop, or its equivalent, is important. In an engineering environment, for example, the draughtsman, the planner, the toolmaker and the fitter must be able to talk to each other, sorting out tolerances and exchanging ideas. For a contrast in style and effectiveness, observe what Platt Saco-Lowell did in Lancashire and South Carolina.

* In America everything took place in the same building. The machines were practical, cost-effective and developed on time. Their manufacture did not call for high levels of skill or job knowledge. Despite its high labour turnover and cost, Greenville was an effective development and production unit with saleable products.

* In Lancashire machines were manufactured in three factories, at Accrington, Oldham and Bolton. Development was done in the village of Helmshore. The conceptual thinking was good but the University of Helmshore, as it was known, designed products that called for skill in manufacture, sometimes overlooking simple factors, like hard anodising rotor housings to prevent grooving in open-end spinning. Every two years, the Stone-Platt board visited Helmshore for a design review. I am convinced the local team didn't change the graphs, slides and charts from visit to visit. Helmshore cost the Group directly about £2m a year, and indirectly its technical reputation among the world's leading textile machinery makers.

In slamming the late Stone-Platt, I am not making a case for economy by eliminating development budgets. Platt needed to update its products, and develop new ones. What it achieved in America was not enough to carry its failure in Lancashire. That, along with other stupidities which we will stumble across in due course, is why the receivers were called in.

We are going to look at patents and licensing later. Here let us remind ourselves that a firm has to protect its intellectual property by ensuring that it owns anything invented at its cost with its resources in its time, and that anyone leaving leaves his secrets behind when he goes. In practice and the world of photocopiers, you cannot prevent some skulduggery. The best way to cover yourself is to provide an environment which keeps the design team happy and motivated – worthwhile projects, adequate resources and publicly expressed appreciation of the value their function.

Because design projects are by their nature unpredictable, their costing uncertain, I give you a prohibition which will be our Twelfth Commandment – Never start a development programme which cannot be funded from current production. That is what The Norman Aeroplane Company did with its Freelance, at a time when the Fieldmaster was not yet fully launched.

* With the dominant Cessna effectively quitting the high-wing single reciprocating aircraft business, Norman's Freelance looked a good prospect. The prototype was attractive and launching production would fill a design and production gap while we migrated the Fieldmaster programme to Yugoslavia. Should we have known that, at a late stage and for the first time on that category of aircraft, the CAA would insist on fail-safe dual controls to the ailerons? Or that, in the toils, someone would delay planning the interior trim? We had allowed for some slippage but, when a project badly overruns, and you have nothing else to sell, and no money coming in, even the soundest concept leads to disaster.

Norman went into receivership because it was unable to certify its new aircraft within the planned time and available funds, despite glittering prospects for the product and an agreed sale of a manufacturing licence in India. Fairey SA in Belgium had products to sell, but in 1976 and 1977 depended on somebody else achieving his development targets. As we were to find out, that squares the element of risk.

* In 1975 Belgium joined forces with Holland, Denmark and Norway to buy a new fighter aircraft. There were three contestants for the order, Swedish, French and American. Fairey SA, experienced in compensation programmes after building Starfighters and Mirages, slotted itself into the favoured position of final assembly and 'stuffing', whichever contender won. He who stuffs picks up the percentages on the avionics, which cost as much as the airframe, and the subsequent spares business. Good news all round.

* After a dazzling display in May at the Le Bourget Air Show by the prototype F16, the contract went to General Dynamics. We in Fairey SA were involved to the extent of at least £75m of work over the next 15 years and much more if, as happened, other foreign buyers also chose the F16. We faced a tough 18 months between the award and the start of production but the Belgian government agreed to provide the finance to carry us through the delay and the build-up period.

* On 8th and 9th September, 1975 the Managing Director of Fairey SA and I went to St Louis and Fort Worth to see how the F16 programme was going. In effect, it wasn't. We found ourselves looking at a new aircraft, based on the prototype, for which tooling had barely started.

* We kept going in the Belgian factory with its 1,700 employees as long as we could by building our own Islander and Trislander aircraft ahead of schedule. The negotiations for the promised interim finance dragged on interminably, only to be completed in August, 1977, which was a few days too late, as things turned out.

With the F16 work still months away, we tried to reduce our labour force, which led to an uproar. Eventually on 26th September, the local management had to ask for court protection to continue trading.

When the receiver has been in and you've lost all your investment, it is little consolation to see that you were right after all. The F16 has been an enormous success and the renamed Fairey plant at Gosselies has shared in the prosperity. I doubt if anybody remembers these days the overrun on the F16 development, or cares.

These anecdotes tell us that development projects need controlling. You may fail without them, but, when they go wrong, you fail even quicker with them. Don't be afraid to pull out and cut your losses. If you have to rely on someone else performing, make sure that their default will not be your downfall. I doubt if anybody else will be smart enough to sell four governments a fighter which hasn't been developed, but they'll come up with something else. It's a tough old life out there.

A final word: stick to development and leave research to the academics. It took massive incompetence and the addiction of the Principal to strong waters for a British Institution of Higher Learning to become insolvent. We industrialists can founder only too easily, and soberly. As you may now appreciate, I speak from experience, on both counts.

CHAPTER 15

Location

'Get place and wealth – if possible with grace;
If not, by any means, get wealth and place.'
                                        Pope

* We had our dissertation on Alexander Pope in Chapter 12. It will suffice here to note his prescient bracketing of wealth and place.

* I make no excuse to those, the majority certainly, for whom these sketches are no more relevant than Grace before a feast, an embarrassing interlude which postpones briefly our getting at the meat. To retain a single piece of knowledge from an entire book is an achievement. How much more, to acquire an interest or habit, such as the study of history. Apart from the pure enjoyment, you will warm to Konrad Adenauer's dictum that 'History is the sum total of things that could have been avoided.'

* You may have sensed I am trying to guide you towards the 17th century. Aside from the richness of its plot, it is the only subject on which Magnus Magnusson asks questions which are simple to answer. If your business fails, you can always fall back on Mastermind.

When the traveller asked the bystander the way, he was advised that, if that was where he intended to go, he shouldn't start from here. The same is true of many factories. However, like the traveller, this is where we find ourselves, and where we stay through a combination of inertia, convenience, tradition and economy. The original justification for siting the plant where it is may have long vanished but the disruption, expense and hazards associated with moving make relocation unthinkable.

So netting is still made from man-made fibres in Bridport because the climate once suited the growing of flax. In Hull, the company Halls, Barton rigged ropes until 1988 to service a whaling fleet long departed, leaving the beasts to be slaughtered by the Japanese under a cloak of scientific enquiry. You find factories everywhere on the streams which once provided their motive power, a matter of little concern until a flash flood rushes through the tar dip, distributing its contents over downstream allotments. (The deposit was surprisingly delicate, like fine plating, each leaf and stem daintily clad in its robe of mourning. The allotment holders were slow to detect the beauty of the phenomenon.)

Most of us stay where we are because we don't think about moving. We know that every move has its hidden costs. Key employees are reluctant to relocate, even at the firm's expense. The severance pay for those you leave behind is crippling. Those who move may not settle down and the marital upsets occasioned by any separation of husband from wife may lead to lost time or lost employees. America is different, the gravitational pull of the local or the wife's mother being absent. The gangster bosses who run the union franchises in the north have failed to penetrate the south, the geographical divide being as Fleet Street to Wapping. There is no federal minimum wage. When you move, you simply 'let people go'. But we are not talking here about the United States, and must remain content to probe the factors relevant to the United Kingdom.

We should not tolerate a poor working environment merely as an accident of history. Once in a while we should ponder whether this would be the right place if we were to start again. If not, what can we do to create conditions closer to the ideal on the same site or in the same locality? The one item we can never cost is the expense of disrupting a skilled and experienced labour force, of recruiting and training its replacement.

For most manufacture the ideal factory is an open rectangle on a single level with 17 feet to the eaves, a strong floor, good insulation, adequate access, plenty of parking and not too remote from a town with its people, its shops and its communications. Movement of work from one floor to another in a multi-storey building costs labour, increases work in progress and complicates supervision.

If you decide to upgrade an old factory, at least engage an architect who understands manufacturing, which is what our old friends James Pearsall failed to do. The next generation of management had to dig deeply into the corporate pocket to rectify the mistake.

* In 1962 James Pearsall decided to build on to an ancient factory an addition of four floors, connected by stairs and a lift. The height of the new shops was eleven feet and the floor loading only enough to carry machinery currently in use. There was no air conditioning but windows opened on to the gardens of nearby terrace houses.

* Fifteen years later larger and heavier machines were cracking the concrete floor beams. The 92 decibels of noise were deafening in the confined spaces and not very popular with the neighbours either, even if the night shift kept the windows shut. To speak of sweated labour in summer was not to use polemical imagery.

Pearsalls couldn't walk away from its old site because braids and threads have to be dyed and the old factory contained a dye-house. If you possess a dye-house, or a plating shop, or any other noxious industrial operation, stay where you are, keeping your head down, placating the neighbours and preventing effluent flowing into surface drainage channels. The cost of meeting modern environmental conditions when you install these facilities on a fresh site is prohibitive.

If you move, choose first a site within the travel-to-work area of your present employees. This varies around the country, depending on commuter transport and tradition. In the south and west people tend to be more mobile mentally and logistically. In parts of the north, any move is too far. The minority anywhere who use a move as the opportunity to claim redundancy are those you hardly want to keep anyway.

Discarding for a moment your constant prior concern for the comfort and happiness of your employees, consider the load a new location may place on your managers and yourself. You have regularly to visit distant sites: keep them in clusters, preferably in places easily accessible by air or train. If you have to rely on driving, say farewell to another segment of your life.

You need to look into the value of the property you are leaving, and its planning status. Where it is in a town, or suitable for housing or out-of-town shopping, you need a property man working for you because you can be sure the developer will only be working for himself. However tempting the sum, you are unlikely to make any profit directly out of the move. You can cost the new site, the buildings, the partitions, the air lines, the conveyer systems, the restrooms, the offices, the heating, the cooling, the car parks and so on. You cannot cost the disruption, the lost production while you untangle the plant from one place and get it producing in another. Just accept that it is wiser to stay put unless the reasons for moving are compelling.

This scepticism may lead to something constructive, like optimising the use of your present site or consolidating two units into one. People work better in concentrated areas, apart from the cost of heating and maintaining surplus space. As we have just seen, Pearsalls went about an on-site expansion in an ill-advised way. In Lolift, when we decided to concentrate, we closed the wrong factory.

* When we bought the company, there were two factories, in Ripon and Knaresborough, with goods being shipped partly completed between the two. There were theoretical savings in overheads of £70,000 a year in closing the smaller factory, bussing key staff to Ripon: and a capital boost from the sale of the empty factory.

* When we had done it, many of the Knaresborough workers, who actually lived in Harrogate, refused to move. The good folk of Ripon, freed from the threat of losing work to a sister plant, became even more obstructive than before. As mentioned elsewhere, before long we closed the business.

When you buy a factory, you tie up funds which may be needed as working capital and you are more committed to that location. When you rent, you may be limited in your ability to knock the place about; the only certainty of rent reviews is that the rents will rise; and, on vacation, you cannot avoid the tyranny of dilapidations however precise the schedule of condition on entry. A lease at a rack-rent can easily become a liability but a long leasehold or freehold is a security lenders will understand, a saleable and inflation-proof asset. The sums may tell you to rent but experience shows it is better in the long run to buy, if you can.

As soon as you become, in the jargon, footloose, you are the target of every regional and national agency, courted by the seductive attraction of towns which you thought bred only demagogic politicians and football hooligans. You may even be unwittingly exposed to the dreaded 'Skem factor', that disabling disease contracted by those persuaded to set up shop in Skelmersdale, the New Town spawned from the slums of Liverpool. The fatalities are forgotten but the survivors, those who stayed in industry and remained sane, will never forget their experiences. In Merseyside, for all its industrial militancy, you might find skilled and responsible workers; but those who moved to the New Town took with them no skills and no responsibility – only the militancy.

Because potential movers study logistics, they gravitate to the south-east. There most manufacturers find easier access to skills, suppliers, customers, ports and airports. Cost and the shortage of labour may force them away from the centre, to settle near a harbour or along the artery of a motorway, where each intersection will provide its cluster of development. Other regional centres strive to build resources to match those in the south-east but the geography of Europe works against them.

The more desirable your preferred location, the slower will be the planning and other processes. Conversely, the less economically attractive, the faster will the trap close around you. It was frustration over bureaucratic delay that pushed me into a flawed decision in 1967.

* In 1967 Taunton didn't see itself as a manufacturing town and barely tolerated the industrial base which underpinned the prosperity which enhanced the aspirations of its professional men and the affectations of their ladies. Those of the élite who shared the onerous duties of Ale Taster or Rhine Ridder in the Court Leat also gave of their time as Alderman or Councillor, keen to save their beloved community from the further despoliation which new factories would bring about.

* Avimo had outgrown the ancient buildings beside the railway, where it struggled to make hyper-clean optical instruments in the dust and vibration generated as the Kings, Castles and Halls thundered by, and lesser creations chugged more sedately past on their way to Barnstaple or Minehead. Offered the choice in Taunton of trying to build on a filled-in quarry or a swamp, we fell for the siren song of the Devon County Council, which lured us to Barnstaple, 52 miles away.

* A major consideration was the availability of labour, and it was indeed available, unskilled and unused to industry, outside the tourist season. Come the summer, off they went to the bars and beaches, where the pickings were richer and the work more congenial. Every specialist, whether storeman, draughtsman, fitter or inspector, had to be imported from up-country.

We survived in Barnstaple by setting up a new type of business demanding lesser skills than we needed in Taunton. The lesson was not to trust local politicians or statistics. The reported unemployment in Ilfracombe, a slightly seedy resort a few miles from our new factory, was $17\frac{1}{2}\%$. On a television programme deploring local unemployment, the incompetence of the government, the ineptitude of British industry and so on, I offered to lay on a free bus between the two towns, paying people from the time they left Ilfracombe to the time they returned. We had two takers: a publican who had wearied of the licensed trade and a holiday-maker from the Midlands who fancied settling in the south-west.

Barnstaple was in a Development Area, a place where manufacturers received incentives to relocate. We didn't go solely for the incentives, but they were a factor in the decision. We should have recognised that no incentive can repay the cost of poor communications, unskilled or bloody-minded labour, remoteness and a non-industrial environment. The newcomer cannot recruit loyal or skilled workers who, by definition, are not themselves footloose. The fact that people are unemployed does not of itself mean that they are looking for work. In short, we should have foreseen our Thirteenth Commandment – Never choose a new location on the basis of incentives.

On the English Industrial Estates Corporation, I discovered that the surest way of restoring some kind of prosperity to a depressed area is by encouraging indigenous firms to grow. If however you have a profitable operation in one of the difficult areas, think twice before investing in any major expansion in the same place. If you do, you may find yourself regarded as no more than a tethered goat in a jungle clearing, but with no hunter waiting in the hide. That happened to Fairey.

* A subsidiary, Tress Engineering, manufactured small hydraulic valves profitably in Newburn out of two scruffy buildings with poor offices and sub-standard workshops. What a propitious location, you might think, with its George Stephenson associations, but in the late sixties, no location in the north-east was propitious for engineering. With the decay in nationalised ship-building and steel, the Amalgamated Engineering Union prevented the recruitment of any trainee or dilutee so long as any holder of a union card was out of work. Plenty of riveters, platers or puddlers were unemployed in Wallsend, Middlesbrough or Sunderland, but that wasn't much help if you wanted turners or fitters in Newburn This condition was described by Harold Wilson as The White Heat of Technology in a memorable and successful election campaign.

* To bid for larger tenders world-wide, we needed to extend our range of valves. That also gave us the chance to build a modern factory with well-lit offices. The white-collar staff, including the foremen and designers, were unionised and the manual workers chose as their convenor an ambitious communist. For three years after the expansion the two unions played box and cox in striking or working to rule. The only way of stopping the losses was to shut the place down, including the two original buildings.

They made a television programme about Tress, which was screened locally. It was billed for showing on the national network too but the BBC cancelled it.

Consider the question of managerial housing and of schooling before uprooting an existing unit and transplanting it far away. Your managers and their wives may decline to live in an area where the council estate is the prototype for all private development. (The only exception may be the doctor's residence: everyone knows that the medico must be coddled as a useful member of society; and that, if you try to make his family live in a council house, you will find the surgery shut.) Nor are ambitious parents prepared to accept regimentation imposed by political bigots when it comes to availability of schools.

If you are compelled to relocate, approach the ordeal with extreme caution. The larger the bribes, the bigger the drawbacks. Those who first agree to move may decide to stay behind, and those who do move may not remain long. You are unlikely to find again the ring of sub-contractors, the stockists and the skills which you used to take for granted. The people you recruit will be the worst of the local labour, ingrained perhaps with habits and practices you never imagined existed.

Bear in mind that you expand most efficiently by using your present site and people more efficiently. Take a fresh look at those 'make or buy' decisions. Accept at face value no blandishment from those trying to persuade you to move. Avoid anywhere with a flat roof: it will leak.

When the arguments for relocation or a fresh facility are compelling, see if there is an existing business into which you can back your own. Anything already up and running will have storekeepers, smithwrights, electricians, supervisors, buyers, inspectors, computer operators, clerks and shopfloor personnel. Its car park will be surfaced and drained, and it may have a covered loading bay. You could also find 3-phase power, a transformer, compressors, air lines and cranes. There could even be a staff canteen for you to shut.

A pristine site has its attractions but the risks are enormous. Relocation is one of those functions we may only do once, learning as we go. Most people never make use of their experience because they swear never to go through such turmoil again. And that is moving or expanding to somewhere in the same country. Nevertheless, a move on to a green field site in foreign parts can be carried through successfully, and the

Japanese in particular have shown us how to do it, even sowing a new work ethic into what might have seemed infertile soil.

We give manufacturing overseas a chapter to itself shortly, along with licensing. All the strictures contained above are equally applicable to a foreign venture, to which other complications will be added. These will be revealed at the appropriate time. In the meanwhile, having skirted around trade unions, let us confront them head on, along with trade associations. We cannot continue to go through life looking only on the bright side.

CHAPTER 16

Trade Associations and Unions

'When bad men combine, the good must associate, else they fall, one by one, an unpitied sacrifice in a contemptible struggle.'

Burke

* Burke enjoyed, with Bacon, the gift of proving with hindsight to have been right on every major issue of his day despite being constantly at odds with other contemporary politicians, writers and thinkers. Any who still hold that the views of a majority are correct and should prevail will benefit from studying Burke's record on the American colonies, India and Ireland; on the freedoms of the press and trade; on corruption and nepotism, slavery and liberty. His famous parting from Fox came because Burke was the first to appreciate that, however pressing the need for reform, the removal of all checks and restraints on political behaviour, as in the early days of the French Revolution, would lead to absolutism.

* Being a man of his time, he was prolix and verbose. He addressed the House of Commons for nine days summing up in the trial of Warren Hastings. He was, as usual, right, and Hastings wrongly acquitted.

* Burke's Ireland had a population two thirds the size of its sister

island and a capital rivalling London in its elegance and sophistication, of which happily the architecture still remains. The English, in times of national crisis, were rightly fearful of Irish strength. As with St Petersburg in October 1917, so with Dublin at Easter, 1916: the architects of revolution were a tiny disaffected minority whose success and failure eventually led them to government. And both in Russia and Ireland, the effects of discarding the rule of law to achieve political ends, about which Burke warned so eloquently, are still with us.

* What became the Irish Republic has also acquiesced in the demise of the native Protestants who once adorned every aspect of Irish life, a class of which Burke himself was a perhaps reluctant member. That, with Partition, is a continuing tragedy for Hibernia, and for us all.

The three employers' organisations to which British firms or individuals belong are the Confederation of British Industry, the Institute of Directors and the British Institute of Management. The breadth of their membership is such that they can only represent industry in the broadest terms. You may get a return on your investment if you positively require the bulletins they circulate. Otherwise you should question whether you would incur the expense of membership if you were not already a member. If the answer is no, resign.

Retaining your membership in the hope of influencing policy is a delusion. Government and Whitehall pay no attention to anyone who isn't a threat to them. They fawn on the media and brush all others aside. As we will see in a moment, there are other reasons for participation in these bodies, but influencing government policy is not one of them.

The Board may nonetheless feel it right that a firm of your eminence should be seen to contribute to the deliberations of the CBI. That, they will say, will provide a forum where other industrialists can be met informally, and the company's views can be conveyed to the corridors of power. The only true advantage is likely to be providing an outlet for someone who is under-employed, and might become a nuisance. The risk is that somebody with important work to do may be seduced by seeing himself joining the ranks of The Great and The Good.

A Chairman should either also be Chief Executive, or have so much work outside the company that he cannot find the time to meddle with its executive management. It is disastrous when he, through want of anything better to do or through conceit, establishes himself as a parallel source of authority to the Managing Director. This results in confusion among the ranks, and a field day for the company politicians. A weak Managing Director will shrug his shoulders, draw his salary, and let things drift: a strong one will fight the Chairman, or leave. Either course is bad for the firm.

The Chairman who is hyperactive (which, by executive definition, involves turning up at the office when there isn't a Board meeting) can be encouraged to trudge round a golf course in working hours or write unpublished letters to *The Times* only to a limited extent. If you engage his energies in the CBI and other public bodies, he is unlikely to do the company any harm and the semblance of activity will satisfy the participant, enabling the real managers to get on with managing.

Attending committees, councils, enquiries, conferences and the like passes the time amiably, and is no more harmful or beneficial than an afternoon at the bridge table, playing for toy money. The practice only becomes dangerous when someone with executive duties comes to see such activity as part of his job.

We are talking about a slippery slope, which the sportsman can only leave by deliberately throwing himself to one side, at great peril to both pride and person. The invitation to join the county committee of the CBI is harmless enough. Nor can you really deny a senior executive a monthly afternoon off as a member of the Regional Council. Soon the toboggan is moving faster: County Chairman, Regional Chairman, membership of the national Council itself, with the concomitant committees and commitments.

Before long there are Garden Parties and an invitation to Number 10. A leading industrialist cannot cry off those important functions where bankers, insurance people, road hauliers and other groups meet annually, or refuse to travel the county to shake a princely hand. One day that same hand may pin something to his lapel, or even tap him on the shoulder.

But what of the shop? Before long an important merger in America is being postponed, because of the demands of public life. Troubled managers are being met half-way in hotel rooms to save more time-consuming factory visits. Too late we receive a Queen's Award, that harbinger of doom.

Genuine trade associations provoke more difficult questions. In the days when the unions threw with legally loaded dice, no engineering employer could afford not to belong to the Engineering Employers' Federation, who were as tough and uncompromising a bunch as their union counterparts. So long as the curse of national pay bargaining persists, somebody has to negotiate on behalf of the employers and you need to know what line they are taking. If they agree to pay too much, you are the one who does the paying: if there are strikes because of a niggardly settlement, or no settlement at all, again you pick up the cost.

You will also find a trade association better than a lawyer at an industrial tribunal, and very much cheaper. Some control access to major exhibitions, like the Society of British Aerospace Constructors at Farnborough or the International Textile Machinery Association's four-yearly extravaganza. Others adjudicate on the allocation of quotas, as, for example, the export of wire rope to the United States. If you economise by not joining or staying away, you cannot complain when a dominant manufacturer makes decisions binding on the whole industry.

You can run into trouble when customers blame your firm for an unpopular decision taken by a trade association, just because a member of your staff happened to be in office. As you might expect, it was Brownell who demonstrated this.

* The West Coast of the United States houses the world's biggest fishing fleets, many reaping the rich harvest in Alaska whose coastline is longer than that of the rest of the Union put together. Brownell dominated the twine trade, selling through stockists from San Pedro to Seattle, not on price but on brand reputation.

* Netting imports into the USA were subject to quotas as well as duty, to protect domestic industry. There was however no indigenous manufacturer of monofilament gill netting for the salmon boats, nobody therefore to be protected, and the stockists bought from the Far East without too much attention to technicalities like quotas. This did not deter some busybody on the Twine and Cordage Institute peaching to Washington about it, presumably on the basis that if his firm had to live with quotas, so should everyone else. Washington takes these infringements seriously, unless you have a senator rooting for you. They dropped hard on the gill net importers, fining them heavily and thereafter seeing the quotas were enforced.

* Brownell's then president was also president of the trade association. As such the importers saw him, and Brownell, as being responsible partly for their comeuppance. They at once looked around for another twine supplier and before long a look-alike product had captured not merely the West Coast business but much of that in the Gulf too. Twine for the fishing industry then ceased to be the most predictable and profitable of the Brownell products.

They tell me the former president of Brownell is doing very well these days, as a realtor and volunteer fireman. Brownell finally handed over its Gulf operation to a competitor who demurred when it came to paying for the inventory, and later closed its operation on the West Coast.

Where a product is subject to an approved Standard, as in the medical, aviation, telecommunication and a host of other businesses, the appropriate trade association is likely to have a committee advising the government body concerned. In that event, your representative on the committee should be technically strong and commercially aware. You have to be sure that whatever recommendations go forward do not involve redesigning your product, or give an advantage to a competitor. In a perfect world, the Standard would be written around something you have patented, which is the kind of dirty trick a competitor will try to put across you if you are not alert.

Having a competitor effectively able to rewrite the specification for a product can cut you out of the business. Again it was Brownell in 1986 who saw how these things are done.

* Brownell made commercial twine and nets. It then contrived to supply twine to a manufacturer of nets used as a base for camouflage and, when landed with excess stocks due to a broken contract, obtained US government approval to manufacture the nets themselves. The big profits lay in converting the nets into the final product, by adding treated scrim, edge cord and so on. This business was dominated by two large corporations who had no intention of letting in a price-cutting minnow. One of them had two lobbyists and ten lawyers on the project and the other probably fielded a similar team. Naturally, it would have been a breach of the anti-trust laws if they had so much as spoken to each other: or exerted any improper influence over the officers responsible for the tender in St Louis.

* From its British parent, Brownell knew how to meet the specified standard of radar reflectivity and prepared its bid on that basis. Suddenly both large competitors devised a way of enhancing the radar performance still further, although the military

application of this was questionable. Clearly the American soldier is entitled to nothing but the best, the State of the Art, as they say. So the specification was changed, even if it had the unfortunate effect of excluding Brownell from bidding.

* Boeing, from its AWACS, knows a lot about radar. Faced with a visit from government scientists who wished to check Brownell's competence at the new standard, Brownell enlisted Boeing's help. The Boeing team flew to New England for the meeting, answered all the questions satisfactorily and headed back for Seattle. No sooner were they airborne than the scientists remembered some more technical queries, and of such import that they must be answered within hours. If there were any uncertainties, regretfully Brownell would be struck off the tender list.

* The exigencies of distance require that flights from Hartford to Seattle have intermediate stops. The Boeing team were contacted on their way home and able to clear the new questions. Thus Brownell remained, for the time being, on the approved lists of bidders. There were to be other incidents, like the one concerning the code-marked twine which we noted earlier. Brownell were forced to give up in the end. They ended up by successfully suing Uncle Sam. (Brownell's foray into the U.S. camouflage market brought down prices, as did John Bloom with washing machines and Freddie Laker with Transatlantic travel. When you take on the big boys, remember that they can lower prices too, if they have to. Bloom, Laker and Brownell learnt this the hard way.)

In summary, ask your accountant to give you a list of the associations and pressure groups to which the firm belongs, look at the costs, check how much useful management time is being absorbed by your membership. Cut out those from which you see no tangible benefit, replace any working delegate by a deadhead, if you have one, or your personnel manager, if you haven't. Check the technical competence of those on committees concerned with standards, quotas and the like.

In the days of the cartel, there were many good reasons for

meeting your competitors regularly, and a trade association was as good a venue as anywhere else. Today, if you want to indulge in price-fixing, do it in a remote and secret place, and keep no records.

Anybody who was in management before 1979 can be forgiven for thinking that Burke's 'combination of the bad' was aimed at the trade unions. We might have been more sanguine if we had recognised, with Burke, that tyranny inevitably leads to absolutism, which eventually destroys itself. The true architects of the Thatcher revolution on union law were Scanlan, Jones, Foulkes, Gormley and the other tyrants, although that is not why many of them ended up in the House of Lords. One incident comes to mind.

> * In the early 1970s Fairey Engineering had a request from Gormley's National Union of Mineworkers for its famous band to turn out at the head of some march by the miners. The bandmaster, who was also company secretary, declined. He then had a very senior member of the NUM on the phone threatening a strike and blacking of the firm if the band failed to appear.

While dealing with a British union was like playing soccer against William Webb Ellis (except that our opponents were not merely disregarding the rules, they were making them), most of us were pusillanimous in failing to stand up to or speak out against the situation. The people you knew, on your own shop floor, were nothing but cannon-fodder, thrown reluctantly into successive political battles. The penalty for desertion was the loss of union card, of job and even of the prospect of working at their trade in future. The employer was faced not merely with a strike but with all manner of coercion through secondary action which was quite legal, like blocking supplies in the docks or blacking the receipt of goods by a customer. Any agreement was enforceable against the employer but not against the union. Small wonder that power went to their heads.

We are fortunate that foreign managers had more guts. The first company publicly to stand up to union violence was the American-owned Roberts, in Stockport. Then the Indians of Grunwick faced out a mob larded with woolly-minded politicians. South Africa, Canada and the United States sent us the managers to restore some discipline, pride and purpose in British Leyland, Shipbuilding, Coal and Steel. Fleet Street had long been above the law, out of bounds even to the Inland Revenue: there our salvation came from an assortment of Iranians, Czechs, Australians and Canadians.

Today there has to be a ballot before a strike, there are virtually no closed shops, intimidation of workers and their families is rare and only the more eccentric politician poses for the cameras on the picket lines. If you have union trouble, it's probably because of bad management. All the same, there are some good habits from the old days you should keep in mind.

Remember that a union negotiator only has the power to say no, to refuse anything. Do not therefore expect him to initiate or propose things. The very attributes which would make a good shop steward or convenor are the same as those which we seek in a manager. Those able to choose either career almost always opt for management, and when a steward or convenor shows signs of maturity and leadership, he will before long find himself accepting a supervisory post. We should not therefore be surprised that people who remain as shop stewards are either unintelligent or politically motivated, and cannot be relied on to act rationally or to take a long view, however patiently things may be explained to them.

A union negotiator will welcome the chance to go over the head of the responsible manager. If you permit that, you destroy the authority of the manager. Every minor disagreement will turn into a confrontation and land on your desk. Settle any dispute at plant level if possible. As soon as paid outside officials are involved, you may find yourself faced with someone who wants conflict, with consequent publicity for himself and the union. ACAS may then lower the temperature, but not always.

Faced with disruptive tactics short of a strike, like a go-slow or work-to-rule, you should decide immediately whether to give in or precipitate a walk-out, which you do by suspending the ringleaders. Few strikes last more than three weeks but all leave scars on the souls and holes in the pockets of everyone involved. By giving in to a go-slow, you invite repeated use of the same weapon. As the old biscuit advertisement said, 'One bite invites another'. The way to react to an overtime ban is to ban overtime. Institutionalised overtime is inefficient anyway.

When you are faced with a strike ballot, you have to stand aloof unless the falsehoods and distortions become too blatant. Ignore the hate-ridden diatribes which appear in Socialist Worker, Militant or the union's own broadsheet; the majority of those at whom this stuff is aimed are also sickened by it. If you have to correct a lie, send your letter to each worker at home but do not complicate things by restating your case. You should have put that across before things reached this state. Whatever you do, tell the truth. You may not be able to tell all the truth, or nothing but the truth, but you must never lie.

At no stage become involved in fighting a dispute through the press. Journalists thrive on dissension and trouble. Peace and reasonableness are not just bad news: they are non-news. You should nominate someone acquainted with the facts to talk to the media, and be the only spokesman. If a cub journalist with a diploma in social science distorts things too much, have a word with his editor. If the BBC shows bias against the firm, as it will, write to the Director-General, with a copy to your MP.

Our pious platitudes about treating your employees as individuals need restating here. They must have mechanisms whereby they can bring their ideas, fears, aspirations and complaints to your notice. An elected company council is a better forum than a mass meeting in the car park with a union official deciding policy on a show of hands. If you are blessed with a union-free shop, take care that nothing is done to give your employees cause to invoke union protection. Conditions in a union-free company ought to be, and can afford to be, better than in a unionised shop.

We have been short on anecdotes not because there is none. The converse is true. I have seen and been involved in waste, closure, the loss of jobs, the transfer of manufacture abroad, stupidities and cruel injustice through strikes, blacking, black-mail, coercion and other once legal but monstrous practices. I have seen sleepers introduced into good firms, to stay quiet for six months before they emerge to incite discord. (When the one in Avimo left, he said to me, "It's no good here. You've got them brainwashed.") I've had a Managing Director who insisted on dealing with every union matter himself, and we ended up with a closed shop. Because of the unbridled exercise of union power, jobs and capital have been wasted; production has been transferred abroad or imports taken over. Society as a whole has been the loser.

Those of you who have tried to deal with the unions in India, Belgium or Spain will have your own horror stories. The Teamsters, too, take some beating, but at least they discipline their members once the deal is struck. As we are moving next to overseas manufacture and licensing, we cannot escape the subject entirely, for which I can do no more than apologise.

CHAPTER 17

Overseas Manufacture and Licensing

'Chase brave employment with a naked sword
Throughout the world.'

Herbert

* George Herbert died of tuberculosis in 1633, when foreign trade was less significant than today, but we have come to expect prescience in poets, and especially when they are also men of the cloth. The use by industrialists of the naked sword has gone out of fashion, although Anglican clergy still warm to the occasional freedom fighter, eschewing the harsher soubriquet of terrorist.

* One of Herbert's duties, when not cloistered with his Muse, was to attend James I at the races. His mother was a friend of John Donne and he of Francis Bacon. He was persuaded, against his better judgment, to accept a living by that doyen of greeters and joiners, William Laud, who survived him by over a decade until the archepiscopal head went on the block in 1645.

* Prominent people continued to know each other and meet regularly until the end of the 18th century. Boswell tells us of a conversation on 3rd April, 1778 in which the other participants were Sheridan, Burke, the Doctor, Reynolds and Edward Gibbon.

You wonder sometimes how they found time to put pen to paper, or brush to canvas.

British manufacturers have to export because their home market is often too small to support economic production. Whether we will ever enjoy the whole of the EC as a home market is questionable. The French and Italians show no signs yet of curtailing their chauvinism and dismantling their non-tariff barriers.

With certain categories of merchandise, you can hold your foreign markets without the complication of sourcing abroad. These include some branded goods, especially clothing and liquor: complex products, like specialist machinery: and items which are mass-produced so efficiently that it is not worth duplicating the investment. There are cases too where you can pick up your fixed charges at home and sell at marginal cost abroad. When foreigners do that to us, it is described as dumping.

We cannot hope to emulate the Taiwanese, whose low wages are coupled with ruthlessness and industrial efficiency; or the Japanese with their vast, rich and protected home market. Our Empire which enjoyed Imperial Preference – some enjoyed it less than others – is gone. We remain inventive and wax indignant when base aliens steal our ideas. If we want to get back at them, we can manufacture off-shore, or sell someone a licence. Let us look at off-shore manufacture first.

The rules we noted about expansion on a new site at home apply also to setting up shop abroad. Back into an existing organisation if you can. The differences of language, law, taxation and so on are obvious. The hidden snags are more dangerous, like the political and cultural climate in Quebec in 1976, when Bridport-Gundry and British Ropes decided to start manufacturing soft ropes in Canada. But Canada is a tolerant and advanced society. Nobody is suggesting surely, that prejudice and racism scar the face of that fair land. Read on.

* The partners jointly owned an importing and distribution operation which took its name from the Scottish town of Gourock. We were already in Montreal and decided to put in the rope-making machinery in the nearby town of Boucherville. At the same time, the provincial government embarked on an anti-English campaign, egged on by de Gaulle and others. The memorial to Wolfe's death was removed from the Heights of Abraham and, among various petty and spiteful acts, employers were forbidden to take on any worker who was not a native French speaker.

* The rope-making started but, there being no Québecois rope-makers, we were unable to recruit an experienced manager or any technical staff. Extruded fibre littered the floor like candy floss. Production was sporadic, the losses horrific.

* On 4th March, 1976 I landed at Mirabel airport to chair a crisis meeting of the board. All the British and German first-class passengers were segregated from the rest. After holding and questioning us for two hours, long enough to ensure we had missed the transport into Montreal or anyone meeting us (which in my case was Larry Robillard, the French-Canadian fighter ace from the Battle of Britain), we were allowed entry into Canada for one day.

* One day was enough. Bridport-Gundry pulled out. Eventually our partners, after struggling to continue, had to close the plant.

There are worse places than Quebec. At least I was allowed out. A fellow Stone-Platt director visited J. Stone and Co. (India) Ltd, a public company in which, from 1973, we had owned 60% of the equity. He was roughed up and imprisoned by some of the striking workforce, the experience leaving him with a regard for the Indian police not dissimilar to mine for the Quebec immigration officials. And I expect Union Carbide wish they had never set foot in Bhopal.

Another hidden reef below the waves is accountancy. You can check the local rules, on depreciation and the like. You can even learn some of the dodges, like writing up fixed assets on an American acquisition and having the enhanced depreciation allowed for tax. You will find it difficult to engage a local accountant who understands that, in a manufacturing business, the only estimated figure between inventory counts should be the one relating to stock movement. Within the EC you can introduce your own employee. Elsewhere, and in the United States especially, you have to suffer the indigenous product. We have already seen how a Brownell accountant contrived to inflate the profit by juggling with the stock. His successors also continued to do some silly things.

* In July, 1988 we were negotiating the sale of the Brownell business to its managers, along with two depots in Louisiana but retaining the Seattle operation which was important for our Irish company. As physical inventories had been taken on 30th April – before any sale had been contemplated – that was a good date on which to fix the value of the assets being sold and avoid argument about what stock was slow-moving or redundant. Then we came to verifying the quality of the receivables and payables as at the same date.

* We soon came across a debt of $82,000 which nobody owed. Remember, this was July. For three months Connecticut had reported this specific debt was collectable on behalf of the New Orleans depot. Ah well, it wasn't a debt really. At the April stocktaking, there had been a surplus of $82,000 on the New Orleans inventory. That's all right then; cancel the receivable and add it to inventory. No, we can't do that. Seattle wasn't doing too well and so we transferred the credit to them, to improve their figures. And by leaving the phoney debt on the books, overstated profit by $82,000.

But it was worse than merely overstating profit. Instead of

investigating the surplus, they fouled up the figures in three locations. The concealment of a loss in Seattle meant that policy decisions were being taken on false assumptions. Misleading management accounts are worse than none at all. The management buy-out was never completed and Seattle was later sold. The imported trawl business on the West Coast which Bridport Gundry Ireland had pioneered was thus handed over to their Irish competitor who is reputed to have exported 50 mid-water trawls to Seattle in the first nine months of 1990.

Before making a move, check the local tax rules and double-taxation agreements. Beware of taxation disguised as social charges and levied on the payroll. Stay away from California, which likes to attribute world-wide earnings to the local outfit, and from France, where a foreign company needs almost a presidential decree before it is allowed to lay off staff, and countersigned by the Pope if it is British. Make sure you can remit dividends and repatriate capital. Where Exchange Control exists, which is almost everywhere, obtain approvals before sending money abroad and retain the evidence of what was sent, when and how.

Obvious stuff, you may conclude. But too many people cut corners, especially when the Big Boss starts managing dynamically. People who own sound businesses seldom want to part with them cheaply, and especially not to foreigners. It took Stone-Platt at its worst to buy an unsuccessful firm with an unfamiliar product in France using borrowed money against the advice of the only director who knew what a lousy trade they were entering.

* The Hayward-Tyler subsidiary was a leading British manufacturer of pumps, with minor operations abroad. Vannes Lefebre was an unsuccessful family-owned French manufacturer of valves. Pumps and valves share engineering properties and look alike, but the markets are dissimilar.

* Many of the members of the Stone-Platt board had convinced themselves that growth did not lie in solid, unexciting, basic businesses within the United Kingdom. With inflation an irreversible fact of British life, and the cost of borrowing nothing in real terms, you could grow by buying any high-technology business, especially if it were abroad. The sum at risk with Vannes Lefebre was 'only' £300,000. It cost about £1.6m eventually to unload it.

(A second director joined me in a subsequent vote against paying £700,000 for a business we never actually took control of. Years later I used to run into the two partners who sold it. They couldn't believe their luck, keeping both the cake and the halfpenny. At least, with Vannes Lefebre, Stone-Platt took possession of the assets, for a time. Perhaps it would have been better for everyone if they hadn't.)

You may think these anecdotes of no particular significance. But the cash was.

Do not overlook the possibility of the half-way house to overseas manufacture, the joint venture. The local investors will share your losses and may even pay you out if you want to escape. At the same time, it is likely that their own interests will come before yours, and they are closer to the till than you are. You will find, I regret to say, that outside northern Europe there are few places where you will be allowed to go about your business with the freedom and security that you enjoy at home. Involvement in South Africa may give fanatics an opportunity to prolong your Annual General Meetings, but there are many worse places in the world than that.

This counsel of despair is meant to be more a plea for caution. Too many companies have taken the plunge without first testing the depth, temperature and cleanliness of the water. Before you agree to move in, study carefully what it will cost you to move out. And ponder deeply our Fourteenth Commandment – Never pledge the credit of your parent company to support an operation abroad.

Now Licensing, that high road to receiving a regular income without effort, that by-pass which gives you new products without developing them. This is a subject on which many books are written, seminars held and experts proliferate. It is second only to the sale of arms in spawning advisers, specialist lawyers, middlemen and opportunists, some of whom are honest and competent and others of whom are not. The potential advantages to both licensor and licensee are obvious. Why then are so many in either camp unhappy about their experiences? We stick, as usual, with the things that go wrong.

As licensor, your product has to be readily saleable in the territory you are ceding. Your licensee is likely to be already in the same business, a potential, albeit less successful, competitor. You are now proposing to hand over to him what has given you the technical or commercial edge. Once he has this knowledge, he may cheat, and the law may encourage him to do so, especially in the EC where a licensee can sell virtually anywhere within the Community, however tightly you try to pin him down.

Ideally, you retain control over an integral part of the product, like a magneto-restrictive strip at the heart of an alarm system. Practically, you negotiate to receive as much money up front as you can, and then induct your licensee into the know-how and full manufacture by slow stages, first having him import the finished product, then buying sub-assemblies before achieving full local manufacture. Retain ownership of any brand name and secure the right to any improvement to the product which the licensee may introduce. Set the royalty at a reasonable rate; if you put it too high, the honest licensee will not sell much product and the dishonest will have another excuse for cheating.

It is easy to forget that many countries tax licence fees and royalties at source. They also make difficulties over paying in other than the domestic currency, which may be unconvertible without Central Bank approval. In India, for example, the tax rates vary and the speed at which government business is transacted would turn a sundial into a stopwatch. Then there is the corruption. Someone has to fund the political parties, I suppose, but the methods are unsubtle, as Bofors can explain to you in more detail, if the subject grabs you.

Before granting a licence, especially to a backward country, check the record of the applicant with previous licensors. If remittances can only be changed to sterling or US dollars with official approval, at least arrange for the cash to be lodged in your name at a local bank while you are waiting. Sometimes a licence provides that you, in the fullness of time will have to buy the product back from the licensee. It is advisable then to fix a labour rate in US dollars, based on the times achieved, after learning, in your home factories. Apart from having a cheap manufacturing source, if you can overcome quality problems, this will at least give you some chance of controlling incursions by the licensee into your export markets.

Much as we deplore having to use lawyers, licensing is one activity where reliance on common sense and experience is not enough. Often, to get the cash out, the licence has to be subject to the law of the licensee. If he speaks another language, the documents have to be translated and notarised. As you need a lawyer with an office or good correspondent in foreign parts, you have to go to one of the larger international firms. You hope to pass their costs on to the licensee, but often that is not possible. I thought, from my years on the other side of the fence, I knew all about lawyers' fees, but I found I still had lessons to learn.

* Delta Communications negotiated a useful sale of telecom equipment to Venezuela, based on the formula of selling completed product, then sub-assemblies, then components and finally a full licence. To get the cash out, the documents had to be certificated in Spanish and the contract was subject to Venezuelan law. This meant our employing a top international lawyer, and I was happy to know one such, the senior partner of an enormous firm, an honest and able man with whom I sat on another Board. The deal was done most efficiently, and the fee paid.

* We had another possible licence deal in Greece. I suggested to my friend that, as he had never met his clients, he might care to break one of his regular trans-Atlantic trips at Shannon to spend a couple of hours getting to know them. He kindly did so, and sent us a bill for $5,000.

À propos of nothing in particular, I remember a feature of the Venezuelan deal which made me thankful that most of my international business originated in England. Our Irish bankers, one of the largest, were unable to see any value in two rather insignificant bits of paper, countersigned by a bank in New York. I stuffed them in my wallet, flew back home, walked into the branch of Lloyds Bank in the small market town of Bridport and was immediately credited with upwards of US$250,000. You have to know a confirmed bearer credit when you see one.

When you hold other assets in the licensed territory, check your product liability cover. A local judge will find it hard to concede that incompetent manufacture, installation or operation have made a good design dangerous. Because of the sad state of United States civil law and crazy awards of damages by juries, steer clear of any licensing there. You can be caught even if you don't grant a licence, as Stone Manganese Marine discovered in a suit bizarre even by American standards.

* SMM patented in the United States its formulation of metal used throughout the world in the casting of ships' propellers. An American manufacturer, without SMM's knowledge, permission or licence, copied the formulation and cast a propeller which eventually failed. The cause of failure might be cavitation, caused by the vacuum induced when the propeller moves through

the water: or that the formula had been incorrectly mixed: or the propeller was badly cast: or it had struck something: or the design was wrong. The shipowner carried no spare and suffered considerable loss while he waited for the replacement.

* SMM were joined in the proceedings on the pretext that, by patenting the formula, we had held it out to be suitable for use in the manufacture of propellers. The court action cost us around one million dollars.

You consider becoming a licensee yourself when you have surplus manufacturing or selling capacity, but no product: or when you are threatened with action for infringing a patent and dare not risk going to court; or when someone brings to the market a damaging innovation which you cannot or dare not copy. Do not be tempted to see a licence as a cheap way of stealing a better product; our commercial judges are swift to sniff out roguery and show no prejudice to the home team. Be careful to avoid the traps with which you try to ensnare your own licensee: up-front payments, the liability to buy kits of parts or tooling from the licensor, any bulk import of the completed product and any commitment to minimum sales or royalty figures.

In 1966, I made many of these mistakes with a product which seemed a good idea even though it wasn't our type of business. Honda have since proved what might have been.

* Avimo, still largely a jobbing sub-contractor, was desperate for products. Our Munich agent was selling a portable compressor designed for use in house painting. A distributor in the north of England gave us an introductory order, which we unwisely doubled on the manufacturer before tooling up for production under licence.

* Although the compressor made a better job of painting large surfaces with less labour and material, the British decorator continued to prefer his brush. I never understand how it is that

distributors seem able to cancel orders when things go badly; perhaps refusing to pay is as telling a method as any. We were soon left with a store of compressors and a much reduced cash balance.

* My eldest son was awaiting a berth as a deckhand on a bulk carrier, as a cheap ride to Canada. He surprised us all by selling the compressors in the horticultural trade, where they proved perfect for spraying inside greenhouses.

The best advice I can give you, if you want to stay in control of your business, is to be content with manufacturing close to home the products you have developed and understand, exporting them so long as that is profitable. Licences nearly always turn out to be a form of gambling and those who become involved, as with other speculators, only tell you about their winnings. If you are obliged to participate, trust no licensee and make no extravagant commitment to any licensor. Never mind that your lawyer hasn't met his clients. Always consider the downside risks, and then you are less likely to be disappointed.

CHAPTER 18

Incentives and Profit Sharing

'What is it, trow you, that makes a poor man labour all his lifetime, carry such great burdens, fare so badly, macerate himself, and endure so great misery, undergo such base offices with so great patience, to rise up early, and lie down late, if there were not an extraordinary delight in getting and keeping of money? What makes a merchant that hath no need, satis superque domi (enough and to spare at home), to range all over the world, through all those intemperate zones of heat and cold; voluntarily to venture his life, and be content with such miserable famine, nasty usage, in a stinking ship; if there were not a pleasure and hope to get money, which doth season the rest, and mitigate his indefatigable pains? What makes them go into the bowels of the earth, an hundred fathom deep, endangering their dearest lives, enduring damps and filthy smells, when they have enough already if they could be content, and no such cause to labour, but an extraordinary delight they take in riches?'

Burton

* Prophecy of this quality is not looked for in an Oxford man, even one in Holy Orders. But Robert Burton was remarkable too in calculating the date of his own death, and contriving to die when

it came around in January, 1640/1. His timing was unfortunate as he lived through the overture to the Civil War but missed the performance.

* He first wrote a comedy based on the pretensions of the professors at the University, an easy target for the satirist then as now. His Anatomy of Melancholy has had the distinction of remaining in print, on and off, for nearly four centuries, for the convenience of the many eminent scribes who have mined its endless veins of precious ore. Even Dr Johnson acknowledged it was the one book which induced him to rise from his bed betimes.

* A modern employee is less inclined to macerate himself than those of yesteryear, being reluctant also to rise up early and lie down late. When the sage speaks of the discomfort of travel and the inadequacies of airline catering: or of the perils of diving in the North Sea after oil, we can only marvel at his powers of divination.

We have already observed that pay ranks second to security in most people's minds. The more confident and capable employees pay the less regard to protecting themselves with service contracts; they know they can readily find another job. These are the ones you have to attract and retain, as employees. You must then decide what more must be done to get from them that extra effort and commitment normally to be found only among the self-employed.

We will deal first with the handful of managers in each unit able significantly to affect its profitability and return on capital. For them we need an incentive scheme which gives them many of the rewards of running their own business. That involves paying attention to status – titles, directorships and, regretfully, cars – pandering, but not excessively, to the relevant deadly sins: envy, gluttony, avarice and pride. They must also be able to supplement their basic pay through exceptional performance.

The incentive scheme for these people should take into account the use of working capital as well as the amount of profit. We all know how to pump up profits in the short term by building excess inventory and adding back the overhead recovery. Next year we have to cut production to absorb the surplus stock but not everyone worries about the future when the past has produced a bumper bonus.

You can agree the principles on which bonuses will be calculated but it is wrong to fix the annual targets too far ahead because we operate in a climate of uncertainty, our business lives constantly affected by things beyond our control. Many managers worked harder in the tough early Thatcher years, containing losses and staying afloat, than in the boom years which followed. Give an employee contractually a long-term right to commission on a fixed basis and you may find it impossible to move him. One of the perks of bank managers used to be the commission on insurance. Customers frequently had life policies forced upon them as a prerequisite to a loan and some managers declined any move or promotion because that could mean the end of a sideline as profitable as their salary itself.

To avoid these traps, the profligate use of working capital or the abuse of a privilege, agree with your managers each year their budgeted profit and use of capital. The bonus is then based on achievement of these budgets, enhanced by any excess profit but factored by any reduction or increase in working capital. They then build for stock or give too much credit at their own expense as well as yours.

Could you spell that out again please? Certainly. Say the budgeted profit is £450,000 before tax and after interest. If they achieve £500,000, the management team gets 10% of the profit, or any excess above £450,000 up to the £500,000. If the average working capital is £2m, the profit-based element of the bonus goes up or down by 1% for every 5% of working capital movement.

198 Thinking About Management

Still unclear? On the above budgets, they make £550,000 but use £2.4m of working capital. On profit, their 10% bonus comes to £55,000 but by using 20% too much cash, it is reduced to 6%. If they had made £500,000 and only used £1.6m, they would have been better off with a bonus of 14%, 10% on the profit and 4% increment for good use of working capital. And the firm is better off too, because it has the use of that extra cash.

Remember that with this scheme the targets must be fixed each year: it certainly makes for prudent budgeting. And the division of the spoils between the senior manager and his colleagues must be settled at the same time.

The scheme is less effective when there are inter-dependent separate units within a group whose profits depend on arbitrary transfer prices. If your object is a 30% margin on everything, you cannot achieve that where the same product passes through up to four different plants, because the customer won't pay it. You then find preference being given by individual units to outside customers who will pay the higher mark-up for the part-finished product. Even when you install a scheme where part of their bonus depends on the group result, parochial attitudes will prevail.

I dislike share options because they are selective and unfair. If people in a public company want to buy shares, they should use their own money and not ask the shareholders to dilute the equity. This egalitarianism was the cause of adverse comment when I left Bridport-Gundry.

* One of the non-executive directors about to be elected on my leaving told a large shareholder whom he knew socially that I was the worst director of a public company he had ever come across, not judged by my management record but because I wouldn't sanction any benefits limited only to senior managers. What he would have said if he had known I owned the car I used for business and opted out of the management BUPA scheme, I dare

not think. The shareholder, having seen the price of his stock rise by some 15 times while I was Chairman, phoned me, being puzzled at this judgment. The price fell 80% in two years under the new dispensation and I did not bother to canvass his views further.

The contrary argument in favour of share options, which is supported by most institutional fund managers, is that they benefit other shareholders because they induce senior employees to work harder, remain loyal to the firm and perform better. There is no other mechanism, it is said, through which a salary-earner can accumulate capital without too heavy a tax burden. Bosses should eat their fill while they have access to the trough. A director is penalised if he uses his savings to buy shares in the company because he is subject to such stringent rules against insider trading that he cannot get his money out except by resignation or retirement.

Distributing shares in an unquoted company is less of an incentive unless there are positive plans, and a good enough record, to make a public issue before too long. Because directors of such companies reserve the right to refuse to register transfers, the shares are virtually unsaleable except at an artificial price within a restricted circle. The best way out is to allow employees to offer shares among themselves by tender. The intending seller posts a notice saying how many shares are on offer; sealed bids are sent to the company secretary and the successful bid price is posted openly. It's all pretty artificial but better than no market at all.

British managers have come to look on a range of other goodies as their right, apart from greater security and higher pay. These include free life cover, health insurance and the company car. Life and health cover can be justified but the cost of cars is disproportionate to their benefit to the employer, unless used by people who have to travel daily as part of their job. Those without cars become jealous and those with, extravagant, wasting the firm's cash or credit by changing them regardless of need, usage or commercial sense. Whatever stringency you impose on capital expenditure, someone will contrive to sneak through the routine replacement of cars. By standing aloof and buying your car out of your own pocket, you can take a high moral tone, lead by example and so on. Nobody will take any notice however, or consider you other than as slightly eccentric.

Any attempt to restrict or limit the privilege of a company car will combine disparate forces into a cohesive lobby. Persist, and you face open revolt and threats of claims for constructive dismissal. If the firm is solvent, the problem can be approached gently, as by advising each beneficiary how much his car is really costing, offering the same money in a salary increase; or by giving him the car to buy out the abuse. If the company is terminally sick, drastic surgery is recommended.

> * In July, 1983, I became involved with John Williams of Cardiff at the behest of the Chairman of the Welsh Development Agency. Within days one of its several bankers demanded repayment: I preferred not to ask to whom it had been Listening on that occasion. The company was very sick but there were over seventy cars in the hands of the employees, former employees and close relatives of former employees, all drawing their running expenses, including free petrol from the company's garage.

> * All inessential cars went about the same time as the Financial Director. We closed the pumps and leased the garage to the fitters, who then ran it as their own business. John Williams didn't go into receivership, and that, as I keep pointing out, is a Good Thing.

As noted earlier, in Avimo and Globe, we had a simple profit-sharing scheme where everyone with a year's service benefits pro rata to the annualised gross salary. This automatically compensates for different levels of responsibility, and for working shifts or part-time. The rules must be clear and so simple that everyone can understand them and see how individual shares have been worked out. A trigger point of 10% return on capital and sharing 10% of the pre-tax trading profit after interest seems to work, but once the scheme is in place, you can only improve it. If you decline to participate yourself, you can adjudicate on the many hard and testing cases which are bound to arise.

This kind of bonus has to be calculated by the auditors, to ensure fair play. There should be two payments annually, with no accruals for people who leave voluntarily during the period when the bonus was earned, or before the pay-out, except in cases of sickness or retirement. The important payment is the one in early December, in good time for Christmas shopping. The other should be immediately before the summer shut-down. When the employees start touching real money, they become as cost-conscious as the boss, and better placed to see where much of the waste happens.

You can set out details of any bonuses and so on in a company manual, but do not include in any statutory Contract of Employment more than the bare minimum because once you do, the additional rights and benefits may be held to apply to everyone. No standard contract can prevent enhancement of benefits for individuals. It is absolutely fundamental that managers must be able to dismiss employees if the business is to prosper, or even to survive. The problem with state education in Britain is not the syllabus, or cash, or the influence of television, or the social tinkering taught in Training Colleges, or the administrative waste, but the inability of the employers to dismiss rotten teachers. Just as bad coinage drives out good (*pace* Gresham), so do bad teachers. The salvation of a firm, and the preservation of some jobs rather than the loss of all, may hang on the ability of the management to cut back without ruination. In Lancashire Stone-Platt, by fecklessness and arrogance, had once again dug its own grave.

* My diaries for 1980 record our agonising over the major factories in Accrington, Oldham and Bolton. The change in the pattern of world demand for textile machinery and a pound bloated by excessive interest rates made our British factories uncompetitive. The firm had agreed with the union, and enshrined in binding agreements, generous severance pay for any employee who left involuntarily – not as generous, perhaps, as providing free accommodation in the town for the mistress of a former director, but I only found out about that later.

* Eventually we faced up to closing one of the three main factories, and that at Oldham – the one with the new but unused cranes – was chosen. Companies have to provide in the Balance Sheet for the estimated costs of closure and, when we did so, the change in ratios triggered a banker (yes, effectively the same one which toppled Fairey) to demand repayment. Stone-Platt was on the long, bumpy slide into receivership.

* Why then, with the wounds from your Fairey experience still open and suppurating, did you not ask questions about the effect which raising reserves for the Oldham closure would have on the Balance Sheet, and on the ratios? A better question would be: Why did you accept the answers you and the Board received from the Financial Director and from the senior partner in the company's auditors to those specific and pointed questions? Why indeed!

However much you may distrust non-standard service contracts, management recruits will expect them. Whatever the period of notice specified, the employee is unlikely to honour the commitment once the decision to leave has been taken. In public companies, it has become fashionable to write into the contract a double period of notice which becomes effective should a hostile bid succeed. This golden parachute is yet another example of how managers look after themselves. If anyone needs it, you do, as the boss, because you are the person most likely to be handed his running shoes the day the predator moves in. And, whatever you do, check the rules of the pension fund to keep that out of his clutches: but we are moving too far ahead.

Most of the time, when people want to leave, let them go: and don't take them back. If they are going to a competitor, get them out of the place as fast as you can and keep them away from copying machines, although the horse will almost certainly have bolted, along with drawings, parts lists, customer details and any other useful documents they have been able to lay their hands on. As soon as you start offering inducements to persuade someone to stay, you walk into a minefield. You are going to upset other managers who have remained loyal by showing either that you are susceptible to blackmail or have been underpaying them: which may well be true, but you mustn't advertise the fact. Always remember that biscuit advertisement – One bite invited another:

Wages and salaries remain the biggest incentives of all. Wage levels are critical in retaining and recruiting good employees but, even where there is no agreed rate between an Employers' Association and a union, supply and demand indicate the kind of level you should aim at. For managers, the problem may be more complex because you need individual assessments, but at the same time not to cause resentment among those less generously treated. The surveys published by headhunters are a useful guide but must be approached with caution. On the downside, the information is usually a year out of date but this is offset by the fact that most of the statistics come from larger, higher-paying companies and are more than what most people are getting, or what firms can afford. Headhunters like publishing high salaries because that means easy assignments and big commissions.

The people we tend to overlook are the ones in the middle, the foremen and chargehands. I joined a company in August, 1988 where the foremen took home, before tax, between $1\frac{1}{2}\%$ and 2% more than those they were meant to supervise. The nomenclature was inexact, but we all pay junior managers badly, having allowed the differentials to erode over the years, mainly through weakness in the face of union pressure. Low pay and inadequate differentials have led to a widespread inability to recruit or promote to supervisory grades, and so to poor management on the shop-floor. The day all foremen are graduates, or ex-warrant officers, and paid accordingly, would herald a new industrial era, but I anticipate the Second Coming first.

They say that if you pay peanuts, you get monkeys. It isn't entirely true. Most bad employers get much more than they pay for, and much less than if they paid better: which brings us to our Fifteenth Commandment – Never overlook anyone who performs well in a junior function. However tempting it may be to leave people where they are, you may find that they are carrying an immediate superior and you are wasting managerial talent. It is too late to recover the situation when they tell you they are leaving.

The corollary for the individual is not to stay too long doing a junior, responsible and difficult job. Good managers should not lose good employees, but should work at developing their potential. You should respect their areas of responsibility and avoid taking decisions which are properly theirs. If you visit a far location, warn them that you are coming. Managers must be respected, and backed until they are sacked. It is only when they have to be replaced that you find out how the market has moved against you, how much you have to jack up everyone's package to match what you are being forced to offer the new recruit. But if the newcomer is too greedy, whatever the attractions, find someone else.

Let us end with a final tale of suffering, which Longclose faced when two managers, whom no inducement would have retained, left to go into opposition.

* We took over Platt Sizing shortly before Stone-Platt failed, transferring the operation across the Pennines from Bolton to Leeds. In the confusion of the receivership every piece of technical data concerning these huge and complex machines was wiped off the computer storage disks in Bolton. Two of the employees who had come to us with the product then left to set up a business selling spares for our machines.

* We had virtually to start from the beginning, without parts lists or knowledge which customer in the past had bought what. Spares are the most profitable side of this kind of business. Losing all the job knowledge was a cruel blow; losing much of the spares business to our new competitor even crueller.

It is time to move on to less harrowing things, although there is plenty over which to lament in our record on training and safety, as we shall see next.

CHAPTER 19

Personnel, Training and Safety

'There is a great deal more learning in the world than there was formerly; for it is more universally diffused. You have perhaps, no man who knows as much Greek or Latin as Bentley; no man who knows as much mathematicks as Newton: but you have many men who know Greek and Latin, and who know mathematicks.'

Dr Johnson

* Isaac Newton needs no introduction but you may be wondering to which of the contemporary Bentleys the Doctor alludes. Not Nathaniel, also known as 'Dirty Dick', despite his claim to the first glazed hardware shop in London. Nor to that eminent classicist, Thomas Bentley, but to the renowned scholar about whom we read in Pepys's diary, the cantankerous Richard. Learning Latin at his mother's knee, he went to Cambridge at the age of fourteen. His long career as Master of Trinity was remarkable for the extent and breadth of his scholarship as for his unremitting squabbles with the Fellows. He also fell out with Hobbes but was able to deduce, from Newton's discoveries, the existence of an intelligent creator, for which theological virtuosity he became not Bishop of Durham but Archdeacon of Ely. He was twice up before his Bishop during his 38 years as Master, and twice condemned to be dismissed from office. On the first occasion the Bishop died before formally

delivering judgement; the news of Queen Anne's death coming the next day then put an end to the proceedings. The second judgment, in 1733, also went against him but he ignored it on a technicality, continuing his stormy rule for another four years.

* We can but speculate on what Johnson would have said of learning today, the sum of human knowledge being so much increased but its diffusion diminished to the degree that scholars seldom expect Greek, Latin or mathematics among themselves and never among businessmen: nor are they often disabused.

The Personnel Manager often organises training and usually keeps a statutory record of accidents, which allows us to bring three topics into one chapter. He is not a line manager, to be used as a communicator with the shop floor; nor is he an arbitrator between workers and management. He is likely to hear of any niggles in time to sort them out, and should always be consulted before a change is made which alters the environment in which people work, even as trivial as shifting a drinks machine. Recruitment and dismissal are his responsibility. Selling the employees your version of events is not.

Even in a small factory, someone has to keep the records and deal with all manner of queries covering anything from maternity leave to pension entitlement. Union negotiators have nothing to lose by stringing out meetings, and somebody has to be on the other side of the table. Various statutory returns have to be made promptly and, if individual dossiers are not kept up to date, it may cost you dear when you are taken before a Tribunal. The personnel function, with its expense, is one you may deplore but cannot ignore. It will cost even more if you call it Human Resources.

Recruitment is no longer the simple task of putting a notice on the gate or in the local paper, sifting out the applicants and taking on the one who has the best qualifications. As we have already observed, the only people against whom you cannot discriminate these days are fit, white males. Society has encouraged everyone else to suppose that their rejection for any post has been based on prejudice, especially against sex or skin pigmentation. Your advertisements, if truthfully and carelessly drawn, may invite criminal prosecution. Unless you keep meticulous records of interviews and aptitude tests, you may find yourself excoriated as a sexist or racist.

Let the expert within the firm handle appointments for routine vacancies. In any district, personnel officers will maintain, if not a black list, one which incorporates shades of grey. You pressurise them to take on those they would otherwise reject at your peril, as a fellow director of mine once did, to my cost.

* Our personnel officer rejected an application from someone she knew to be of limited intelligence and troublesome disposition. He had a relative who worked in some domestic capacity for the family of one of the directors who overruled the personnel officer and took the man on.

* The factory had enjoyed harmonious labour relations, apart from an incident at the turn of the century when the workforce objected at being forbidden to leave their machines when they needed to urinate. Nobody wanted a union job, except the newcomer. After he became Convenor, there was nothing but hassle which wasted everyone's time and benefited nobody. It took years to shift him.

Before you sack anyone, look at the legal position first. As the firm is likely to end up before a Tribunal however justified the dismissal, make sure that procedures are followed and records kept. Even then you may have to pay up, but not so much. Do not expect any sympathy because the person you dismissed made it impossible to run your business. Citing examples is painful because it is too revealing about our culture as a supposedly industrial society. Where else in the world could an airline cabin attendant turn up for work late a dozen times in eight weeks, claim wrongful dismissal, arrive late for the Tribunal and be awarded more than £2,000? Yes, in Britain, in November, 1990.

And this will continue until costs follow the cause, so that frivolous appellants, or their unions, have to pay your expenses if they lose. At present our system emulates the United States where civil suits can be brought unadvisedly, lightly, or wantonly, like brute beasts that have no understanding. (A church which prefers the language of the streets to a poetic liturgy four centuries old cannot complain of plagiarism.)

It was in the United States that we managed for once only to chalk up a victory against the sanctimonious and hypocritical do-gooders who devise and administer these silly regulations.

* Safety is a Connecticut corporation manufacturing equipment for rail cars, and was the best acquisition Stone-Platt made in my time. As there were not many black people around and women couldn't handle the heavy components, we had problems filling our employee quotas. Before long a young lawyer arrived from Washington to warn us of the wrath to come if we failed to mend our ways.

* Relaxing over a drink with the president of Safety that evening, he confessed that the rules were difficult for a firm like ours, and hard on 'us Wasps'. The president, a distinguished World War II bomber pilot, confessed that, as a registered American Indian, he had no hang-ups about employing people on merit rather than racial origin.

Your personnel office is also going to handle pensions, sick pay and absenteeism. Pensions we will talk about later. Sickness is a problem, striking as it does on Mondays, Fridays or when Newcastle United are playing at home in the week. Paying a visit to the victim, with or without grapes, is more likely to achieve a cure than sending him to Lourdes. Persistent invalids or absentees – the distinction is a fine one – must be moved on. We have said elsewhere that everyone in a company is important. If on direct work, resources have to be kept in place to support them; if on indirect, some important function is being neglected while they are away (or, if not important, should be cut out). You may not be able to build up a Tribunal-proof case for the absentee, or for someone you know to be cheating the firm. It is cheaper in the long run to dismiss them, to say nothing and pay up.

Everyone knows education and training are Good Things to which our society gives insufficient attention because of someone else's short-sightedness, niggardliness or stupidity. This received wisdom is tied to a number of assumptions which are best brought into the open if we want to face our problems objectively:

* We have a right to enjoy a higher standard of living than foreigners, even if we work shorter hours and less hard than them, because we are British and (mainly) white and won two World Wars.

* We are a naturally inventive race which led the world in industrial development, breeding men like Brunel with his ships and railways, Bramah with hydraulics, Marconi with the wireless and so on – (two French and one Italian, but no matter).

* We have a unique mastery of financial matters.

* Our illiterate and unskilled are entitled to the same standard of living as everyone else in the United Kingdom rather than that enjoyed by those of similar attainments in, say, the Indian sub-continent.

* Nobody should be required to acquire any skill or contribute to the creation of wealth.

* It is degrading to be 'in trade' or to work in industry.

With these and other hang-ups, it is not surprising that our industrial training is abysmal. Charting where we went wrong would take another volume but we must mention the abandonment of the old-style apprenticeship, which followed the granting to teenagers of full adult wages before they had completed their training; and the ending of the Higher National Certificate, which called for a mixture of experience, scholarship and determination now hard to find in a society obsessed with television and satisfied with mediocrity.

You can try to row against the stream, and benefit your business, by taking as many apprentices as you can reasonably absorb. Ask their parents to an interview and assess how much support they will give before making a final decision. Despite the cost, give apprentices as much of the old-fashioned treatment as you can, passing through all departments and attending college for both Ordinary and Higher National Diplomas. These people, and your graduate recruits who need much the same treatment, are your next generation of management. Many of them will move on but you can look on them not as wasted expense but as an investment in society. You may also be able to poach similar people trained at someone else's expense.

Much factory work calls for dexterity or familiarity rather than skill. That kind of training is best done on the job or, where several trainees are involved, in classes where you can use test pieces, videos and an experienced instructor. If you have repetitive work which demands concentration throughout the day, women are far more likely to do it consistently well than men.

In recruitment, you will find that some applicants come from an environment which does not predispose them to settle down to hard work in an office or factory. Children straight from school or college have not acquired the bad habits which a few weeks on the dole or kicking around the streets may have inculcated. Anyone who has worked in a public sector office is likely to be taken unaware by the tempo expected in a private firm. And vice versa: one of my daughters-in-law, who had worked for IBM, took a clerical job with an admiralty establishment in Taunton. After doing almost nothing the first day, she started asking when someone was going to give her some work. She was at once visited by the Convenor who said she wasn't welcome. People don't complain of having nothing to do if they work for the Navy, and it is positively anti-social to rock the boat.

You should ask supervisors to attend courses. Special training makes them better managers and improves their morale by indicating that their status is recognised. You should also ask who is interested in acquiring formal qualifications, and do all you can to smooth their path by granting examination or study leave and tailoring their work to suit the particular discipline.

Training for more senior managers is usually a mixture of formal education and experience, with too many of us only learning through our mistakes. There is a plethora of books for people to study, some more readable than others. Seminars and courses are said to help those who cannot assimilate the written word, although most of them profit only their organisers. I suppose some of those who attend, if they cannot absorb what they read, obtain some benefit but a course or symposium is usually nothing more than a very expensive day out.

We have said before that in business you are only as good as your performance. The possession of awards, degrees and diplomas may be prima facie evidence of knowledge but, outside a specialised discipline like accountancy, it is little else. Letters after a name or a doctorate before it do not provide an inside track. We enter the world of management as we entered the world itself, naked. That may be why so many of our graduates prefer teaching, the learned professions, government employment or the City. It's tough to have to compete on level terms with people who don't recognise that they are inferior.

Factories are dangerous places and accidents happen in a flash: one moment, the familiar, comfortable, noisy environment and the next, mutilation or death.

My first two experiences were vicarious. I was consulted by a young man working in Trant's flour mill in Kingsbridge whose finger was torn off when a ring was caught by a proud rivet on a conveyor belt. Then a girl working for the London Rubber Company was scalped when her hair was tangled in some rotating machinery. I never liked male jewellery and I saw that scalping was as nasty, if not as fatal, in the East End as in the Wild West.

Those are two of the classics, wearing jewellery at work and not covering long hair. The others are unguarded pillar drills, especially when the object being worked on catches in the bit: guillotines and presses, however guarded: welding flash: picking out swarf by hand: and machining metal without wearing goggles. The only prevalent industrial accident to view with suspicion is 'back trouble', the onset of which usually coincides with spring digging. That said, too many people lift loads with their knees apart, scorning to use hoists or trolleys: and then drop things on toes unprotected by safety shoes.

We are all responsible for each others' safety and, however much people resent your being fussy, if you see a dangerous procedure, say so at once. If I hadn't kept quiet, two Belgian ladies would, in due course, have been able to attend the Resurrection with a full complement of digits.

* In 1970 I was in a factory making sintered metal components near Charleroi. The process involves the compression of powder in moulds, which are then baked. To speed up production, many of the operators were using hydraulic presses with the guards permanently propped up. I suggested, as Chairman elect, that this might not be a good idea, even if using the guards slowed things

up and led to lower bonuses. On my next visit, five weeks later, the guards were all in use. In fact my suggestion had been ignored but two accidents, involving respectively a thumb and two fingers, had proved more compelling.

* (My predecessor in the chair was a German, a Herr Doktor Doktor, who boasted that he had managed a factory of 6,000 people during the war, with only 16 Germans in charge, and achieved standard rates of productivity. I didn't press him too closely about the nature of his incentive schemes.)

However vigilant your staff, however safe your methods, someone will try to beat the system – either thoughtless, smart, forgetful or lazy. And when, having deliberately cancelled all the safety devices, they have broken a limb or been scalded, you and the company are still to blame. If you are concerned about any process, you can always ask one of the approved officials to come and have a look. These people – inspectors for Factory, Health and Safety, Environmental Pollution, Hoist and Crane, Boiler, Nuclear – have draconian powers. They can give you helpful advice, sometimes. They can also shut you down and prosecute you. Or they can cover their backsides by firmly straddling the fence.

* Langdons store 3-tonne reels of paper which normally are delivered on curtain-sided vehicles but occasionally turn up in a container. It is easy to offload from an open trailer but awkward from a container as you have to manoeuvre some of the reels before the lift truck can grab them. Two experienced warehousemen, having off-loaded a container one week, refused to touch it the next. Their reluctance may not have been unconnected to the recent ending of lucrative Saturday morning overtime, although they attributed it to qualms about safety. After being instructed to proceed, they refused to work and were suspended.

* Langdons offloaded the container with other staff in the presence of an official, whose superiors declined to give a ruling on the

methods employed until they had seen another demonstration. But there might not be another container for weeks while five or six curtain-siders a day needed off-loading and vehicles have to be turned round. What about the suspended warehousemen? Ah well, that's your problem. (Naturally, Langdons were eventually sued for wrongful dismissal and duly punished. The Authorities eventually suggested a modification to the method of packing the reels of paper in the containers in Finland, which might have cured everyone's problems if, having persuaded our customer to persuade the Finnish manufacturer to comply, we could also have persuaded Neptune to prevent the rolling of the ship during the intervening sea voyage.)

And another cautionary tale.

* Fairey Engineering machined magnesium, which is flammable. After three years' accident-free operation, we invited a Factory Inspector to monitor our methods and precautions. She issued some eleven summonses against us.

Remember too the accidents which do not maim. Happily I have never worked with asbestos but solvents, noise and dust are common hazards. The refusal of employees to wear ear protectors or face masks won't stop them suing you when they have contracted tinnitus, chronic bronchitis or emphysema. At least make sure the equipment is available and your insurance premiums are paid.

The days when you needed fifty householders or a fiat from the Attorney-General to tackle a public nuisance are long gone. Today even non-residents can have a tilt at you. An adjacent school cost Globe a fortune by objecting to the occasional smell of acetic acid. Nor did the ecologists thank us for the rare fungus which appeared on the banks of the Exe, half a mile downstream from our plant.

Although a well-insured blaze without any casualties can have its consolations, you should periodically review your fire precautions. Gangways should be free of clutter and properly marked. Never stack rubbish inside a factory and if you allow old cardboard boxes and pallets to accumulate against an outside wall, someone will set light to them, as happened at Bridport. However much you want to keep intruders out, remember that a fixed external fire door keeps victims in. I suppose everyone puts wedges under internal fire doors: at least remove them before the Fire Officer does his rounds.

Still on the subject of fire, there is now more public awareness of the stupidity of smoking, although non-smokers are still subjected to the harmful emissions of others in many workshops and offices. People who smoke in non-smoking areas should be disciplined and, if there is any danger of fire or explosion, summarily dismissed. Let us hope that, ere long, we revert to the Victorian convention whereby those who wish to pollute the atmosphere in this way do so only in secluded apartments.

A fellow-employee maimed or killed is a disaster of a different magnitude to any pecuniary loss. You can set the climate in your firm by your own awareness of danger, how you personally comply with regulations and what actions you initiate. You have not only to be seen with, as appropriate, a hard hat, goggles or ear muffs (coloured external ones rather than plugs, so that everyone knows you are protected): you must also be ready to pull up publicly anyone who is breaking the rules. Sometimes you will be too late.

* The Belgian engineer at Fairey SA who climbed under the rubber press to see why it had stuck never learned the answer. Eighteen years later I saw in the garage a Langdons' driver working on his tractor, fitting extra lights. He couldn't raise the cab fully beyond the point of balance because the ceiling was too low, and he was relying on the vehicle's hydraulic system to keep it suspended as he worked beneath it. '*Plus ça change*', as the Belgian might have remarked, had he been spared.

'You ask too much,' I hear you cry. Of course you can't see to all these things yourself. But you have to know about them. In a big firm, personnel, training and safety tend to turn into somebody else's problem, until a ferry capsizes or an arm is ripped off. Neglect these functions and you have at best an inefficient business; at worst someone is killed and you end up in court. We don't want that to happen, do we?

Then let us repeat the truism. Everything you achieve depends on people, and they need even more looking after than plant and equipment.

CHAPTER 20

Advertising, Publicity and Product Support

'If a man write a better book, preach a better sermon, or make a better mouse-trap than his neighbour, tho' he build his house in the woods, the world will make a beaten path to his door.'

Emerson (or Hubbard)

* Attribution poses a problem when the record depends on so unreliable a witness as Sarah Yule and her recollection of when she recorded Ralph Waldo's words in her handbook. Certainly Elbert Hubbard never conceded that Emerson came up with the goods first.

* Equity demands that we give the credit to Elbert. Of his 'A Thousand and One Epigrams', the thousand are gone, leaving only the one – 'Life is just one damned thing after another'. At the very least we should add the mot about the Mousetrap, and make it two. Emerson can afford to be generous. Nobody, apart from the Bard, was ever more quoteworthy although, as he remarked on another occasion, 'Every hero becomes a bore at last'.

Why, you may ask, should anyone want to claim the parentage of an assertion which is so demonstrably untrue? Passing over books and sermons, you can be sure that, however superior your unbranded mousetrap, it will be buried by the 'Little Nipper' and other established makes. It may in due time be copied and sold in volume by someone else, but that is different.

In 1961 I was green enough to suppose that you could launch a good unbranded consumer product and people would buy it on its merits.

* We were scratching around in Avimo for a consumer product with an optical slant. Someone lashed up a camera lucida, a device which uses a semi-silvered mirror to project on to a drawing board the image of any object or view at which the eye-piece is directed. The concept was not original. Just as you can thank Oscar for any epigram, so any optical discovery can be attributed to Leonardo. Our Cameraboard, as we called it, helped children to draw accurately without tracing paper or talent. For their grandparents it was the perfect gift, inexpensive, educational, durable and original.

* We couldn't sell it. We had no marketing expertise, no contacts with the toy trade and no brand name. Wiser and poorer, we went back to batch production of military hardware, leaving the children and their grandparents with their expensive tat.

Spenders of money are conservative, distrusting the unfamiliar. They like to recognise a name before they rely on the integrity of the product or its manufacturer. We observe the phenomenon in the market acceptance of textiles and fashion goods so long as they are branded with the logo of some hairdresser, designer or sportsman with whose name, through achievement in other, often unrelated, spheres or through the pages of the popular press we have become familiar. I too have bought for one of my children a Jimmy Connors tennis outfit, knowing that he was no seamstress.

Conversely, the manufacturer sells by reputation rather than quality or price, although those two elements eventually make up the reputation: which is what makes brands so valuable. You've probably forgotten our First Commandment – Never sell a new product to a new customer. The corollary of that is you can't sell new products to new customers, so don't waste resources trying. Even when you have a reputation in one market, it is unlikely it will carry across into another.

It follows then that most of your advertising should have the object of promoting a brand image. With consumer goods, 'advertising' includes the use of logos and trade marks, packaging, presentation and point-of-sale display just as much as the space you buy in journals and your intrusions into the homes of the zombies watching the hypnotic screen. Most of us are insufficiently objective and skilled to handle advertising in-house and waste money until we decide to pay for expert advice.

The decision about how good your product should be is not one which should be left to the design office. Quality costs money, but so do promotion, presentation and packaging, and the market may not be prepared to pay for both. There are also products which the customer does not want to last too long. Take those Avimo refrigeration absorption units which we couldn't persuade the public to buy, even in the easy days of the early sixties.

* An absorption unit exchanges heat for cold by circulating on a thermal cycle a mixture of ammonia and hydrogen gas, to which heat is applied at a fixed point. Added chromate inhibits the build-up of sludge in the labyrinth of pipes through which the gases circulate. We used 4% chromate – far more than our competitors. We never had one return from our production of 5,000 units. But we couldn't compete with competitors with household names whose reliability depended on turning the unit upside down when it ceased to work, giving it a good shake, and hoping it would carry on for a while before it had to be thrown away. We had made the mistake of investing solely in quality, leaving nothing for promotion.

Of course a product should be sufficiently reliable to outlive its guarantee or keep after-sales rectification within budget. An example of paring things too fine was the lead-acid accumulator. The car battery's life was, like the absorption unit, determined by sludge. The lead plates were therefore suspended internally above the bottom of the container with a clearance finely calculated to ensure that the sludge shorted them out a few minutes after the warranty expired. The battery makers who did this fell on hard times when damned foreigners introduced a product free of this deliberate design defect.

If your product is bought by the public direct, leave copywriting – advertisements, brochures, instruction leaflets and so on – to the agency, checking only the technical content. Don't start editing what they write, despite your anguish at the verbless sentences and other solecisms. Listen to what they tell you about your potential markets. Remind yourself that these are the people who persuaded a nation of beer connoisseurs to pay a premium for lager. And note our Sixteenth Commandment – Aim your publicity at customers. It sounds obvious, but lots of people don't.

* Having sorted my Fairey papers when I changed offices, I resolved as a penance to keep only the files relating to corporate advertising. We ran a series highlighting a product from each operating company, and took full pages in the *Economist* for 11 issues. Everyone knew the name Fairey, so we had no need to promote that. Who else were we trying to convince, and about what? Were we trying to tell our shareholders something, or to sell anything? The pictures were brilliant and the captions snappy, but it was a total waste of money. Happily the advertising of individual operating companies, in which I was not involved, was better thought out and more sharply focused.

As with the style and content of your publicity, so with the choice of medium and the packaging. The path to the pockets of your customers is through the programmes they watch, the papers they read. It is the customer who elects to pay a premium for knitting needles in a redundant plastic tube or soap with layers of packaging so dense that you wonder if you are back in the parties of your childhood playing Pass the Parcel, where the final unwrapping eventually exposes the prize.

You also have to persuade the distributor or retailer to stock your product rather than, or in addition to, your competitor's. Point of sale presentation should be left to the experts, but it doesn't do any harm to visit retail outlets and see what the result is. It is just another facet of selling that we present our goods in a way which makes it easier, or less trouble, or more profitable, for the middleman to push them.

Unless there are special reasons like resisting a bid or trying to get on the Honours List, publicity aimed at projecting the firm's image or hiking its share price is almost invariably a waste of money. Taking space in the City pages to announce your results is unlikely to boost your market rating nor will the editorial staff, whose comment can be important, give you much credit for your gullibility and fecklessness. Those who want to study your Report and Accounts are likely already to be shareholders and, if they are not, know where to lay hands on a copy.

The creation of a cult of personality around the boss may be something he has to enjoy, or suffer, according to his modesty or vanity. Because a successful businessman tends to go on being successful, having survived and learned from past mistakes, his identification by bankers, shareholders and the City with a firm can improve its rating and its credit. At least three of my knighted friends, through their high profile and reputation, saved quoted firms which were for a time insolvent. My failure at Fairey in 1977 owed much to my facelessness, my aversion to publicity stemming from a wish to keep my family and business lives apart.

Editors of technical journals are always on the look-out for copy. If they suggest that an editorial mention or article is a trade-off for paid advertising, think twice before participating. The piece is more likely to be printed if it is illustrated with clean line diagrams or black-and-white photographs. As with all selling, make it easy for the target to buy.

We may recoil intellectually from sponsorship, being mindful too of the fee which inflates the cost without improving the product. Forget these scruples. Familiarity with the sponsor leads by transference to product acceptance and that, as we have noted, leads to public awareness and so to enhanced sales. Obviously much of what is termed sponsorship should be regraded as charity, or blackmail. You are unlikely to enhance your sales as a result of a child negotiating ten lengths of a swimming pool. If you sponsor a sportsman, pick a winner: if an event attended by the public, make sure you have potential customers among the onlookers, in person or through a cathode ray tube. If sponsorship fails to produce results, drop it.

Public Relations has an image engendered by the suspicion that, if we were hearing the truth, no intermediary would be needed. 'Hand-out' has become synonymous with con. Yet we must once more bottle up our prejudices. As with advertising, few businessmen are objective or experienced enough to select and present material to third parties in an effective way. The most cost-effective solution for the small firm is to retain a local journalist; he knows where best to plant stories and, who knows, his retainer may induce him to make a more sympathetic view of your affairs when the dirt is airborne and in public. The medium-sized firm should retain a specialist, often in double harness with packaging, design work and brand promotion. The big fellows run their own PR departments. Make sure they concentrate on the products. Some seem more intent on promoting the boss, realising that flattery will get them everywhere.

An in-house Public Relations Officer can help distance other managers from the press, which is usually interested only in scandal, internal disputes or bad news. He can also organise exhibitions, supervising stand design, translation of literature, availability of exhibits and models, invitations to customers, catering arrangements, hotel bookings for those condemned to man the stand and the myriad other tasks which nobody else has the time, knowledge or inclination to see to.

'Hospitality' – now there's a word: not, for the manufacturer, the entertainment of visitors and guests 'with liberality and goodwill', as the Oxford English Dictionary tells us. The Faber Dictionary of Euphemisms is closer to the mark with 'free intoxicants', as anyone footing the bill for a tent or chalet at a trade show will soon discover. People are greedy, and none more so than junior civil servants out for a jolly, with just enough clout to harm your business if you offend them. Those of us who have had boundless opportunities to gormandise at someone else's expense tend to view without charity the behaviour of those whose opportunities are infrequent. You contain the damage by admitting to your private bar only people with invitation cards, but many of those have companions from whom they would consider it an insult to be separated. Others simply infiltrate themselves to a barside position while your gaze is averted and, attaching themselves to bona fide guests, receive every assistance from the hired catering staff in guzzling and drinking copiously. Apart from the cost, they squeeze out real customers.

I inadvertently used the same technique in Plymouth recently.

* Having travelled far and wishing to enjoy a family wedding service in comfort, two females in the party requested we make a stop before attending the service. The facilities of a public house hard by the church were dismissed out of hand and we drove to an

hotel where I escorted them into the foyer. There I was greeted by the maître d' who, seeing my fancy garb and the rosebud in my buttonhole, insisted I should not delay in availing myself of the drink and canapes laid out in the room behind him.

* I had noticed a wedding party in the grip of a photographer on the steps of a nearby chapel and, as he was clearly no more than warming to his work, I had no fear of being surprised, glass in hand and a smoked salmon roll jostling other delicacies on my plate. I prefer not to relate the subterfuge by which I extricated my charges and myself. There is however one watering hole to which I will only return in deep disguise.

Let us pause for a summary. Address your publicity at potential customers. Employ experts for public relations and advertising. Build up and protect your brands. Pay attention to packaging and point-of-sale displays. When business is sluggish and you need to economise, the last place to start cutting back should be on product and brand promotion. Unfortunately, it is often the first.

The quality of your product support is important in building up or protecting your brands. As appropriate, you need clear technical instructions and literature, efficient repair and servicing arrangements, prompt access for customers to spares, and training facilities for people being introduced to complicated or specialised machines. The spares and servicing need not be cheap but, if you try to cheat people, be reconciled to losing their custom next time round. The firm which encouraged its fitter to sell my wife a phoney warranty which was no more valuable than the guarantee with the product lost more than my domestic business when it refused to make a refund.

Obviously the location and scale of spares depend on the product. To take an extreme case, if you sell an aeroplane, the failure of a component means that it will be grounded until the approved spare is available. You encourage the operator to hold spares of consumables, like filters and brake pads. Your local distributor should carry anything which is likely to need routine replacement, especially tyres, batteries, instruments and radios. In the factory you hold those bits of the airframe which get damaged most often, like ailerons and flaps; and expensive items like struts for undercarriages or propellers. Nobody expects you to hold spare wings but somebody has to stock engines. Whatever you do and however much your recommendations are ignored, if there's an AOG, it's the manufacturer's fault. And though other manufacturers don't suffer the traumata of an 'aircraft on ground', their customers are just as clamant if the absence of a spare part causes loss or inconvenience.

Make sure that you keep an accurate record of which customer bought what to which build-standard. We have already seen the problems which ensued when the Stone-Platt receivers allowed the records of Platt Sizing to be erased from the computer.

It is becoming increasingly difficult to persuade skilled and experienced fitters to travel the world installing machines and trouble-shooting. If you delegate the job to your agent, he is unlikely to know what parts have been pirated to keep another machine running, or to recognise the damage caused by constantly operating at above the rated capacity. Obviously it pays to build into the product as much reliability as is economically feasible, and to make it user-friendly. But some users aren't friendly, and the further away they are, the more unfriendly, stupid and helpless they become. That is why sensible exporters carry a line in their budgeted costs called After Sales Rectification.

You accept that customers will cheat over spares and repairs for anything under warranty, or where outstanding bills have yet to be met. Sometimes you have to say you will soldier no more, having first cleared your lines with ECGD, if they are involved. Just occasionally you run across a mill owner who is not really interested in production and specialises in claims that whatever machine he has bought is below specification, resulting in vast losses; and there are one or two governments which have a tendency to call Performance Bonds unreasonably. Your Technical Director and a team of your finest fitters can demonstrate that you have honoured the contract in every particular but, if their performance cannot be instantly replicated by unskilled and illiterate recruits, the machine will be held to blame and you asked to pay.

It depends on the country and the customer. The communist states used not to cheat, perhaps because, so far as the operators were concerned, it wasn't their money anyway. A rule of thumb is that the expertise developed by a country's businessmen in formulating spurious claims is in inverse proportion to that country's attainments in other realms of human endeavour. Unless you know positively that you are dealing with rogues, it is worth taking an informed look at the problem. Three Avimo instances, where our customers were honourable people, come to mind.

* The long pitot dual-static heads for the VC-10, attached to the side of the fuselage, gave spurious readings in flight, which was traced to malalignment and bending of the tubes. When our technician entered the flight shed at Weybridge, there was a ladder leaning against the delicate and unsupported instrument, to facilitate the cleaning of the pilots' windscreen.

* The Israeli army urgently needed some binocular-periscopes for its Centurion tanks during one of its ding-dongs with its neighbours. Weeks later we had a complaint that the sights had misted internally due to imperfect sealing. (They are normally filled with dry nitrogen at 10 psi to obviate any moisture entering the instrument.) The sealing could only have broken down if the instruments had been subjected to extreme conditions, like being

flown in the unpressurised hold of a civil aircraft at 30,000 feet. It is against IATA regulations for aircraft on civil flights to carry war material.

* Some 'Pop' valves for pressure control on Swiss steam locomotives leaked because they were failing to reseat properly after blowing off. Our fitter waited by the tanks from which the boilers of the engines were replenished. Before long he saw the firemen washing the grit off their shovels in the same tanks.

Ah, well. You don't lose them all. But, if you lose too high a proportion, or concede too many claims, or gain a reputation for bad service, or make too many of the mistakes I have made, you will fail, and so will the business. On which gloomy note, it is time to move on to a more cheerful subject, transport, which is an area most of us Top People seldom think about. Perhaps we should.

CHAPTER 21

Transport and Distribution

'A truly pious mind receives a temporal blessing with gratitude, a spiritual one with ecstasy and transport.'

South

'Of great riches there is no real use, except it be in the distribution.'

Bacon

* Two quotations, but for two subjects. Bacon's turn will come with Chapter 22, including his fatal contretemps with a dead chicken. South is less well-known, although the aspiring junior manager might learn much from his career. The term 'brown-nosed' is of later provenance but nevertheless springs to mind.

* He studied at both Oxford and Cambridge, was offered the see of Rochester in England and an archbishopric in Ireland, trimmed his way deftly through the Civil War and Restoration and dallied with Rome when that was the fashion, but remained a protestant. His verse on Peace with the Dutch delighted the great Oliver while the Merry Monarch was equally smitten by a sermon. 'Odds fish,' the King said to South's patron, 'Your chaplain must be a bishop.' And no doubt he would have been, if there had been a see vacant within the royal concentration span.

* One of South's tricks was to learn his sermons by heart in the

days when others used the equivalent of the autocue, shuffling their notes and losing their thread. Born 300 years later he might have trodden the boards or hosted a chat show; but would not have been accorded the resting place in Westminster Abbey which his remains still occupy.

Before moving away from the past, let us recall how an industrial society is created by and operates through transport and distribution. Some scholars suggest that the economic stagnation of the Roman world sprang from the crudity of its mathematics – the inability to multiply MDXVI by CL, for example, or even to divide XXVI by II. Others advert to the moral turpitude and corruption of its people, which augurs ill for the Western world today. However the real block was their inability to transport goods in bulk other than by water, which remained the constraint, despite the 18th-century canal boom, until we scarred and serried the countryside with railways. Even in 1850 only one British settlement was able to support more than 3,000 inhabitants unless it was on sea, river or canal; and when the Devon village of Lynton got its railway on 11 May, 1898, there was no larger community not already connected to the system.

It is a truism to note that mass production can only develop where the resulting goods can be efficiently and economically distributed. The ideal situation is when customers turn up in their own transport to carry the goods away just as they are ready to be shipped: outside the pick-your-own-fruit business, that seldom happens. The next best solution is to deliver to people who pay you – wholesalers, retailers, main contractors or whoever – in line with your planned production rate. When your customers won't take the stuff fast enough and you can't turn off the tap, you have to consider storage or consignment stocks. That's where things become messy and dangerous.

Despite our earlier comments, placing consignment stocks

with third parties is the least satisfactory way of getting them on the market. You don't get paid until after the goods have been sold, sometimes a long time after, and the stockist has little incentive to look after the goods or to keep the inventory down. If you are not careful, a bailiff or a receiver can grab them. All you can do is to reserve title, ensure that the storage conditions are adequate and check that the stock is rotated. If anything is damaged or slow-moving, ship it back home.

Halls Barton, in the last days of its independence, kept its production moving by what turned out to be an excessive use of consignment stocks.

* Many rope customers do not want it in massive coils but cut to length and spliced to meet a specific requirement. Halls Barton only had two depots where these services could be provided and, with an attenuated sales force, faced increasing difficulty in matching a minimum production rate with diminishing demand. The wire rope factory in particular was kept going by heavy dispatches to distributors who only held consignment stocks.

* The rope located in British ports was easy to check and control, although it would have been better to have had the cash. The stocks in the Faroes and Iceland were likely to be paid for in due course and the cash tended eventually to find its way back to Hull. It transpired that the rope in Newfoundland had been there up to four years, stagnant rather than slow-moving, constantly added to but never written down. That in Panama caused questions to be asked whether its sending had been actuated by commercial or charitable considerations.

* Bridport-Gundry secured a few payments from Panama, and recovered some of the rope. The Newfoundland position was only resolved by buying the business of the distributor, and then closing it. We made what had seemed excessive reserves against these consignment stocks hoping, as with all acqusition accounting, to bring them back as profit later, but the outcome was – how shall we say? – disappointing.

In pricing consignment stocks, remember that you are financing certain outward delivery and in addition the possible cost of returns. You have to carry interest on the value of the stock for an indeterminate period. You have to find the expenses of the person who is monitoring the stocks for you and, however much that comes to, it will be cheaper than not monitoring them.

Distributing through your own depots is safer than entrusting third parties with stock but again you meet the snag: until someone buys the goods, you don't touch any cash. The depot doesn't have to be in a town centre. If your product range is too narrow to bear the full overhead, carrying someone else's complementary lines can ease the burden and bring more customers into the store. If you can persuade them to let you have consignment stocks, so much the better. At least you can insist on proper stock and credit controls in your own stores. If you are running several, you can concentrate buffer stocks in one place, feeding the others on an ad hoc or daily basis. That helps keep down your working capital.

If the public buys from your depots, you will meet pilfering and cash discrepancies. Put the tempting and portable items in full view and make sure your cash registers have a locked 'Z register', which the people handling cash cannot access. If the register records transactions in 2-hourly cycles, it is not hard to detect discrepancies and find out who is milking the till. Electronic Point of Sale (EPOS) computers allow stock records to be kept efficiently, providing useful information like stock turnover on top of the accountancy function. It is a sure bet that, when you introduce them, they will speak a different language to your existing equipment. Never mind: someone has to keep the software houses busy.

You should compare the performance of each depot regularly, especially as to volumes and margins. If most of them are hovering around the 38% bracket, but one can only achieve

34%, keep digging until you find out why. Too often I have failed to be sufficiently persistent. A sum of £5,000 pilfered from inventory or cash requires £100,000 of new business to make good the deficiency.

Cyclical businesses – anything from garden furniture to tumble driers – can often only run efficiently if you pile up stock in the slack period so as to have it available when the season comes round. You have to stay in production to keep your staff, your outlets won't take the stuff off you even on consignment and having warehouses of your own would involve keeping them empty for several months of the year. Assuming you can fund out-of-season production, the most cost-effective solution is to do a deal with a storage specialist. Let him worry about security, thievery, fork-lift trucks, insurance, dilapidations, warehousemen and so on. He can take away the stuff as it comes off the line; then, when the season arrives, he can pick it and deliver to your order. A word of warning: if you are aiming for the Christmas trade, the cost is likely to be more than for the rest of the year.

Apart from local or van deliveries, you will save always on carriage by using a haulier. The majority of 'company' fleets are simply operated by hauliers in the customer's livery. That form of advertising is useful but, for standard equipment, you can be paying for it three times over: in the price of the livery, in the additional cost of reduced flexibility and in having to take a long-term contract rather than constantly picking the best spot prices. Of these, the reduced flexibility is the killer. However much you swap the tractors around, the rigid vehicles or the trailers in livery are not going to run better than half their mileage fully loaded.

The Channel Tunnel will change things but until then railways are really only useful for bulk mineral traffic and if all the other freight they carry were transferred to the roads, it would increase volume there by only 1%. No trans-shipment and securing return loads are the keys to efficient transport. Running light, as most company vehicles do, is another way of losing money without thinking.

Consider what you are competing against. The efficient haulier looks for an 80% loaded factor, and even then makes less than 5% on turnover. Each cab has a telephone so that the traffic controller stays in touch with his vehicles and can pass them any relevant information about road conditions from his constantly updated computerised maps. If the drop is to be early, or late, the customer is warned. When there is a delay in loading, he will leave you a trailer to be picked up as soon as it is ready and, if you have problems in the yard, will send in a shunter. When inevitably you are forced into a change of plans, a haulier is flexible enough to absorb some or all the costs, as Langdons did on 21st July, 1989.

> * We had a contract to take 14 loads of large pipes a day on flats from Taunton to Bude. Faced with a drought, the South Western Water Authority suspended deliveries for three weeks. The same hot weather which caused the drought increased the public's thirst. Langdons had no problem in switching the tractors to pull soft-drinks in curtainsiders.

> * Suppose Stanton and Staveley, the pipe manufacturer, had picked up the costs of the moratorium – 14 drivers' wages, £700,000 of capital lying idle, vehicle excise duty, insurances and so on. That's £20,900, without other overheads. Perhaps they could have claimed against the Water Authority, but how much better it was not to have to find out.

Whether you are regularly delivering parcels or trailer-loads, it is wise not to rely on a single haulier. An element of competition, as always, keeps the pencil sharper when it comes to pricing and you avoid being embarrassed if your haulier suffers a labour dispute. The contractor with good equipment kept clean may be slightly dearer than a local cowboy but is almost certain to be more reliable. Keep a weather eye for too close a friendship between your shipping manager and the transport firm he favours. A bottle or two at Christmas or a day's golf are routine but some firms go much further when it comes to 'inducements', and, as ever with bribery, someone else – you in this instance – eventually picks up the bill.

You may choose, or be forced, to use your own drivers and vehicles. You will find that their productivity is about two-thirds of those driving for a haulier, many of whom will be self-employed despite their working for only one company. Company drivers, especially if in the same union as the workforce, can make the Bar look like a bunch of amateurs when it comes to protecting privilege, time-wasting and excessive earnings. All drivers must by law restrict their stint behind the wheel, parking up when they run out of hours. If stranded away from home, they receive an overnight allowance. When, to compound their problems, they are stranded on a Friday night, they usually get a guaranteed four hours' wages on Saturday, at time-and-a-half or even double-time. I wonder how many of your drivers run out of hours twenty miles from home each Friday, park up, spend a night in uxurious comfort and complete the journey next morning? If you check your overtime sheets, or the appropriate lay-bys, you will find out, and at least be aware of what the drivers' jargon 'dodgy nights' means.

Until I became Chairman of a transport company, I would drive the motorways without much thought for the stream of commercial vehicles coming towards me or rolling with me on the inside lanes: unless it were raining, when I might mutter darkly about the spray from the wheels. That fellow in shirt sleeves may well own his £50,000 tractor, for all the company logo. His 38-tonne trailer cost anything up to £48,000 and his load may be worth a quarter of a million. Paying for his services, and all those other vans, tankers, spiders, skeletals, flats, rigids, curtain-siders, Tautliners, artics, fridges and so on takes a large slice out of your overhead and profit. But for them we would within weeks revert to cottage industries and starvation. These were the individuals who made it possible for Mrs Thatcher to break the monopolistic tyranny of the state corporations – coal mining, rail, steel and scheme ports. Civil servants, local bureaucrats, the law, medicine and education must cherish their immunity from a similar threat.

We all use pallets and we all lose them. The firm which loses least is the one which keeps a computerised record of every transaction. Your vehicles should have an underslung rack or some similar place where a driver can pick up a replacement pallet when the receiving storeman refuses to offload palletised cartons. Indeed, with shrink-wrapping, you don't want them off-loaded because your 'POD' – the universal Proof of Delivery note – cannot be qualified if the shrink-wrapping is intact.

A few years back, there was a great deal of fuss about salmonella and other types of food poisoning. While medical pundits pontificated and political breasts were beaten, nobody bothered to stroll through the streets near the reception areas of public cold stores or hypermarkets to count the vehicles parked up, refrigeration at full blast, getting the container below zero so as to make a delivery. It takes a lot of fuel to keep a container down on a long trip, especially where there are intermediate drops. If then you have perishables to transport, ensure that chilled and refrigerated are segregated – it costs much more to refrigerate than to chill. And then insist on a recording of the internal container temperature covering the whole journey. If your haulier can't do that, change hauliers.

Apart from your pallet losses, you also have to pick up the cost of other packaging, particularly cardboard boxes. Despite the fact that these can be obtained at short notice, many firms choose to keep several weeks' supply, consuming both space and cash. Have a look round your own stores, if you disbelieve me. It happens because the storeman usually requisitions the supplies, and nobody checks his inventory. Standardise on carton sizes and cut out printing where you can, but don't send fragile cardboard on long sea voyages, unless it is further protected by shrink-wrapping or being tightly packed into a container.

Export deliveries generally fall into two categories – using the channel specified in the order and Letter of Credit, or making your own arrangements with a customer or distributor who is only concerned that the goods arrive on time and undamaged. Letters of Credit often name the ship and ports to be used, which is a bind even when the nominated vessel plies between those places; when, as often happens, the ship decides to use Rotterdam instead of Felixstowe, or to delay its voyage until the documents have expired, you can only hope that the customer wants the goods enough to amend the Letter of Credit. In cases where the delivery route is for you to choose, check the cost of air freight. The saving in time and packaging may offset the increased fare, particularly if the goods are not bulky. If you decide to deliver overland, use a haulier who regularly makes the trip: other considerations apart, he is likely to have a return load. And don't try to get away on a long haul with the skimpy packaging you use when sending the stuff just down the road.

There is nothing in these paragraphs about how to run a haulage business, and as I am still learning, there are other word processors better qualified than mine to undertake that task. Besides, as I keep reminding you, this book is about staying solvent, and you will have to pay more for trade secrets. However, as someone bruised by a life of manufacturing, I can tell you there are consolations in operating a business such as haulage, where there is no such thing as stock and work in progress. As soon as a haulier makes a trip, it goes straight across to debtors.

Nor have we enlivened the pages with edifying stories. Again the lapse is not due to a paucity of candidates. My memories remain vivid of saturated and tangled rubber thread in cardboard boxes on a Moroccan quay; of shrink-wrapped pallets deliberately pronged by forklift drivers to keep the families of storemen in Christmas cheer over the festive season; of castings cracked and instruments damaged by being packed loose; of hob-nailed boot marks on the enamelled surface of an engine-room annunciator system, with dials broken and instruments ruined; of five successive, and successful, raids on jeans in a city-centre warehouse: of James Pearsall's thread appearing at below manufacturing cost on a stall in Taunton market.

To see if the absence of anecdotes has resulted in lapse of concentration, shall we set a simple test? All questions to be answered. Write neatly on one side of the paper only.

* how many days' usage of cartons do you hold in dispatch?

* what percentage of miles do your vehicles run light?

* how many pallets do your fridge trailers hold and what is the EC limit?

* how many hours a week are your drivers actually driving?

* what is your proportion of tractors to trailers?

* do your tachometers have sealed fuses?

* how many blue pallets are you short each year and at what cost?

* how much did your transport manager pay for his wife's new car?

* when did you last introduce a new haulier to your business?

* what are the different VED rates for 1, 2 and 3 axle trailers?

* did you really know what a POD was? Do you now?

* if you saved 15% on transport, what would that mean in cash and profit?

* have you fitted devices to stop owner-drivers braking only on the trailers (ruining your tyres but saving their own)?

If you find this test searching, or fail to pick up the significance of some of the questions – about the 'blue' pallets, for example – it's time you went back to school: or moved on to something less embarrassing, like Negotiation and Take-overs.

CHAPTER 22

Negotiation and Takeovers

'It is a common error in negotiating; whereas men may have resources to persuade, they strive to use them all at once, which weakeneth them.'

Bacon

* Bacon, like Burke two centuries later, was right on almost every topic, his thinking contrary to received wisdom at the time, which is normally enough to blight a career in public life. It is not surprising he exasperated both the Virgin Queen and the artful Scot who succeeded her. His relationships with their respective favourites were also far from deft, although he managed to distance himself from Essex before that unfortunate nobleman got the chop and was lucky with the timing of the hand which stuck a knife into Buckingham.

* He accepted bribes, as do politicians worldwide in the early days of nationhood. We must of course except from that calumny the saintly More who, as Lord Chancellor, returned the £40 hidden in the gloves Mrs Croaker gave him. Perhaps he might have been beatified sooner if he had returned the gloves as well, and kept details of the incident to himself. Bacon eventually overdid his venality and what is surprising is the size of the fine Parliament levied on him. £400,000 in those days was a lot of money.

* It is anticlimactic to record that Bacon died as a result of catching cold gathering snow with which to stuff a dead chicken.

In negotiation, as in selling, you find the winning hold and hang on to it. Failing that, select carefully the point where you can stand and fight with confidence. As Bacon says, it is counter-productive to deploy a sequence of arguments when a single point is decisive. Having marshalled the facts, you can decide what is your objective and then plan your campaign. Agree with your Board your limits of authority – nothing is more galling than to have them refuse to ratify a good deal – and then let the negotiator get on with it.

* The Rolls-Royce receivership caused enormous cash problems to its suppliers. I was asked to make an offer for one such, Kontak Engineering in Grantham, a manufacturer of hydraulic pumps and motors which exactly complemented our business at Fairey Hydraulics. We could have had it for the amount of Bacon's fine, £400,000. My Chairman and Commercial Director thought this was £25,000 too much. That caution or cheese-paring killed the deal and was later to make the Chairman of Kontak's holding company a very contented man, as he never failed to remind me when we met.

Anyone who has lived through a series of disasters during which things have consistently got worse is likely to be ineffective as a negotiator. The Board of Fairey had been run ragged by the nightmare of having agreed to guarantee the construction of a nuclear power station for a fixed sum. They were wise to bring a fresh mind to the problem in April, 1970 and he was fortunate in detecting a winning hold.

* The Fairey Company and International Combustion jointly owned Atomic Power Constructions (APC) which had contracted to build the Dungeness B nuclear power station at a stated price.

Both parties had compounded their folly by guaranteeing the performance of APC. The customer, the Central Electricity Generating Board (CEGB) was claiming damages of £47m jointly and severally against both guarantors, a modest assessment as it was to turn out when the full extent of the debacle became known.

* The CEGB, advised by (Sir) Philip Shelbourne, was negotiating with the guarantors only to the extent of deciding how much it could extract from them without forcing them into receivership. Having just joined the Fairey board, I was asked to take over as their negotiator. We met in the headquarters of CEGB where Shelbourne tabled a demand against Fairey for £7m, some £4m more than it had reserved in its accounts, payable if necessary by instalments with any balance secured by a debenture. It was said to have been the largest claim ever made against a British firm and I couldn't help feeling a trifle pensive.

* On closer examination, the CEGB was in a deeper hole than Fairey. It had already spent millions on the power station, and it needed APC to get it finished. Suppose I were to join the APC board: as a director of a company which was clearly insolvent, it would be my duty to place it at once in receivership. The receiver would be bound to repudiate the onerous contract and that would involve CEGB in finding a fresh main contractor. It would then have to renegotiate some 3,000 sub-contracts, and not just the big ones with Fairey Engineering and International Combustion.

* I declined to negotiate jointly with International Combustion or to deal further with Shelbourne. By 13th July, 1970, the Chairman and Finance Director of CEGB were able fully to appreciate my possible dilemma as an invitee to the APC Board. Fairey was released from its guarantee in return for relinquishing its worthless APC shares. Fairey Engineering received an unexpected £3m for excess costs already incurred, and a fresh contract on acceptable terms worth £13.1m.

* The news was kept quiet for a time to allow the CEGB to reach its accommodation with the other guarantor. I had planned to

invest heavily in Fairey shares and, although in those days there was no law against insider dealing, I delayed my purchases until the news was out and the price had doubled. Others with similar information were less scrupulous, or less stupid.

Unable to learn from experience, I was later to allow guarantees to be given by Fairey to support a venture larger than the company could sustain, to continue to lead a negotiation when I had been worn down by months of stress and then to achieve a saving deal which some of my Board in effect rejected. Thus my leaving Fairey was to be marred with regret and temporary penury, if not with bitterness, as we shall see shortly.

In a big negotiation you either make a proposition which you feel is the most the other side will accept, and stick there; or you give them something to knock off. Haggling is a way of life in many places and a negotiator may feel frustrated if you merely accept his terms and walk away. It is also a mistake to strike too hard a bargain. By asking a little too much for Delta Communications, we ended up being paid much too little.

* The Irish government decided to industrialise by supporting the chemical and electronic industries. Their forays into chemicals have not proved entirely happy but a number of international electronic firms were induced by lavish grants to set up factories, among them the Canadian telecommunication prodigy, Mitel. When Mitel in March, 1984 decided to shut its Irish plant employing 280 people, I was asked to see if some less drastic action might be taken. The company ended up with a management buy-out, based on halving the staff, relocating, and developing its own product range. We called it Delta Communications and I ended up as Chairman.

* By November, 1988, after some false starts, we were the only Irish-controlled electronics company of any consequence, the English connection being voiced in muted tones, if at all. We had

good products and an international customer base but raising cash in Ireland for working capital was not something to which its banks had yet turned their minds nor were our mainly English backers content to watch their investment mature slowly. Of our four suitors, we liked the Chicago-based Tellabs best. On 12th December, 1988 the Managing Director of Delta and I agreed a price of IR£10 a share, subject to what is known over there as 'due diligence'. As we were giving no warranties, that was fair enough.

* Inevitably during the investigation there was some covering of backs. In the end, we had to take IR£6 a share – still 6 times what the employees had invested but not as good as the IR£7 or IR£8 we should have had if we'd set our sights lower. So Ireland lost the ownership of its electronic White Hope and Tellabs had an extremely good purchase because everything we had said about Delta turned out to be correct.

Most deals have legal angles but most lawyers are bad negotiators. On opposite sides, they like scoring off each other. On your side, they tend to interfere. Commercial law is by and large common sense. If you start floundering, you can adjourn and get advice. And always break off if the talks become stalled. I learned this, along with much else, in Bucharest.

* We were building Islanders in Romania. Our counterparts had very limited authority but would never admit it. As soon as they started filibustering or constantly consulting among themselves in Rumanian, we asked for an adjournment, which let them ring their bosses without losing face. (We used to work through interpreters, except at dinner where we spoke French or German. One day in the formal meeting the Romanians started talking to each other in an incomprehensible gabble. That evening I discovered it was a Transylvanian dialect. I had carelessly let them see their Romanian was not entirely incomprehensible to anyone with a smattering of Italian and Spanish.)

In any important deal it is unwise to meet the other side on your own. You may miss a point or they may misrepresent what you have agreed. As soon as you have a satisfactory deal, draw up Heads of Agreement right away and then keep on the pressure until the formal and binding contract has been signed. Twice, in Fairey and in Stone-Platt, I lowered my guard after signing Letters of Intent which would have resolved the problems. If you show a banker a port after a stormy trip, it is possible to understand if not to condone his making a dash for shore. So it was with Stone-Platt.

* By early 1982 Stone-Platt could only survive if it dumped its Lancashire textile machinery operations. Fortunately the American card-maker, John D. Hollingsworth, wanted to buy them, and the factories in South Carolina and Spain, and had the £17m or so it needed to do so. Over four days we hammered out a complex and detailed agreement covering the transfer of assets and liabilities in many countries and dealing especially with the complications arising from extensive outstanding buyer credits. At 6.55 on the afternoon of the 12th February, I signed the agreement. John D. wanted to wait a day for some superstitious reason but in effect it was all tied up. I had a hole in my shoe, no spare underwear and wanted to get home. The deal, along with a sale and leaseback we had agreed with Hunting Gate, meant Stone-Platt could pay off its bank debt and in future trade profitably with its remaining businesses.

* By appointing receivers before the confirmatory, and binding, agreement was signed, the banks saved John D. some £5m when he eventually completed his purchase. Hunting Gate bought the Crawley factory from a management buy-out team and the only people to suffer in the end were Stone-Platt's directors, creditors and shareholders, some more deservedly than others.

Like Stone-Platt, Fairey was a *cause célèbre* of receivership. The senior receiver told me on the eve of his moving in that he thought the move quite unnecessary: he was right, but the saving Heads of Agreement had not been converted into a binding contract, nor did he put undue pressure on the bank to change their decision.

* As we have seen, the delays in (and overstocking for) the Venezuelan bridge contract for Fairey Engineering and the F16 programme for Fairey SA had made the Group short of cash. (Sir) Philip Foreman of Shorts wanted the successful Islander and Trislander programmes, and suggested buying them with an immediate down payment of £10m, with up to £6m more to come after the details had been threshed out. On 8th August, 1977 he told me he would resign if the Northern Ireland Office, which financed Shorts, blocked the deal. We agreed the terms and signed a Letter of Intent on 16th September. My family, of whom I had seen little for many weeks, had booked a holiday in Cos and I was confident enough of Fairey's future to go there for the first week.

* I should have stayed home. Not everyone on our side, or in government, wanted the Shorts deal to go through. Some preferred the offered embrace of the National Enterprise Board to that particular form of self-help.

For most businessmen, conducting a major negotiation is like buying a house; you don't do it very often and you have to learn on the job. If you employ someone who is good at doing deals, let him take the lead. He doesn't have to be a lawyer or accountant but he needs to have enough confidence not to be overawed or browbeaten by them, even by so commanding a figure as the famous Shelbourne. Buying from a receiver demands special care, because he won't provide any warranties. Here you need to identify assets, which you can see and touch, rather than a company which may have hidden liabilities. For all their sharpness, many receivers do not have the time or background to comprehend the value of what they are selling, added to which they have the limited objective of raising enough cash to pay their fees and the bank. Some of my best acquisitions have been from these hard and faceless vendors.

Bidding for another firm is a voluntary choice, made after close study of the market and the victim. If your target is a private company, the main considerations are the price and what it will cost you to sort it out.

You then call on the Chairman or principal shareholders and take it from there – just another negotiation until it comes to shifting family members out of the way. A management buy-out involves the same considerations, except that you probably know the business better than the vendor and the price is usually discounted because he can't charge you for the promise of your own future services. Launching a bid for a quoted company is a different matter.

Study, surprise and secrecy are the ingredients of a success-ful contested bid. You want the price of the target company to be as low as possible when you make your play. If you like to appear gentlemanly, tell the target after the markets close on a Friday that you intend bidding. It is useful to build up a stake in the victim before the bid, if only to finance the expense should it fail. The rules governing this become ever more stringent and in any event sustained buying in the period before you pounce makes the offer look less generous and so defeats the purpose. You may then have to be content with the Dawn Raid.

A cash bid, or alternative, is always more compelling than paper and if you offer your own shares, you can expect the defence to make every effort to talk them down. When in turn you decide to bad-mouth the target, don't go below Board level. If you appear too critical, people will wonder why you are bidding for such an outfit, and if you win, you have to live with the rest of the management for a while, even if you decide to fire the directors.

You are likely to win a contested bid if you carry the Institutions with you. Some of them, unit trusts particularly, favour short-term gains. Others, and especially insurance companies and pension funds, have a slight pro-incumbent bias. They will be influenced by what they read in the financial press. You must therefore nobble the key journalists and keep things simple so that they can report what you say without having to interpret it. Above all, show confidence in victory, until the price runs away or a White Knight appears, when you can retire from the field with your dealing profit intact and your reputation untarnished.

When the bid succeeds, do not rush headlong into reorganisation of the victim. You should not have embarked on the enterprise without a team of accountants ready to move in, to assess your prize and install your types of control the day victory is conceded. Apart from that, leave things as they are for a few weeks. The management needs time to settle down after a change of ownership and you must constantly remind yourself of the cliché about babies and bath-water. The halcyon days when you could make an instant grab for the surplus in the pension fund are now over, which is one less thing to have to worry about.

Being on the receiving end of a bid is a pain. Win or lose you devote several weeks of your life to a sterile and costly exercise during which it is difficult also to give enough attention to the business. You best avoid bids by running the company well and keeping your shareholders happy. Keep in touch with analysts in your sector and the Institutions controlling big blocks of shares but don't pester them. Before long pestering makes them nervous and they'd rather you were minding the shop than wasting their time. You can't do much about your share price anyway; over time it will represent the sum of how the market rates your performance. A Chairman who becomes paranoic about every share movement or any new nominee name on the register not only unsettles the team and diverts resources to an unprofitable activity. They can also unwittingly talk up a bid.

A well-run company has its defences in constant repair, with its assets adequately valued in the Balance Sheet and rolling forecasts of profit and cash generation readily available. Even if the offer is reasonable, dig in your heels for more: if in paper, press for cash. You are free to attack anyone in the predator's camp, subject to the law of defamation, and if you can expose the vanity of a fanciful entry in Who's Who, that can swing support your way (as it did on one celebrated occasion).

Time works against the aggressor and for the victim. When John Williams was first under attack from Wyndham Engineering, their increased second offer led to a net reduction in acceptances, so vigorous had our defence been – any change in bid terms entitles those who had previously accepted to withdraw. The speed of response to circulars is important, although your advisers, wishing to cover themselves with boilerplate, will slow things down if they can. Remind them that they'll still have a job if you lose, while you'll be left reading the Yellow Book in enforced idleness.

The biggest direct expense of a bid is the money you squander on the mandatory advisers – lawyers, merchant bankers, surveyors, PR consultants, accountants and other hangers-on. In each case choose the man rather than the firm, and insist he stays with the job in person until the end. With solicitors, you may get better service from the provinces, and specifically from Leeds and Manchester, than from the City, and at a fraction of the cost. Listen to your advisers but make your own judgments. You know much more about the business, and about business, than they do. Just as with any other purchase, specify what services you want and then agree the charge, or the basis of charging. If a professional man finds such a commercial approach beneath his dignity, find someone else because you are going to need at your elbow someone who has a commercial attitude.

As it happened, my worst experience of being ripped off was not my fault.

* A troubled quoted company based in Yorkshire owned a loss-making engineering subsidiary on eleven freehold acres near Heathrow airport. The manager, threatened with closure, asked me to help him in a buy-out. An insurance company was ready to pay £500,000 an acre for the site, or part of it, and, for reasons which would take rather a long time to explain, we were able to see a deal in which my client ended up with the business and a douceur of £2m, provided we could find some interim finance.

* Unfortunately the lawyers and merchant bank I was using decided that this gift horse needed extensive oral examination. Notwithstanding the evidence of a keen prospective buyer, the bank asked me to obtain a verbal valuation of the site from a specific firm of West End surveyors, which I did, one hot and sweaty afternoon, without finding anyone who would discuss their fees. They sent someone to walk over the property who confirmed verbally that it was worth what was on offer. Their fee was £10,000.

* While we were dickering, a wealthy individual offered to provide the finance and took over the deal. The business was saved. The insurance company went ahead with its purchase. I was paid a modest fee. My client seemed happy. So, no doubt, were the surveyors.

You are certain to be taken to the cleaners if you are put in the position of having to meet another party's costs. If, for example, you are obtaining grants from a Development Agency on terms which entail your paying their professional advisers, you can expect to be ripped off, with no recourse, fees being a matter between the professional man and his client and not to be questioned by the third party even if he has been landed with footing the bill. And when you are taking on a lease, insist that the landlord pays his own costs, or at the very least agree the amount in advance.

Still on the subject of lawyers, in my youth (said the sage) I used to have an 18th-century plaque behind my desk, showing two farmers pulling respectively the horns and tail of a cow, and a lawyer sat milking it. As I forbore to steal it when I left the firm, I can't show it to you as I did to countless prospective litigants. But I can give you a Seventeenth Commandment – Never engage in contentious litigation. Naturally you must try to recover debts or resist silly claims, but going to law is bad, bad news for everyone but a handful of crackpots who enjoy it, and the legal profession. No lawyer can tell you you are going to win and, if he does, he's too reckless a man to listen to.

It is appropriate to discuss patents while our thoughts are turned towards the avoidance of incurring professional charges. Outside the drug industry, there are very few 'new and original' inventions. Most of the designs which people patent, from friction spinning to horizontal dyeing machines, were drawn and described decades earlier. The wheel has been around a long time and if all those who swore affidavits in support of patent applications were to be prosecuted for perjury, the jails would be insufficient to hold a tithe of those convicted.

Two things happen when you apply for a patent. You involve yourself in irrecoverable expense in the form of fees and you allow your competitors the luxury of studying the specification rather than discovering for themselves how it was done. You may, however, find yourself in the unhappy position of having to see off some bogus claims made by a competitor which, if left unchallenged, could damage your sales. There are almost always valid grounds for rebutting any application or patent, of which prior disclosure or non-originality are the most common. But, like any legal action, it will all cost money because patent agents don't come cheap and patent lawyers are even more pricey.

If you hold a patent and wish to warn off a competitor or his potential customer, proceed with caution. You may properly draw their attention to your claims but any additional threat may constitute both a civil and a criminal offence. This is one letter which you should ask a lawyer to draft for you.

So much then for corporate piracy and employing members of the learned professions. We move next to Sources of Finance – which may indicate how to fund these expensive tastes.

CHAPTER 23

Sources of Finance

'Let it be no bank, or common stock, but every man be master of his own money. Not that I altogether mislike banks, but they will hardly be brooked in regard of certain suspicions.'

Bacon

* Bacon again! It's as well he's out of copyright.

No borrowing and no common stock – what bliss! No lenders wanting repayment or investors wanting dividends. As soon as we accept money from outsiders, we move out of the Garden of Eden. For most of us the Fall happened long ago. Let us then consider the options open to us once we have been thrust out of Paradise into this cruel and greedy world.

The step on the borrowing ladder below using entirely your own cash is to finance the business through equity. There is no obligation to refund capital or pay interest: the only blemish is the wish of shareholders to receive dividends which, in normal times, you need only pay out of profits and subject to having enough working capital. If you own more than the magic 50%, you can even afford to ignore the minority, unless you want to change your Articles or compulsorily buy them out. They can huff and puff and disrupt General Meetings, but that is about all.

The flip side is not to invest as a minority shareholder in a private company without the protection of a suitable shareholders' agreement. My father didn't think sufficiently about this when he bought shares in the Chelmsford Golf Club Ltd.

* In 1923 a company was formed to buy land and construct a golf course on the outskirts of the industrial city, then market town, of Chelmsford. The Club over the years acquired most of the shares in the Company and its members now operate it exclusively for their own benefit, ignoring the interest of the outside shareholders. The auditors, heedless of complaint, describe the Company as a 'mutual organisation' and reduced tax is paid by the Company on that basis. I suppose, if they are golfers, the auditors and the local taxman declare their benefits in kind, or play elsewhere.

* A recent Balance Sheet tells us that the net assets of the Company are £148,398 but as there has been no revaluation of its freehold land for nearly 70 years, the figure is probably understated by a huge factor. Ownership of 4 of the 900 shares in issue, for which an equivalent in today's money of £2,000 was paid, has not so far proved a good investment.

When you have equity shareholders you can give them the choice of taking more shares in lieu of dividends. That doesn't produce fresh cash but never mind – a penny saved and so on. If you want more capital, you can have a Rights Issue, reflecting that by so doing you dilute your equity; and having to pay dividends on the extra shares will hit cash in future. Shareholders don't like Rights Issues, especially if the bucket has been back to the well before. When you offer new shares at a heavy discount, many shareholders will sell the rights, leaving you perhaps with unwelcome strangers on the Register. Nor can you rely on the Institutions backing you, whatever they may have promised. 'I'm sorry, Chairman, but after taking a detached view in the light of our overall commitments and bearing in mind our responsibility to our investors/ pensioners/

stockholders....' Or in plainer speech, 'We decided to cash in.'

A Rights Issue, like anything involving a Circular or Prospectus, is a device for enriching your professional advisers. That does not mean that you don't end up writing most of the document in-house, apart from their disclaimers of liability. You don't have to be quoted to issue a Prospectus to the public (in effect more than 20 individuals), but there are some quite stringent rules to observe. Happily I forgot that when we bought Crewkerne Textiles.

* Bridport-Gundry owned a minority of the venerable Crewkerne sail-maker and webbing manufacturer in whose shops the sails of the Victory were woven, a bullet-torn fragment still to be seen framed in the reception area. When we decided to make an offer to the great-aunts, fifth-cousins and assorted relatives among whom the majority shares were distributed, our London lawyers sent out a 59-page document, including various undertakings and warranties, which immediately gave the prospective vendors the vapours. A locally-based firm, less versed in or daunted by the legalities, then sent them a short note which they could understand, and, through turning a blind eye to some of the relevant sections of the Act, the deal was saved. I'm sure the Admiral would have approved.

An unquoted firm can also apply for funds to a 'venture capitalist'. These people have their quota of losers, and the winners have to carry all, which makes it a very pricey operation. Their 'arrangement fee' is no more than an opening shot. You will end up paying for their solicitors, and your own: their accountants, and your own: stamp duty, registration fees, security printing and, if they can get away with it, underwriting commissions as well. Happily I have never been savaged in this trap but once I was approached to give first aid to a victim.

* Some years ago I was asked if I would consider being Chairman

of a high-technology company in Bridgwater which had recently raised £900,000 from a 'venture capitalist' at a cost of £130,000 in fees, the imposition of two non-executive directors, various onerous options to the new investors, a retainer to the broker for 'financial services' for at least 5 years at £10,000 a year and various other impositions. I said I could do nothing unless the package were renegotiated and, hearing nothing after five weeks, returned the documents. They were good people, with saleable products; and in due course they went bust.

These are the points to watch out for if you are raising outside money for the first time, for an existing business or a management buy-out:

* agree in advance a basis for fee charging and other expenses

* ask for more cash than your business plan suggests you will need

* reserve the right to veto any director appointed by outsiders

* settle in advance your policy on dividend levels and cover, and on going public

* stick to the standard of Articles for a private company if you can, including the right for directors to block share transfers

* don't accept any unnecessary retainers to third parties once the deal is done, especially sinecure directorships to merchant bankers or brokers.

With a management buy-out you are doing investors a favour by letting them in on a proven business. It is usually accepted that ordinary shares issued to the managers at par will be taken up by outsiders at a premium and that the newcomers may have to provide long-term loan capital, often at a subsidised coupon, in addition to their injection of equity. Here too you must expect restlessness among the tribes when they see the grazing on that particular patch has been exhausted. Three of the firms featured in these pages – Longclose, Delta and Langdons – performed well after buy-outs from respectively receivership, the threat of closure and heavy loss-making. In each case, despite their subsequent performance, the managers had before long to face outside investors anxiously looking for the exit.

Except when they want to get out, investors are unlikely to bother you so long as the company performs and they receive a return on their money. Those based in the City are loath to leave its confines except to massacre hand-reared driven birds on a wind-swept moor or stand thigh-deep in icy water not catching fish which are readily available on city slabs. If then you hold your General Meetings more than ten miles from the Square Mile, the attendance will at best be sparse and the proceedings brisk.

There are many ways of introducing fresh capital into a business from outsiders other than through the simple ordinary share. Do not be put off by convertible loan stocks, debentures, preferred, deferred, redeemable or preference, fully- or partly-paid stocks and shares and other non-junk bonds just because you were keel-hauled by a preference shareholders' defence association that time you had to increase your borrowing powers; we cannot blame them for seeking retribution for those years of a minuscule coupon further annually eroded by inflation when their moment in the driving seat arrives. Carefully used, non-ordinary share issues can satisfy both lender and borrower, sometimes even at the expense of another, as we contrived at Globe in 1982.

* Globe Elastic Thread was one of the 'just survivors' of the Howe/Thatcher onslaught of 1979-81, although the American parent never ceased to believe it had all been my fault. Knowing that capital gains can be set off against trading losses only in the year in which they occur, in our last year of loss we sold our freehold factory to a foreign company, took a gain on the sale and then leased it back. We then capitalised the gain by creating a class

of Redeemable Ordinary shares which were issued pro rata to existing shareholders.

* With the return of prosperity, we bought the factory back and in due course redeemed the Redeemable Ordinaries for cash, which, unlike ordinary Ordinaries, did not need the consent of the court. Among other things, we saved £180,000 in tax, which, as they say, sure beats working. I have to confess the parent company seemed to take this feat of legerdemain for granted, never ceasing to remind me how wretchedly I had performed when I first came into the business in '79.

For most of us most of the time, borrowing means the clearing bank, its local manager a mixture of friend, counsellor and supplier. If what we want is within his discretionary limit, it's all very gentlemanly, apart from occasional haggling about rates. If it's too much for him, Region always seems to take his advice. And for most of us most of the time, everything works out fine.

However, we are talking about not going bankrupt, and most of the bankrupting is initiated by banks. Don't be misled by the charm of the manager, or even by assurances from the upper echelons. On 28 July, 1977, over a City lunch, the Chief Executive of National Westminster assured me that the bank would 'see Fairey through'. When it named the receiver on 10 October, his office was in the very building where we had taken lunch. Ten weeks is a long time in banking. Forget the ad men's soubriquets – the 'Action' bank, the 'Listening' bank, your 'Friendly' banker, the 'Sign of the Black Horse' and so on. These fellows want to make as much as they can out of interest and charges, and at all costs to avoid write-offs. The hatchet-man from Head Office won't be friendly or listening although, to be fair, he will be taking action. And the Black Horse may, if alarmed, end up taking you for a ride.

As your manager approaches retirement, so your peril

increases. He wants to leave a clean portfolio and the apparatchiks become more watchful as the sand rises in the lower glass, ever mindful of the Bard's warning that the evil that men do lives after them.

So, before talking to your bank about borrowing, reread chapters 1 and 3. It really does help to know what business you ought to be in and to budget properly. If you are financing losses, it is better to find out before the bank does.

You cannot borrow more cheaply than on overdraft (unless you indulge in some fancy footwork in foreign currencies), with interest being paid only on the uncleared daily balances. Overdrafts should only be used for working capital. It is unsafe to mop up the facility on an expense which will not be fully recovered over 12-months' operation. Whence our Ninth Commandment – Do not tie up your working capital in fixed assets, which could also be written as Never use an overdraft for hard-core borrowing.

If you operate on an overdraft, check the figures daily – the bank balance, the cash book, the uncleared balances either way and especially the direct debits. If you are going to need more cash, warn the bank in advance. Nothing upsets a banker more than having to honour or return cheques which push you over the limit. This leads to an Eighteenth Commandment – Never exceed your overdraft limit without first warning the bank.

For longer term borrowing there are a number of sources and devices – sale and leaseback, factoring, hire purchase, convertible loan stocks, mortgages on specific properties and so on. Always tell your banker what you have in mind, even if he isn't getting the business. If rates are low, accept a fixed rate of interest; and negotiate a variable – so much above base – when they are high. With American-style options available, don't overlook the chance of term borrowing in a foreign currency; the insured cost will be 3% of the loan but the savings can still mount up. Make sure that you can redeem early without being skinned. Despite the Common Law ban on clogging the equity of redemption, there seem to be plenty of ways for lenders to do it.

In a private company where the balance sheet is of less importance, it may pay to acquire equipment on short-term hire with the right to buy after a period for a nominal sum. The inflated hire charge is usually allowable for tax and you end up with hidden assets which the Revenue has helped you buy.

When a bank, especially an American bank, says it wants its money back, they aren't bluffing. There were many things which contributed to the unique instance of Fairey, a profit-making, cash generating company, being forced into receivership. We have touched on some and the law of defamation has muted comment on others. The camel's back was broken by the behaviour of Citibank.

* Having made a play for the business of financing the Belgian F16 programme in November, 1976, in February, 1977 the American bosses of Citibank refused to back their Brussels office. Meanwhile Brussels had lent Fairey SA £2m or so in Belgian francs and, to keep the loan, we had to guarantee that from the United Kingdom. I had been reappointed Chief Executive of Fairey on 16 July 1977 and, by chance, things had started to go right; but paying off Citibank was not the top of my priorities. They were secured and I could hardly ask our lead bankers to take them out until the other deals which had been agreed were in place. Our lawyers strongly advised that I should cease dealing direct with Citibank, and foolishly I listened to them.

* On 12th September, Citibank obtained judgment in Belgium for the immediate payment of the equivalent of £2m. The proceedings were ex parte, which meant that no notice had been served on us as the defendants. This made every other loan, even term loans, immediately due. They were of course quite entitled to pull the trigger, having pointed the gun, but from there on it was downhill into the pit.

If a bank asks you for security, try to avoid giving a personal guarantee. The point of having a limited liability company is that the proprietors don't go broke if it fails. Banks routinely ask companies for fixed and floating charges secured by debentures. Make sure the debenture is discharged when you move back into permanent credit: the bank won't remind you that it no longer needs security. Where you have several bankers, they may want negative pledges, to stop any one of them having priority over the rest. They will also stipulate various ratios they require you to comply with, of liquidity, net assets, interest cover and so on. American bankers monitor these ratios rigorously and often elect to demand repayment if any of the conditions is broken, even though the breach may be merely technical.

Stone-Platt may have got wnat it deserved, but it wasn't just the pulling of the rug when the banks decided to cut and run, but the vehemence of the twitch, which opened my eyes.

* The accountants, Ernst and Whinney, had prepared two reports on Stone-Platt for the Midland in September and December, 1981. Things certainly looked black for the Group then, although I didn't agree with all they said. The events of 12th February, 1982, when the Hollingsworth Letter of Intent was signed, changed the situation fundamentally. But under the terms of the debenture, the Board needed the bank's approval to complete both that deal and the sale of the Crawley property where the contract was to be signed and the sale completed on 19th March. Let me remind you – the proceeds of these deals would virtually eliminate the bank borrowings.

* Having been in on both sets of negotiations, I was at the Stone-Platt office in London on 17th March when the Chairman went to see the Midland Bank about approving these two saving deals and to ask for continued support for the time – days in one case and weeks in the other – which it would take to complete them. Before the Chairman returned to the office or communicated with anyone,

the company secretary received a call from a financial journalist on the *Guardian* asking for confirmation that the bank had decided that a receiver should be appointed. She also spoke to an institutional shareholder in the same sense, revealing to him off the record the name of the institution from which her information came.

* Once a bank gives you notice to repay its loan forthwith, you need a few days in which to get your act together, and a few days without the blare of publicity: otherwise you are guilty of trading while insolvent. A French bank might well have supported the group while the two deals were being completed if the threat of receivership had been postponed for a week, or even kept quiet for a couple of days. But it wasn't. Our friendly bank manager told me he was sure the bank had not tipped off the press, and I believed he was sure. But somebody somewhere spoke out of turn.

It is a blemish on the accountancy profession when a firm which prepares a report on a company for a bank is allowed to accept a subsequent receivership. A big receivership is a licence to riches. The prospects for the creditors of Stone-Platt when partners in Ernst and Whinney were appointed its receivers had become infinitely better in March, 1982 than they had been in December, 1981, when the second Ernst and Whinney report, prepared at the company's expense, was submitted to the bank.

A sign that your bank is getting edgy is when it demurs about giving advance payment, bid and performance bonds. Strictly, these bonds involve the bank in 100% liability: in practice, bid bonds end with the lodging of the bid, advance payment bonds are covered by the advanced payments and performance bonds should be insured as to 90%, 95% or 100% with ECGD. To stay with Stone-Platt, when we bought the Longclose subsidiary from the receivers, we confidently handed over a banker's draft to cover all their bond liabilities, knowing that within 12 months they would have worked their way through the system.

Most British clearing banks behave so well that we cannot believe they will ever act badly. To protect yourself, don't give them the chance. Just assume the worst. I worked for some years in Bridport-Gundry with a former trawler skipper, renowned for his honesty as for his fishing skills. Consider how he was served.

* John Day decided he needed a larger vessel and made arrangements with a shipyard to build it. He had a small mortgage, some £6,000, with the White Fish Authority, on his existing vessel which was worth over £100,000. He paid the first draw on his new boat amounting to £34,000. When it came to the second draw, having heard some rumours he asked the surveyor whether the builder was sound and was assured there was no problem. He therefore paid £14,000 more cash and asked his bank, one of the Big Four, to lend him £20,000 to make up the balance, taking a second charge on his existing boat. The bank said, incorrectly, that it could not take the second charge on technical grounds. Nonetheless it seemed keen to see that the second draw was paid, as no doubt was the banker of the boatbuilder which would then touch an additional subsidy of £68,000 from the White Fish Authority. To avoid delay, John's father thereupon stumped up the £20,000.

* The boatbuilder then collapsed. John Day resorted to modifying his old boat, supported by his bank which found that, after all, it could take a second charge on his boat along with security on his house and a guarantee from his wife. So when he was unable to work out of the trough into which his losses had flung him, both he and his wife were bankrupted.

* John Day and the shipbuilder banked with the same bank. There is of course no suggestion that the manager of one branch of the bank was in communication with the manager of another branch. The bank has recently been running advertisements boasting about its services for small businesses, but they haven't featured John Day yet.

Remember what Bacon told us about bankers: 'they will hardly be brooked in regard of certain suspicions'. Even if you meet them at Rotary and they play off 14.

CHAPTER 24

Directors and Direction

'Himself stood director over them, with nodding or stamping, showing he did like or mislike those things he did not understand.'

Sidney

* We are inclined to think first of the romantic soldier, courtier and scholar Sir Philip when we run across the name Sidney. If not him, then perhaps Robert, the first Earl of Leicester; or Henry, who became Earl of Romsey; or another knighted Henry, the Lord Deputy of Ireland. With such distinguished relatives, Algernon might be seen to limp home at the back of the field. Yet what tumultuous years he saw, and how much better can we feel for the 17th century recalling his life.

* The child painted by Vandyck served in Ireland as a Captain at the age of 19 and again at 24 as a Lieutenant-General, being badly wounded at Marston Moor in between. Like so many of his contemporaries, he was a supporter of order but an enemy of despotism, and was arrested by both Roundhead and Cavalier for supposed sympathy with the other. His first parliamentary career ended with the clap of Colonel Harrison's hand on his shoulder that fateful 20th day of April, 1653, sitting at the Speaker's side when Cromwell finally lost patience with the Rump. That didn't prevent him later becoming a member of the Commonwealth Council of State.

* The Restoration found him mediating in Scandinavia between the Kings of Sweden and Denmark – so influential had Oliver's realm grown – after which he thought it wiser to go and live in Rome on 5 shillings a day than chance his luck back home. When, after conspiring with Louis XIV to set up a Republic in England, he eventually recrossed the Channel, he was again returned to Parliament, despite winning one election and having the mortification of seeing the returning officer proclaim the loser. Arrested on a trumped-up treason charge, he came up before James's henchman, Chief-Justice Jeffreys, and was executed, to the unrestrained glee of the King, on 7th December, 1683.

* Apart from Algernon's exploits, his travels, his wars and the people he knew, his experiences remind us of the civilised liberalism of the 17th century. Even the despots, James II excepted, tolerated independence in that homogeneous world yet untainted with nationalism. Although his literary style was turgid and prolix even for those days, the chance American reader might like to recall that it was Algernon who helped Penn draft the constitution for the State of Pennsylvania.

No 'nodding and stamping' for the modern appointee to the Board: the first thing most of them do is order a business card, with a coloured logo for the extrovert or, for the fastidious, an embossed black type across which overseas customers can run a sensing finger. Certainly, your first Board appointment indicates that you are either arriving or arriviste, and, if to a subsidiary of a larger firm, little else. However, becoming director of any company should impose obligations as well as status.

In a public company, the restrictions on share dealing are designed to deter insider dealing. In practice, although you can buy shares during the relevant periods following the announcement of results, it is frowned upon if you sell them at any time. In 1977, members of my family watched their fortune diminishing and then disappearing as I told them they must not sell their Fairey shares. Happily the investors advised by the company's merchant bank were not subject to the same constraints, it seemed, nor were the bank or the firm's solicitors acting improperly when they received substantial payment of fees when the receivership was imminent. At least I wasn't asked to sign the cheques and thus have to concern myself about what might constitute an unlawful preference of creditors.

The same constraints apply to the giving of price-sensitive information to outsiders. It is best to leave that kind of talking to the Chairman; or, if you are Chairman, to instil discipline and procedures among the rest of the Board. Remember that a false market in shares only creates problems when the Institutions have not heard the inside information first.

Most Boards of quoted companies include their general and financial managers, which gives them at least two executive directors apart from the Chairman. Think hard before putting other executives, like managers of operating companies or divisions on the board. If you include only some, you excite various suspicions, most of them justified; and if you have them all, you are likely to end up, as Stone-Platt did, with an excess of mutual support, silence and back-scratching among the executives.

The ideal non-executive director needs to be schizophrenic. His Chairman wants someone experienced, independent, forthright, respected, knowledgeable and with enough time to keep up with what's going on. But not too experienced or he may start interfering: nor too independent or he may vote against the Chair: nor too forthright or he may come out with some home truths: nor too respected or he may become a rival: nor too knowledgeable or he may ask awkward questions: and so on. The real test is that he can afford to walk away from the job if he doesn't like what's going on.

Bear these things in mind when you become a non-executive. D'Arcy Biss, whom I had removed from the chair at Fairey in October, 1970, asked me within days of its receivership to join the board of UKO International, of which he was then Chairman. It was a double kindness, the offer and the timing, from someone who owed me no favours.

* UKO was badly run and, after my decade at Avimo, I knew the optical business. Unfortunately I lacked tact and quickly upset most of my colleagues. Within months, on 21st July, 1971, d'Arcy asked me to resign. It was the more embarrassing because at the Annual General Meeting a week later, he was to express in generous terms the contribution I was making.

* The rule is that if you're asked to leave, you go. The sad thing was that if I'd behaved with greater moderation, UKO might still be an independent company. It was a measure of d'Arcy's bigness that some time later I was sent a generous cheque ex gratia, without any prior discussion. I confess I was less saintly when my principal critic in UKO later sought a job with a company where I was sitting on the Board.

It is unwise to have any of your professional advisers on your board. It doesn't even achieve the object of getting professional advice on the cheap. You lose the freedom to change advisers and you deny yourself access to objective help when you really need it.

We talked about what a Chairman should do in chapter 16. There are a few people who have the qualities to act as Executive Chairman, playing in effect two roles. So long as they are good at it, and fit, and things prosper, that's fine. The day may come when someone has to bell the cat, for which there will be few volunteers. In a large company, things go better when the Chairman sticks to his traditional functions – appointing people and, when necessary, firing them; stroking shareholders and investors; keeping bankers happy; providing guidance and leadership to all employees; seeing and being seen; planning for tomorrow, next month and five years ahead; appearing before the world as head and symbol of the firm. The managing director then knows where he stands.

It is always a source of tribulation when the Chairman or managing director start encroaching on the other's territory. Other evils aside, the managers don't know which source of authority to take orders from or, on a more practical level, who is going to win. It happened to me once that, as soon as I was away on holiday, my chief executive initiated a policy of which he knew I disapproved, having set things up without telling me before I left. Despite my remoteness, the word was out within four hours. When I returned from the beach, I had already decided to leave as soon as was convenient rather than stay on to retirement age as Chairman, not from pique but because what had to be a close relationship based on mutual trust could never be fully restored.

You must always be ready to move on. If you accept that we only have one life, which we had better live fully, you should not take on any new job without deciding what you want to achieve and how long it will take to achieve it. If you've succeeded in the allotted time, move on to something else: and if you haven't, you should also consider moving on. Having left, let's try a Nineteenth Commandment – Never go back.

The same rule should apply if you allow yourself to become involved, despite our strictures, in public work. (My lapses from grace are set out in Appendix II.) Set yourself a goal and a time limit. Then resign.

These days directors can no longer walk away from a company's creditors if they trade while it is insolvent. There are times, as with Norman, when success is close and you have to balance the best interests of creditors against the possibility of insolvency. Be sure to record carefully what you are doing, and why. A receivership is painful enough without being followed by a personal witch-hunt.

As soon as you join a Board, check its borrowing powers. In the days before inflation, it was common for the Articles to impose quite low limits on borrowing, based on net reserves or shareholders' funds. You can be sure that the moment a company needs to increase its borrowing powers will be also the time when it can least afford to ask shareholders, preference or ordinary, to pass an Extraordinary Resolution.

The only professional advisers you are required by law to employ are your auditors. In a small firm, your main worries are to see that they don't make a meal of it, overcharge or let you in for paying tax, either too much or too soon (as by bad timing of dividend payments). The auditor of a big firm sees things which may be hidden from individual directors, although, if you've been paying attention, you will have been on the lookout for them yourself; things like computer frauds, overvalued consignment stocks, excessive debtors, slow-moving inventory, slack ordering systems, late invoicing and so on. As with all professional advice, the service will depend on the person and not on the firm. Don't fire an auditor because he tells you what you don't want to hear and don't keep him if he forgets who is paying his fees, as happened once with Rex Brothers Motors Ltd.

* With large showrooms, we spent a fair amount on decoration. During one audit a clerk was observed checking the shades of paint through the showrooms, offices, stores and workshops against various invoices from our suppliers. The audit partner had wanted to check that none of the paint bought by the company had been taken by the directors for their own use.

* The three directors, who owned all the shares, confronted him with this. He told us he had a duty to see that supplies bought by the company were used by the company. A duty to whom? To the

Inland Revenue. And who was paying his audit fee, including the cost of the snooping clerk? Well, he told us, we could only dismiss him as auditor after an Extraordinary General Meeting, which would require due notice. We at once voted to dispense with notice and sacked him, giving him a simultaneous lesson in law, manners and the duties of an auditor. We'd have done the same even if we had been taking some paint. It was our firm. You don't pay auditors to sneak on behalf of the Inland Revenue.

I have already warned you about looking to government for financial aid and you may have observed that this was omitted as a source of finance in chapter 23. Politicians and public officials may promise much but don't, and sometimes can't, deliver. The generous offer publicly made will be so hedged round with provisos and conditions, and, if accepted, so delayed in its implementation, as to be worthless; indeed, you might have contrived to manage the business far better if it had never been promised in the first place. The Belgian government spent months putting together its support package for the F16, which came through a week too late to save Fairey. Norman might have succeeded in recreating a British light aircraft industry like that of de Havilland in the thirties if it had not believed in and relied on various promises of aid from the Welsh Office and the DTI.

It would be too painful to take you step by step through the catalogue of half-promises, broken commitments, delays, deceits and dubious devices by which the bureaucrats – the Welsh Development Agency excepted – led the Norman Aeroplane Company to its doom. Suffice it to issue a mandatory prohibition against relying on politicians or civil servants, not just on promises of aid but over anything. They can't deliver even when they mean what they say when they say it. All that concerns them is that the file should be in order, procedures followed, no precedents set. And just when you think they may at last be coming through, the civil servant

272 Thinking About Management

changes his job, the minister loses his or one of them changes his mind or loses his nerve, which was in short enough supply at the outset. If grants or hand-outs materialise, well and good; but don't build any plans around ever receiving them.

Sad to say, you can't rely on people. Many years ago I spoke of a merchant banker, since called to the great counting-house in the sky, as a friend. My older and wiser accountant told me, 'His definition of a friend is someone who makes money for him'. Friendship and business are different and, in a crisis, are likely to become incompatible. If you try to mix them, it's likely to end in tears.

On your way to the top, you should have learned to differentiate between politeness and flattery. As you may well have discovered yourself, a little judicious crawling can ease the upwards path. But when you become the object of flattery, watch out. You personally are of course immune to it but your spouse may succumb if exposed to a plausible sycophant. So keep them clear. Families and business seldom mix, and the family is much more important than the business.

For most of us, reaching the top of the firm has only been possible because someone else was taking care of the burdens associated with running a home and bringing up children. For much of the time work goes smoothly, you get home for meals on time and manage to be around for the weekend, even if you selfishly go off sailing or for a round of golf. Then everything breaks loose and for days, even weeks, you can't pay attention to anything but your business problems. If you have a happy marriage, that allows you release from other cares until the crisis is past. There are however those who are operating at full stretch all the time. You see the signs in some men: they can't relax even when things are going well. But a married woman in a top management faces a problem much more daunting than male prejudice. The responsibility for coping with a home and a senior job means that she is running in overdrive all the time.

When she needs to shift up another gear, it often isn't there, with a resultant breakdown or inability to cope.

As retirement draws near, you may find yourself paying more attention to the pensions scene than you may have thought necessary when ageing was a process which only happened to other people. It is a subject to which many of us might have turned our attention earlier. Like so many of his other ventures, Robert Maxwell's thefts were remarkable in their audacity and scope. There have been countless other scandals and abuses in connection with pension funds, most of them within the law, which have not achieved comparable or indeed any publicity. As ever, when valuables are left lying around with nobody apparently in charge, there are those willing to find a home for them.

The regulations and legislation are, as I write, in a state of flux, and it would be unwise to make any other than general points. You should ensure that the pension fund is professionally managed quite independently of any employee, and that pensioners and prospective pensioners receive regular reports from the fund managers. It is too much to expect that the trustees, who are in practice appointed by the employer, will understand much of what is going on, but at least try to find someone willing to act who is interested in the subject and who will ensure that the trustees do not consist, as normally happens, of the Company Secretary and a couple of Uncle Toms. When the fund is inadequate, the firm will have to make up the shortfall, and when there is a significant surplus, you can pay tax on it and write it back to profits, so long as the trustees agree. If for no other reason, you need to keep in touch with the fund managers and cast an eye over the actuary's reports.

When a scheme is up and running you tamper with it at your peril, unless you are suggesting more benefits for higher employer and lower employee contributions. Before you let such generous instincts take over on the back of one good year, bear in mind that, as with other fringe benefits, the principle of the ratchet applies: you will never be able to claw anything back and the additional expense will stay to haunt you in the troubled times ahead. The reality is that many pension schemes provide retirement benefits far in excess of what pensioners find they need. Their mortgages have long been cleared, their families have left home, their own extravagances diminished by a combination of age and wisdom. Pressure groups are always able to drum up a quota of malcontents and there will be feckless people in every age group. To discover the reality, look at Saga Holidays, analyse the passenger manifest of any one of the numerous daily off-season flights to destinations such as Alicante or talk to your retired friends.

* Some years ago, Jack Jones, a trade union leader, secured a lot of publicity by pleading hardship on behalf of pensioners. As you might expect, the BBC took up the issue with enthusiasm and partiality. With each news bulletin containing its quota of whinge-ing geriatrics, I found myself on a panel on a weekly national programme called *Grass Roots*, answering questions phoned in by listeners. It turned out to be a half-hour of unrelieved tedium because none of the questioners appeared to have any complaint about their lot. (I remember only one similar experience, when, as a token employer, I had to comment on Roy Jenkins' 1979 Budget speech for the governing Labour Party. I exasperated the producer by having nothing but praise for his measures.)

* I tackled the *Grass Roots* producer after the programme. I was told that we had been given to answer only the most critical of the questions. The vast majority of the callers had said that they had never been so comfortably off in their life and many of them referred to Mr Jones in terms which would not have been appropriate for family listening.

When it comes to your own pension arrangements, as with your pay and other perks, try to restrain your selfishness and greed. When you are at the top, you can get away with almost anything. It is no more than another form of flattery for the Remuneration Committee to vote you a salary increase far in excess of what your employees will receive or you deserve: and don't expect any respect if you tell the shareholders that the award had nothing to do with you – your non-executive colleagues insisted. Greed isn't just bad for the firm and for industry at large; it's bad for you too.

We last saw Mr Shelbourne when we were sorting out Dungeness B in 1970. Let us follow his fortunes with the help of a cutting from the *Daily Telegraph* of 5th December, 1988.

* British Petroleum has stopped the controversial payments of more than £200,000 a year to Sir Philip Shelbourne, former chairman of Britoil.

* The retirement package was agreed between Sir Philip, 64, and Britoil in November last year. BP gained control of Britoil in March after a bitterly contested £2.5 billion bid.

* Under the terms, Sir Philip was entitled to £138,600 annual consultancy fees for a maximum three-day month, £24,000-a-year lunch allowance and £40,000 a year for other expenses.

From an annual lunch allowance of £24,000 and a three-day month, it seems appropriate to move on to the subject of diet and health.

An existence where you are subject to stress, long hours, constant travel, insufficient exercise, over-eating and too much alcohol is not conducive to alertness, let alone longevity. You can't avoid the travel and long hours and you get used to stress, which isn't a killer. The other dangers you can avoid, if you take exercise when you can, stick to a sensible diet and lay off the booze, especially when you are flying.

Watch out for signs of deterioration in your employees. Narcotics and alcoholism are your business as much as theirs.

The fellow who dines well and goes night-clubbing on a trip does more than run up his expenses, even when he has the excuse of dragging along a customer.

In retrospect I was lucky that a wartime illness dictated my diet. You don't need to make a thing about it; nobody gives a hang, or even notices, if you don't drink wine or eat various things. In my entire business life, the subject arose only once (outside medicals), when Arnold (Lord) Weinstock offered me a job in 1971. I never asked him how he found out about it but it spoke well of his thoroughness – less so perhaps of the confidentiality of those who kept my medical records.

So why do we do it? For a living, yes, but it is expense not happiness which increases with income. To establish a dynasty? Not consciously, although some may want to continue one. To become rich? Yes, but then never rich enough, it seems, as greed gains the upper hand. To become powerful? That also, until you realise that the world is composed of infinite centres of power, and in the ultimate, we are each of us on our own. To become famous? I was taught a good lesson about fame by a man who kept goats.

* In the late forties I was advising the prospective buyer of some hilly land in the South Hams. I suggested that it was really only suitable for goats. 'Goats,' he said. 'That's why I want it.' He went on to explain the importance to society of rearing, breeding and milking such useful and intelligent beasts. Indeed, he had won many cups and prizes with his animals. 'I'm a big man in the goat world,' he explained.

Apart from providing for your family, business can furnish rewards which you don't need to share with others. It is satisfying to have helped prevent a failure, or seen employees pick themselves up from the horrors of receivership, regaining both pride and prosperity. Over three decades I have worked for three of the companies featured in these pages – Avimo, Pearsalls and

Langdons – each operating within four miles of my home. In this way I have come to know hundreds of my fellow employees living in the same community and shared in their achievements which have sent ripples of prosperity through West Somerset. I value too my Irish association. The heritage of distrust and hatred which bedevils that country will be broken down by economic development rather than words or weapons. For an Englishman to be involved in successful Irish industry is a double bonus; and they are such ebullient people to work with.

The search for acclaim is a hollow exercise, often no more than a substitute for achievement. If you doubt that, consider how badly most of the Queens Award winners perform after they've gained their recognition. The important thing is to enjoy what you are doing – and if that means you also have the satisfaction of becoming a Big Man in your own Goat World, so much the better.

Those who dislike their work tend to perform poorly. If you find you are losing your zest for it, and not just when a holiday is coming up, get out. Let this be our last, and Twentieth Commandment, If you stop enjoying your job, leave it. You will have already found out, as Joe Hunt told us, that making money isn't that much of a problem and, with Franklin, that the man who does things makes many mistakes.

Naturally, any junior employee who applies all the rules and learns all the lessons set out in the preceding pages will inevitably stand out like the one-eyed man in the kingdom of the blind and receive accelerated promotion. But my intention has not been to ease his path to the top but to stop you throwing it all away once you've arrived. There is a narrow line between the seizing of opportunity and the taking of risks. I've told you what can go wrong. The ideal is to make a fortune and keep it. As I keep telling you, it's no joke going bust.

West Monkton   September, 1993

WELL-RUN COMPANY LTD MANAGEMENT ACCOUNTS PERIOD 6 – APRIL SIX MONTHS

Notes: The handwritten cash report is issued every week. Observe the Financial Director's (almost illegible) comments. The Cash Flow is repeated with the monthly figures.

Everything else except the detailed breakdown of overheads and the statement of capital expenditure (note the cars) appears monthly. The Forecast for the Financial Year is looked at more closely each quarter than at intervening month ends, unless something quite unexpected has happened in the meanwhile.

At the half-year and the full year, it is normal to take physical stock, which means that the critical stock adjustment figure – the Joker in the Pack – is only exactly right twice a year. All the other figures are actuals, other than certain accruals for bonuses and the like.

Where orders can only be delivered and paid for subject to import licences, buyer credits or other contingencies, they are classified as 'Awaiting Commercial Clearance'. They don't achieve mention at all unless they are almost certain to be received.

As it turned out, the profit for the full year was £445,000, midway between the forecast after 6 months, and the budget.

WELL-RUN COMPANY LIMITED

BALANCE SHEET AS AT 30 APRIL — all £000s

	£	£	£	Fixed Assets	Cost	Depn	£
Share Capital			200	Land Buildings	298	1	297
Share Premium			705	Plant Equip Motor	648	75	573
Revenue Reserve			1072				
			1977	Investments	946	76	870
				Co. A			9
				Co. B			11
							890

Current Liabilities				Current Assets		
	£				£	
Creditors Trade	700			Stock	1306	
Commission Creditors	95			Debtors	1190	
Sundry Creditors/ Reserves	336			Sundry Debtors	62	
Customer Deposits	65			Bills Receivable	561	
Medium Term Advances	561			St Bills Receivable	67	
St Advances	57			Bank PLC	(17)	
				Deposit A/C	126	
Corporation Tax	142			Tax Deposit	—	3295
Current Tax	74					
Deferred Tax	56					
Dividend A/C	—					
Special Reserves	{ 81					
	41	2208				
		4185				4185

WELL-RUN COMPANY LIMITED   **Period 6 April**

PROFIT AND LOSS ACCOUNT

Sales	Period Act	Budget	Cumulative Act	Budget	Full Year F'cast	Budget
Product A & Spares	188	222	1688	1582	3670	3080
Product B & Spares	191	198	775	938	1250	1870
Product C	59	30	116	180	250	350
Own Sales	438	450	2579	2700	5170	5300
Product D	19	15	73	90	180	180
Merchanted Product A	13	10	51	60	170	120
Merchanted Product B	6	12	27	75	190	150
Total	38	37	151	225	540	450
Direct Material	216	180	1210	1039	2215	2069
Direct Labour	51	50	304	297	630	590
Stock Adjustment	(36)		(167)		(150)	
Gross Contribution on Own Sales	207	220	1232	1364	2475	2641
Manufacturing Expenses	89	86	525	511	1089	1053
Admin.	34	36	204	206	427	430
Marketing	46	49	281	295	592	602
Development	8	7	42	44	89	90
After Sales Rectification	4	4	21	22	44	45
Overdraft Interest	—	—	—	—	—	—
Operating Profit	26	38	159	286	234	421
Merchanted Profit	6	5	24	31	70	63
Interest Receivable	3	3	22	16	34	30
Misc. Income/Exp.	3	1	7	6	12	12
Pre Tax Profit	38	47	212	339	350	526

WELL-RUN COMPANY LIMITED
Period 6 April

SALES	Period Act	Budget	Cumulative Act	Budget	Full Year F'cast	Budget
Product A	157	177	1457	1327	3180	2580
Product B	152	175	667	800	1050	1600
Spares A	31	45	231	255	490	500
Spares B	39	23	108	138	200	270
Product C	59	30	116	180	250	350
Total	438	450	2579	2700	5170	5300
Merchanted						
Product D	19	15	73	90	180	180
Product A	13	10	51	60	170	120
Product B	6	10	27	75	190	150
	38	35	151	225	540	450

Remarks (as appropriate)

ORDERS	Period Act	Budget	Cumulative Act	Budget	Full Year F'cast	Budget
Product A	438	250	1954	1470	3600	3000
Product B	(210)	130	125	800	1000	1600
Spares Product A	99	45	269	250	500	500
Spares Product B	48	20	132	130	270	270
Product C	11	30	166	175	350	350
Total	386	475	2646	2825	5720	5720
Merchanted						
Product D	19	15	73	90	180	180
Product A	10	10	156	63	170	120
Product B	(2)	12	178	72	190	150
	27	37	407	225	540	450

Remarks (as appropriate)

ORDERS UNEXECUTED

Product A	1397
Product B	166
Spares A & B	109
Product C	134
Total	1806

Awaiting Commercial Clearance

Product A	248
Product B	303
	551

Merchanted

Product A	105
Product B	179

WELL-RUN COMPANY LIMITED   Period 6 April

DEBTORS AGE ANALYSIS

1.

Age	Not Yet Overdue £K	Overdue £K	Total £K
0 Current	385		385
1 Month	328	72	400
2 Months	203	13	216
3 Months	63	11	74
Over 3 Months	109	6	115
	1088	102	1190

Not Yet Overdue includes (detailed with any subsequent receipt noted).

2.   **Trade Creditors**

Includes Product D	55
Queries	20

3.   **Personnel Statistics**

	Last Period	Incr/Decr	This Period	Budget
Direct	73	+2	75	71
Indirect	15	—	15	14
Staff	50	—	50	53
	138	+2	140	138

WELL-RUN COMPANY   **Period 6 April**

CASH REPORT

	Period 6 Act	Period 6 Forecast	MAY Period 7 Forecast	JUNE Period 8 Forecast	JULY Period 9 Forecast
Op. Balance	(45)	(45)	(17)	—	(22)
Receipts					
Debtors	495	498	598	350	540
MT Advances	—				
Deposits	8	20	30	20	15
V.A.T.	33	30	15	20	15
Others					
	536	548	643	390	570
Payments					
Creditors	341	288	457	280	270
P.A.Y.E. & N.I.	48	50	40	40	45
Monthly Salaries	39	40	40	40	40
Weekly Wages	50	48	50	48	72
Capital	32	32	—	10	10
Agents	—	5	30	10	10
Rates	9	9	9	9	9
Other					
ACT	29	29			
Dividend					35
Customer Guarantee	60	60			
	608	561	626	437	491
Placing on Deposit					75
Refund from Deposit	100	20		25	
Closing Balance	(17)	(38)	—	(22)	(18)
On Deposit	126	205	128	104	180

WELL-RUN COMPANY LIMITED

WORKS EXPENSES – 6 MONTHS

| | 6 Months | | 12 Months | |
	Actual	Budget	Forecast	Budget
Indirect Premium	50	47	105	99
Public Utilities	43	43	65	70
Training	8	6	16	12
Consumables	12	9	20	18
Holiday Pay	35	38	102	90
Works N.I.	54	51	108	105
Delivery Cost	8	6	14	12
Supervision	14	12	29	25
Storekeeping	16	12	33	28
Maintenance	40	36	85	80
D.O. Prod Control	88	90	185	188
Sundry Works	8	6	18	12
Rates/Insurance	64	64	130	130
Depreciation	76	82	160	165
Leasing	7	7	15	15
Redundancy Costs	—	—	—	—
Sickness Scheme	2	2	4	4
Total	525	511	1089	1053

WELL-RUN COMPANY LIMITED

ADMINISTRATION EXPENSES – 6 MONTHS

	6 Months		12 Months	
	Actual	Budget	Forecast	Budget
Senior Exec.	57	57	118	117
Office Salaries	50	51	105	105
Staff Pension/N.I.	32	32	68	65
Telephone/Post/Telex	15	15	30	30
General Transport	8	9	18	20
Travel	2	4	7	10
Canteen (Vending)	—	—	—	—
Bank Charges	3	4	7	10
Prof. Charges	8	8	16	16
Sundries	12	8	21	18
Loan Interest	—	—	—	—
Printing	10	11	22	24
Special Bonus Payment	7	7	15	15
Total	204	206	427	430

WELL-RUN COMPANY LIMITED

MARKETING EXPENSES – 6 MONTHS

| | 6 Months | | 12 Months | |
	Actual	Budget	Forecast	Budget
Salaries	86	88	177	180
N.I.	9	7	18	16
Travel	33	38	75	80
Agents Commission	95	105	205	210
Credit Insurance	7	6	14	12
Exhibitions	20	20	40	40
Advertising	12	12	24	25
Motor Transport	6	6	12	12
Entertainment	6	6	12	12
Short Term		—		—
Sundry/Guarantees	5	5	10	10
Training Tech	1	1	4	2
Bad Debt Reserve	2	2	5	5
Commissioning	4	4	6	8
Royalties	(5)	(5)	(10)	(10)
Total	281	295	592	602

WELL-RUN COMPANY LIMITED

DEVELOPMENT EXPENSES – 6 MONTHS

| | 6 Months | | 12 Months | |
	Actual	Budget	Forecast	Budget
Salaries & N.I.	24	24	52	50
Sundry	1	2	2	4
Material/Labour	17	18	35	36
Total	42	44	89	90

WELL-RUN COMPANY LIMITED

CAPITAL EXPENDITURE – ADDITIONS

6 MONTHS TO 30TH APRIL

Plant		**£**
Hitachi Seiki CNC Turning Centre		94914.00

Fixtures & Fittings		
Two Plandale A1 Cabinets (Drawing Office)	883.00	
Balance of monorail equipment Paint spray booth	549.48	1432.48

Motor Vehicles		
Rover 827	17317.60	
Sierra 1800LX	8266.00	25583.60

Tooling		
Ordinary	604.00	
For Hitachi Seiki	2397.57	3001.57
		124931.65

WELL-RUN COMPANY LIMITED

CASH REPORT   PERIOD: 10 August

	WK1 Hol?	WK2	WK3 Act	WK4 Est	WK5 Est	Sept Period 11 Forecast £K	Oct Period 12 Forecast £K	Nov Period 13 Forecast £K
Op. Balance	3	(9)	40	3		6	1	14
RECEIPTS								
Debtors	X 539	50	20	40		430	485	475
MT Advances								
Deposits	5	15	5	10		15	15	15
V.A.T.				10		15	15	15
Other Assign.	(20)							
Total Receipts	524	65	25	60		460	515	505
PAYMENTS								
Creditors	5	20	100	180		290	275	290
P.A.Y.E. & N.I.				50		45	45	45
Monthly Salaries			40			40	41	41
Weekly Wages		10	12	12		48	48	48
Capital				5		25	25	10
Agents Comm.				10		30	10	25
Rates		9				9	9	9
Bank Int. (MT)								
Other: Tax/ACT	131							
T.P. Return						58	25	
Dividend								
Other								
Total Payments	136	39	152	257		545	478	468
Placing on Deposit	X 400						24	40
Refund from Dep.		23	90	200		80	-	-
Closing Balance	(9)	40	3	6		1	14	11
On Deposit	X 822	800	711	512		435	460	503

X All 3 achieved and a record! Praise be to Allah!! But don't become carried away as the next 4 weeks is another hill with very little due in.

Enquiries, Committees, Quangos and the like

Regional Board for Industry

This was a wartime relic bringing together industrial managers, trade union officials and senior regional civil servants. I was a member, and then Chairman, of the Somerset Committee. It had no power and I cannot remember any instance when anyone took notice of what we said. I did however enjoy getting to know the regional trade union leaders.

Regional Economic Planning Council

George Brown's reincarnation of the above. It consisted of the same cast with the addition of local politicians and planning officers. Its predictability was illustrated when a blizzard caused many members to arrive late to a meeting. In their absence, I tendered all their views for them. As they arrived, they were asked to speak and were slightly miffed to be greeted with subdued mirth as, in turn, they solemnly repeated my efforts on their behalf. I chaired the Industrial Sub-Committee for a while and was put forward as Chairman of the Council itself, a suggestion which Whitehall received coolly. So long as power remains concentrated in London, these regional bodies are no more than talking-shops.

Committee on the Intermediate Areas

Better known as the Hunt Committee, but today remembered as neither, except by students of regional economics. The membership was one academic, three industrialists, three trade unionists, a senior planner and Sir Sadler Forster from the English Industrial Estates Corporation, each of us coming from a different region. Our assessors, most of whom became Permanent Under-Secretaries and very grand, tried to monopolise the enquiry and to steer us towards interventionist conclusions, in which only the academic supported them. The trade unionists were silent on the occasions when they weren't absent. Our report, the professor dissenting, provided a blueprint for the Thatcher approach to the regions and was anathema to the then Socialist government. It indicated rather than influenced a change in opinion about consensus politics and still reads well a quarter of a century later.

South-Western Regional Council of the CBI

Membership had the advantage that you met other senior industrial managers. When I was Chairman, we published a comprehensive register of the manufacturing companies and institutes of higher education in the region, showing the products and facilities of each. I sent a copy to the Secretary of State for Education, the Rt Hon. Margaret Thatcher M.P., who acknowledged receipt on a buff printed postcard. At the end of three years of proposing or responding to toasts, you can longer commence an address with 'Unaccustomed as I am' etc.

Confederation of British Industry

I had two sessions on the Council, which was too large to be effective. Weaknesses were the dependence of the President on advice and information filtered through the Secretary-General and the dominance of London and its interests. I worked for the setting up of an Advisory Committee for the President and for regular separate meetings of Regional Chairmen. Both of these changes were adopted, although I doubt whether to much advantage in the long term.

On the Regional Policy Committee, I can't remember anyone paying much attention to us inside the CBI or outside it. The committee set up to re-examine Standard Conditions of Sale (for government contracts) was remarkable insofar as its membership included no contract managers familiar with the detail. Its Chairman was also Chairman of a firm which had just been caught out cheating on aero-engine repair. We all accepted his assurances that he knew nothing about it; I suppose a 35% profit margin on turnover had not been enough to excite his suspicion, although another of his directors had been gloating to me about it in licensed premises not long before. The Economic Policy Committee had a strong membership, all of whom might have been better employed running their firms better, myself especially.

English Industrial Estates Corporation

Sir Sadler Forster invited me to become its industrial member after the Hunt Committee, the other members being one each from land agency, accountancy and the unions. Sir Sadler, with the help of two very able officials, the Director-General and Principal Engineering Officer, ran our 700 or so factories faultlessly unless subjected to political interference. I pressed for the construction of small units, a novel concept in those days, and for giving preference to indigenous industry rather than chasing the footloose. The Corporation was in fact well run and profitable, despite political interference. When Sir Sadler died, a less attractive person took his place. Without prior consultation, the two senior officials and I resigned in the space of a few weeks.

Council for Small Industries in Rural Areas

I was county Chairman and then a director, responsible for the south-west. Its main virtue lay in stopping people starting businesses which would fail. Our Somerset campaign for the conversion of old barns for industrial use was frowned on by headquarters which tried to suppress a leaflet we published. That was forgotten when it became national policy. As with most government bodies, its overstaffing and petrification frustrated its making much of a contribution to its stated objects and those who cherished its social aims – local buses, village shops and so on – came to have more influence than those who believe that economic health and prosperity, in the countryside as elsewhere, achieve greater social good than continually tinkering with symptons of decline and decay.

Wessex Water Authority

My membership started when the Authority was well-run and responsive to its market although hampered by its finances forming part of the Public Sector Borrowing Requirement, whence subject to the vagaries and exigencies of the Treasury. I had earlier written to the Chairman complaining that, by charging me by meter for water in a swimming-pool, I was paying twice as the pool was already rated, and in those days water was paid for as a percentage of the rateable value of the property. On joining the Authority, I was told that the letter had led to the charge for domestic pools being dropped, which gives some indication of the style of management. While I was there, we achieved the end of subsidising domestic rates from industry, a proper charge for industry in effluent disposal and the establishment of the same standards in our own sewage works as we imposed on third parties. I became unpopular in Whitehall for advocating privatisation as the only way of raising enough funds to clean up the environment in an industry which had long been dominated by local party bosses paring costs to win votes, and was still refused permission on political gounds to raise its charges or borrow money for necessary capital expenditure because that would count as part of the Public Sector Borrowing Requirement.

University of Bath

When the University was set up, Avimo was asked for a donation. I wrote that we had already given one in our rates and taxes. As a result, I was asked to join the Council and soon became Treasurer, an office I held for a decade: then I became briefly Chairman of Council and finally a Pro-Chancellor. My main object was to ensure a rigid separation of powers, with Council managing the resource and Senate controlling the academic life. A secondary target was to emphasise that universities exist to conduct research and teach students, not to give their employees a comfortable life, and that students matter.

From virtual insolvency, by trying to run the University as a business, the supremely able Richard Mawditt made it the most cost-effective in the country. When he offended people, I backed him, and sometimes I fired the bullets, and forged them too as when alone among university people I supported publicly the increases in charges for foreign students. It soon became apparent that academic success goes hand in hand with efficient administration and the sensible use of resources. I have been fortunate to make many friends among the teaching staff and to obtain some understanding of the mutual inter-dependence of industry and universities.

Committee for Investment Lead Times

I suggested and chaired this. By taking historical examples, we were able to show that most economic policy changes initiated by government or the Treasury were ineffective because the previous policies had not had time to influence events. The findings were taken up by ministers and, I am told, led to a permanent alteration in Treasury economic thinking and planning. If I wasted much valuable time on other committees, this was worth doing, it seems.

Notes on the Companies mentioned in the text

Atomic Power Construction Ltd see under Fairey Co. Ltd

Avimo Ltd

Avimo was started in Taunton as an aeronautical engineer in 1936 by a French industrialist who guessed that France would lose the inevitable war with Germany. He failed to get away from France in 1940 and the company narrowly escaped being taken over by the Custodian of Enemy Property. Its wartime prosperity was tempered by an assessment for Excess Profits Tax at 100%, there being no pre-war history of earnings.

After concentrating on military electro-optics in the early 1960s, we achieved a simultaneous management buy-out and quotation in 1966. In 1971 Avimo and United Scientific Holdings joined forces when USH made an agreed bid. Avimo now employs some 350 people.

I worked for Avimo from 1958 to 1971, declining to join USH as chairman at the time of the merger. With many other employees, I saw my investment in the firm increase by some 5 times between 1966 and 1971.

Bridport-Gundry plc

Bridport-Gundry is a specialist textile manufacturer. Its operations in the Dorset town of Bridport revolve round making nets and converting them for special uses, as for camouflage, fishing, safety in construction work, sports, horticulture, cargo retention and so on. Its Marine division had outlets in many ports. Bridport Gundry Ireland Ltd operated almost as an independent company, with five factories and depots.

In the text we mention other subsidiaries of Bridport-Gundry: Brownell, which was a smaller replica of the UK operations in Connecticut; Halls Barton, an extruder and rope manufacturer in Barton and Beverley; Lolift, a manufacturer of intermediate bulk containers in Knaresborough and Ripon; Jas Pearsall, a manufacturer in Taunton of continuous filament sewing threads and surgical sutures; and Crewkerne Textiles, which wove rigid narrow fabrics.

I joined the Board of Bridport-Gundry in 1974 and was Chairman from 1976 to 1988, taking a more active role after 1981. I stayed as Chairman of Bridport Gundry Ireland until December, 1990. The firm was able to offer stable employment during a tough decade for textiles and shareholders saw their investment appreciate by around 15 times, although there have been major policy changes and disposals since I left in 1988.

Bridport Gundry Ireland Ltd see under Bridport-Gundry plc

Britten-Norman see under Fairey Co. Ltd

Brownell and Co. Inc. see under Bridport-Gundry plc

Crewkerne Textiles Ltd see under Bridport-Gundry plc

Delta Communications plc

Delta was formed in 1984 in Shannon following a management buy-out of the former Mitel assembly plant which was about to be closed. Over four years it developed and sold a range of central office converters and other telecommunication equipment which it added to its assembly on sub-contract and distribution businesses. In February, 1989 the company was sold to Tellabs Inc. of Chicago and renamed Tellabs Ltd.

I was Deputy-Chairman and then Chairman of Delta and remain a director of Tellabs Ltd. The employee shareholders of Delta received IR£6 for every IR£1 share, and outside investors about 40% profit.

Fairey Company Ltd

In 1970 Fairey was described as a 'neatly cored apple' – an aviation company which, after Sandys' assault on the industry, had lost its *raison d'être*. It already owned, or acquired, operating subsidiaries of which the following are mentioned or alluded to in the text:

Atomic Power Construction Ltd
(50% owned) nuclear power stations

Britten-Norman
aircraft manufacture

Fairey Engineering Ltd
heavy mechanical and nuclear engineers

Fairey Electronics Ltd
solid-state relays and cryptographic devices

Fairey Hydraulics Ltd aircraft power controls

Fairey Marine Ltd power boats

Fairey SA aircraft manufacture in Belgium

Fairey Stainless Ltd manufacture of beer kegs

Groves and Gutteridge (East Cowes) Ltd boat manufacture

Roger Laurent SA sintered metal components in Belgium

Tress Engineering valve manufacture

The events of 1977 are described in the text. Only the parent company and the two aircraft manufacturers were put into receivership. The Belgian bankers and government took Fairey SA which has been renamed and prospers with the F16 contracts.The Swiss Pilatus company bought Britten-Norman, later trying to sell it back to the Normans and me. The other companies, with one exception, were sold to the National Enterprise Board, many ending up with the conglomerate Pearson, which later sold Fairey Engineering to Williams Holdings for more than £20m and the Heston operations to their managers, of whom two were original directors of the Fairey Company.

I was Deputy-Chairman and managing director of the Group, and a director or Chairman of most operating companies, from 1970 to July 1975, during which time it seemed we had recored the apple. I was Chairman from November, 1975 to 1977 and unwisely accepted the role of chief executive again in July, 1977, believing on good grounds that I would receive the requisite bank support. Sixteen days later I discovered that I would not. The shareholders received nothing. The receiver paid out the banks and was replaced by a liquidator, one of whose unlikely problems was his liability to capital gains tax on various disposals.

Globe Elastic Thread Company Ltd

Globe in Tiverton was the only surviving British rubber thread manufacturer and the wholly-owned subsidiary of an American parent. After hard times from 1978 to 1981, it became prosperous until a Malaysian manufacturer flooded the market with cheaper thread of equal quality. The factory was closed in 1988 before it went into loss, all employees securing other work before leaving.

I was Deputy-Chairman from 1978 to 1988, acting for part of the time as chief executive.

Groves and Gutteridge (East Cowes) Ltd

see under Fairey Co. Ltd

Halls Barton see under Bridport-Gundry plc

E. Holder and Co. Ltd

My family firm made bed-jackets and trimmings. It now acts as an importer and distributor of trimmings in a small way.

Langdon Industries Ltd

Langdon Industries Ltd is based in Taunton. It hauls, stores and distributes ambient and refrigerated goods. Its main depot also houses the best truck-stop in the country, thus using the facilities efficiently. Langdons was a subsidiary of Tozer, Kemsley and Millburn plc. The City investors who financed half the management buy-out in 1986 were themselves bought out by the managers in 1988 at a 40% premium. I became Chairman in 1986.

Roger Laurent SA see under Fairey Co. Ltd

Lolift see under Bridport-Gundry plc

Longclose Ltd

Longclose manufactures dyeing and sizing machines in Leeds. Always well run and profitable, it was dragged down with Stone-Platt in 1982. The managers bought it from the receivers with City support. I have been Chairman since then.

Norman Aeroplane Company Ltd

Desmond Norman is a genius at aircraft design and an inspired salesman. With the late John Britten he conceived, designed and built the Islander. He then invested his talent and fortune in three other aircraft, the Firecracker, the Fieldmaster and the Freelance.

Mistakes were certainly made in the management of NAC but in any other industrial society, with minimal practical government support, the firm would have survived and prospered. The Firecracker was already certificated as an advanced trainer but the British government foolishly bought a Brazilian aircraft which needed major redesign including a new engine, allegedly to repay help in the Falklands War. The Normans and their backers lost their investment and a skilled and dedicated workforce their jobs.

I was a director and then Chairman of NAC from 1983 to 1988.

Jas Pearsall see under Bridport-Gundry plc

Rex Brothers (Motors) Ltd

The firm was set up in 1952 in Taunton when two brothers walked out of their father's garage business on his remarriage. I played cricket with one of them and was asked to help, remaining involved until 1985. From a modest start the company developed to become the winner of an award as the leading national distributor for a major car manufacturer in two successive years, which made me wonder what the competition could have been like. After two directors married each other, my participation in the business became limited and my contribution negligible.

Stone-Platt Industries Ltd

Stone-Platt had four major divisions manufacturing textile machinery, pumps, propellers and railway carriage equipment worldwide. It also owned or partly owned other firms like Ernest Scragg, in draw texturising machines; Barry Wehmiller in packaging; and manufacturers of plastic mouldings, non-ferrous castings, core-making equipment, fasteners, waste extraction equipment, marine navigational aids, road signs and package boilers.

The decline and fall of Stone-Platt is followed in the text. Almost all the constituent parts have prospered under new ownership, especially the management buy-outs. Sadly, the old Platt textile machinery division in Lancashire no longer exists as a significant manufacturer.

I was a director of Stone-Platt from 1973 to the sad end in 1982.

Tellabs Ltd see under Delta Communications plc

Tress Engineering see under Fairey Company Ltd

UKO International Ltd

UKO manufactured and sold spectacle frames and lenses. It also made stainless steel kitchen equipment for hotels etc. and sold coffee to offices. It is no longer independent. I was a director for a few months in 1978.

West Monkton Advisory Services Ltd

Not mentioned in the text, this is a family firm which gives advice and, in suitable cases, financial support, to companies in trouble. It has been a rule not to accept an assignment from, say, a bank, unless the directors of the company concerned endorse the proposal. We have also found that close involvement as a director of a troubled firm is more likely to lead to solving problems than acting as an outside consultant.

Apart from the financial benefits and the interesting jobs which have come my way through this company, I have also had the pleasure of working closely with two of my sons who have pursued careers very similar to, but less troubled than, my own.

John Williams of Cardiff plc

John Williams made windows, stocked steel and operated a ferrous foundry. I was a director for two spells between 1983 and 1987. The window and stockholding businesses were sold to competitors and the company was then taken over by someone who we hoped would be able to afford the investment which the foundry needed. The foundry has since been sold to its managers.

The Twenty Commandments

1st   Never sell a new product to a new customer.

2nd   Always look first for a customer who isn't spending his own money.

3rd   Never ask for any figures which are not also necessary for running the business.

4th   Never let an accountant circulate any accounts which the rest of the management cannot understand.

5th   Never trust computer-based spread sheets.

6th   Never try to bilk an agent of his commission.

7th   Do not give open credit to foreigners.

8th   Never place an outside order for anything yourself.

9th   Do not tie up your working capital in fixed assets, restated later as Never use an overdraft for hard-core borrowing.

10th   Never commit any resources to plant or machinery without understanding why.

11th   Never expect your juniors to be as smart and dedicated as you are yourself.

12th   Never start a development programme which cannot be funded from current production.

13th   Never choose a new location on the basis of incentives.

14th   Never pledge the credit of your parent company to support an operation abroad.

15th   Never overlook anyone who performs well in a junior function.

16th   Aim your publicity at customers.

17th   Never engage in contentious litigation.

18th   Never exceed your overdraft limit without first warning the bank.

19th   Never go back (once you've left).

20th   If you stop enjoying your job, leave it.

Warner now offers an exciting range of quality titles by both established and new authors. All of the books in this series are available from:
Little, Brown and Company (UK) Limited,
P.O. Box 11,
Falmouth,
Cornwall TR10 9EN.

Alternatively you may fax your order to the above address. Fax No. 0326 376423.

Payments can be made as follows: Cheque, postal order (payable to Little, Brown and Company) or by credit cards, Visa/Access. Do not send cash or currency. UK customers: and B.F.P.O.: please send a cheque or postal order (no currency) and allow £1.00 for postage and packing for the first book, plus 50p for the second book, plus 30p for each additional book up to a maximum charge of £3.00 (7 books plus).

Overseas customers including Ireland, please allow £2.00 for postage and packing for the first book, plus £1.00 for the second book, plus 50p for each additional book.

NAME (Block Letters) ....

ADDRESS...

....

☐ I enclose my remittance for _____

☐ I wish to pay by Access/Visa Card

Number ☐☐☐☐☐☐☐☐☐☐☐☐☐☐☐☐

Card Expiry Date ☐☐☐☐